Related Books of Interest

Reaching the Goal
How Managers Improve a Services Business Using Goldratt's Theory of Constraints

by John Arthur Ricketts

ISBN: 0-13-233312-0

"Excellent writing...a beautiful piece of work. I consider it one of the best books on TOC to have emerged from outside my organization. In fact, I am so impressed that I've asked John Ricketts to be my coauthor for a series of books I plan to write on the concept of ever-flourishing companies."
—Eliyahu M. Goldratt, author of *The Goal* and founder of the Theory of Constraints (TOC)

Ricketts draws on Eli Goldratt's Theory of Constraints (TOC), one of this generation's most successful management methodologies...thoroughly adapting it to the needs of today's professional, scientific, and technical services businesses. He reveals how to identify the surprising constraints that limit your organization's performance, execute more effectively within those constraints, and then loosen or even eliminate them.

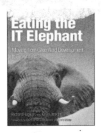

Eating the IT Elephant
Moving from Greenfield Development to Brownfield

by Richard Hopkins and
Kevin Jenkins

ISBN: 0-13-713012-0

Most conventional approaches to IT development assume you're building entirely new systems. Today, Greenfield development is a rarity. Nearly every project exists in the context of existing, complex system landscapes—often poorly documented and poorly understood. Now, two of IBM's most experienced senior architects offer a new approach that is fully optimized for the unique realities of Brownfield development.

Richard Hopkins and Kevin Jenkins explain why accumulated business and IT complexity is the root cause of large-scale project failure and show how to overcome that complexity "one bite of the elephant at a time." You'll learn how to manage every phase of the Brownfield project, leveraging breakthrough collaboration, communication, and visualization tools—including Web 2.0, semantic software engineering, model-driven development and architecture, and even virtual worlds.

Listen to the author's podcast at:
ibmpressbooks.com/podcasts

Sign up for the
ibmpressbooks/

D0415865

Related Books of Interest

Implementing ITIL Configuration Management

by Larry Klosterboer
ISBN: 0-13-242593-9

The IT Infrastructure Library® (ITIL®) helps you make better technology choices, manages IT more effectively, and drives greater business value from all your IT investments. The core of ITIL is configuration management: the discipline of identifying, tracking, and controlling your IT environment's diverse components to gain accurate and timely information for better decision-making.

Now, there's a practical, start-to-finish guide to ITIL configuration management for every IT leader, manager, and practitioner. ITIL-certified architect and solutions provider Larry Klosterboer helps you establish a clear road-map for success, customize standard processes to your unique needs, and avoid the pitfalls that stand in your way. You'll learn how to plan your implementation, deploy tools and processes, administer ongoing configuration management tasks, refine ITIL information, and leverage it for competitive advantage. Throughout, Klosterboer demystifies ITIL's jargon and illuminates each technique with real-world advice and examples.

 Listen to the author's podcast at: ibmpressbooks.com/podcasts

Implementing ITIL Change and Release Management

by Larry Klosterboer
ISBN: 0-13-815041-9

For the first time, there's a comprehensive best-practice guide to succeeding with two of the most crucial and challenging parts of ITIL: change and release management.

Leading IBM ITIL expert and author Larry Klosterboer shares solid expertise gained from real implementations across multiple industries. He helps you decide where to invest, avoid ITIL pitfalls, and build successful, long-term processes that deliver real return on investment. You'll find detailed guidance on each process, integrated into a comprehensive roadmap for planning, implementation, and operation—a roadmap available nowhere else.

Related Books of Interest

Intelligent Mentoring
How IBM Creates Value through People, Knowledge, and Relationships

by Audrey J. Murrell, Sheila Forte-Trammell, and Diana A. Bing

ISBN: 0-13-713084-8

For today's enterprises, few challenges are as daunting as preparing tomorrow's leaders. Mentoring is one of the most powerful tools at their disposal. But not all mentoring programs are equally effective, and not all companies have learned how to sustain mentoring. One company has: IBM. *Intelligent Mentoring* reveals how IBM has done it—and offers specific guidance and best practices you can use to achieve equally powerful results. *Intelligent Mentoring* shows how IBM has fully integrated a diverse portfolio of formal mentoring initiatives into both talent development and innovation promotion. Whether you're a business leader, strategist, Chief Learning Officer, training specialist, coach, or consultant, this book presents a state-of-the-art framework for making mentoring work. Drawing on IBM's experience, the authors demonstrate how to build a diverse portfolio of effective mentoring programs... use mentoring to strengthen organizational intelligence...build sustainable communities of mentors and mentees...promote collaboration across differences... and above all, link mentoring to strategy and use it to sustain competitive advantage.

Can Two Rights Make a Wrong?
Reger
ISBN: 0-13-173294-3

RFID Sourcebook
Lahiri
ISBN: 0-13-185137-3

Mining the Talk
Spangler, Kreulen
ISBN: 0-13-233953-6

The New Language of Business
Carter
ISBN: 0-13-195654-X

SOA Governance
Brown, Laird, Gee, Mitra
ISBN: 0-13-714746-5

Service-Oriented Architecture (SOA) Compass
Bieberstein, Bose, Fiammante, Jones, Shah
ISBN: 0-13-187002-5

The Greening of IT

The Greening of IT

How Companies Can Make a Difference
for the Environment

John Lamb

IBM Press
Pearson plc

Upper Saddle River, NJ • Boston • Indianapolis • San Francisco
New York • Toronto • Montreal • London • Munich • Paris • Madrid
Cape Town • Sydney • Tokyo • Singapore • Mexico City

ibmpressbooks.com

IBM Press Program Managers: Steven M. Stansel, Ellice Uffer

Cover design: IBM Corporation

Associate Publisher: Greg Wiegand

Marketing Manager: Kourtnaye Sturgeon

Acquisitions Editor: Katherine Bull

Publicist: Heather Fox

Development Editor: Kevin Ferguson

Managing Editor: Kristy Hart

Designer: Alan Clements

Project Editor: Jovana San Nicolas-Shirley

Copy Editor: San Dee Phillips

Senior Indexer: Cheryl Lenser

Compositor: Gloria Schurick

Proofreader: Water Crest Publishing

Manufacturing Buyer: Dan Uhrig

Published by Pearson plc

Publishing as IBM Press

IBM Press offers excellent discounts on this book when ordered in quantity for bulk purchases or special sales, which may include electronic versions and/or custom covers and content particular to your business, training goals, marketing focus, and branding interests. For more information, please contact:

U.S. Corporate and Government Sales
1-800-382-3419
corpsales@pearsontechgroup.com

For sales outside the U.S., please contact:
International Sales
international@pearson.com

Library of Congress Cataloging-in-Publication Data

Lamb, John P.

  The greening of IT : how companies can make a difference for the environment / John Lamb.

    p. cm.

  Includes bibliographical references.

  ISBN-13: 978-0-13-715083-0

  ISBN-10: 0-13-715083-0

  1. Data processing service centers—Energy conservation. 2. Information technology—Environmental aspects. 3. Green technology. 4. Social responsibility of business. I. Title.

  TJ163.5.O35L36 2009

  621.39028'6—dc22

                              2009001397

Pearson Education, Inc.
Rights and Contracts Department
501 Boylston Street, Suite 900
Boston, MA 02116
Fax: (617) 671-3447

ISBN-13: 978-0-13-715083-0

ISBN-10: 0-13-715083-0

Text printed in the United States on recycled paper at Edwards Brothers in Ann Arbor, Michigan.

First printing April 2009

Pearson employed a 100% green production method for the publication of this book.

This book was produced with paper made with 30% post-consumer recycled fiber. Using this type of paper saved:

6,288 lbs wood
A total of **22 trees** that supply enough **oxygen for 11** people annually

7,951 gal water
Enough water to take **462 eight-minute showers**

15mln BTUs energy
Enough energy to power an average American household for **61 days**

1,916 lbs emissions
Carbon sequestered by **23 tree seedlings** grown for 10 years

1,021 lbs solid waste
A total of **35 thirty-two gallon garbage cans** of waste

For Penny and Jack

Contents

Preface

Info-Tech's 2007 Green Index indicates that one-quarter of IT leaders in the United States are either "very" or "extremely" concerned about energy efficiency and environmental responsibility, yet only nine percent consider themselves to be "very" or "extremely" green. The index surveyed more than 700 people in North America during February 2007. The market research firm said that dedicated green budgets for IT initiatives might, in turn, influence vendors and suppliers to meet similar green mandates. Large players, such as Dell, HP, IBM®, Cisco, and Sun, have jumped on the green bandwagon, and Info-Tech anticipates a significant increase in the amount of green-focused products and marketing collateral as green adoption continues to gain traction. According to the market research firm IDC, by 2010, for every $1 spent on hardware, 70 cents will be spent on power and cooling. By 2012, for every $1 spent on hardware, $1 will be spent on power and cooling.

At this time, most companies are considering the effects that their Information Technology (IT) architectures and installations are having on the environment. This book outlines the major issues they face. It also describes, through case studies, how the green IT experiences of many different organizations can be leveraged for *your* company. Although IT and data centers are inherently technical, this book is intended for the nontechnical audience, as well. That's because data centers and IT in general (including our laptops, PDAs, the Internet, and so on) are significant contributors to greenhouse gas pollutants and global climate change. Recent UN and White House sessions on climate change have emphasized the environmental importance of green projects. Although controversial, Al Gore's film and book, *An Inconvenient*

Truth, have raised awareness worldwide to the effects of emissions on the environment. Other books, such as Thomas Friedman's 2008 *Hot, Flat, and Crowded: Why We Need a Green Revolution—and How It Can Renew America,* continue to sound the wake-up call. Green IT is one significant step in providing a solution to the crisis. As discussed in Chapter 1, "The Importance of Green IT," many companies are emphasizing the Corporate Social Responsibility (CSR) aspect of green IT. In 2009, Google plans to open a data center in Council Bluffs, Iowa, close to abundant wind-power resources for fulfilling green energy objectives and proximate to fiber-optic communications links. Going green also inspires us at the individual level. Because I grew up in North Dakota, I emphasize in Appendix C, "Comparison of Different Power-Generation Methods," that North Dakota is the top wind state (in potential) in the United States. When I visited my small farm community home town in eastern North Dakota in July 2008, I was proud to see the wind turbines springing up around the state. The Great Plains area of the United States has even been referred to as the Saudi Arabia of wind. This overall awareness, sense of responsibility to contribute, and pride in contributing will continue to be very important for our success in driving toward green IT.

Green IT is the study and practice of using computing resources efficiently. Typically, technological systems or computing products that incorporate green computing principles take into account the so-called triple bottom line of economic viability, social responsibility, and environmental impact. This approach differs somewhat from traditional or standard business practices that focus mainly on the economic viability or economic benefits rendered by a computing solution. These new focuses are similar to those of green chemistry: reduction of the use of hazardous materials such as lead at the manufacturing stage, maximized energy efficiency during the product's term of use, and recyclability or biodegradability of both a defunct product and of any factory waste.

A typical green computing solution addresses some or all these factors by implementing environmentally friendly products in an efficient system. For example, an IT manager might purchase Electronic Products Environmental Assessment Tool (EPEAT)-approved hardware combined with a thin client solution. As compared to a traditional desktop PC configuration, such a configuration would probably reduce IT maintenance-related activities, extend the useful life of the hardware, and allow for responsible recycling of the equipment past its useful life.

The U.S. government is going green. President Bush signed an executive order in January 2007, mandating government agencies use of green technology and processes. See http://www.whitehouse.gov/news/releases/2007/01/20070124-2.html. If corporations want to sell to the federal government, they now must have a green plan.

Many technical groups are also now involved in the effort toward green IT and green data centers. Governments, electric utilities, engineering societies, and all IT vendors are involved. For example, in May 2007, IBM unveiled Project Big Green, a redirection of $1 billion USD per year across its businesses to increase the energy efficiency of IBM products and services. The goal is to reduce data center energy consumption and transform customer technology infrastructure into "green" data centers, with energy savings of more than 40 percent for an average data center.

Green IT and green data center technology cover a broad spectrum, from efficient cooling towers and variable speed blowers, to the use of energy-efficient IT systems such as virtual servers, blade servers, and virtual data storage. These topics are covered both as general areas of concern and in more detail in later chapters. This book was written to have a wide appeal to many types of readers (that is, not just a technical group), as it has been written in a more informal writing style than the typical technical book. The target audience consists of CEOs, CIOs, VPs of IT, system architects, and sales and marketing people. Most of this book is on the level of "Here's what you can do" and geared to the target audience. Some of the appendixes and parts of chapters go into additional technical detail and help respond to "Here's how you can do it."

The competition fostered by these global issues has inspired energy-efficient products and energy-efficient technology services across the globe (for example, Sun, Dell, HP, Fujitsu-Siemens, APC, Liebert, and so on). That competition, along with regulation and standards for measuring energy efficiency, will continue to rapidly drive energy efficiency across the board. We will all benefit.

Green IT is an ideal way for most companies to make a significant step toward environmental preservation. Because IT equipment is continually refreshed as a matter of company policy to remain competitive, the opportunity is there to emphasize energy efficiency for the refreshed equipment. Replacing the IT equipment with energy-efficient systems with concepts such as virtual servers, blade servers, and virtual data storage can easily reduce IT power consumption for the replaced equipment by 50 percent. However, virtual server and virtual data storage technology are methods to enable you to significantly reduce equipment and system management costs for your data center. So, data center green technology is based around a solid business case without even considering the savings due to a reduction in energy costs. Of all the green projects out there, green IT is truly a "win-win" direction for all companies to pursue.

Finally, although the main intent of this book is to examine the business benefits of going to green IT, we should not lose sight that green projects are also socially responsible. Of course, going green also gives a corporation a potential financial benefit. The recent book *Green to Gold: How Smart Companies Use Environmental Strategy to Innovate, Create Value, and Build Competitive Advantage* by Daniel C. Esty and Andrew S. Winston shows how companies benefit financially by emphasizing environmental responsibility and following the "green wave" (to use the author's term). In 2009, with Steven Chu as U.S. Secretary of Energy, going green will get another significant boost. Secretary Chu was director of the Lawrence Berkeley National Laboratory and a strong supporter of alternative energy development, along with a strong belief in encouraging energy efficiency and conservation for all our current infrastructure.

How to Use This Book

This book is organized largely around the two basic reader groups for a book of this type: 1) CEOs, CIOs, VPs of IT, sales and marketing people and 2) system architects, IT architects, engineers, and other technical groups. If you're more involved in the business aspects of your company, you might be most interested in the early chapters on "what to do" in the area of green IT. The following bullets give an overview of how this book is organized and will help serve as a guide for your reading.

- Chapters 1 through 5 give a background on green IT and should be of interest to all readers. These chapters give information on the green IT challenge and the importance of collaboration across a wide array of technical and regulatory groups.

- Chapters 6 through 11 look at some of the technical equipment and strategies for saving energy in IT. Chapters 9 through 11, the case study chapters, are intended to emphasize the "lessons learned" aspect of green IT. The case studies include universities, energy utilities, and large and small companies and span the globe to give guidance based on country or regional green regulations and issues.

- Chapter 12, "The Future of Green IT for Corporations," is the summary chapter and also takes a look at the future. This material should be of interest to all readers.

- The appendixes give details on checklists for green IT, tools for power and cooling estimates, emerging technologies such as grid and cloud computing, background information on the pros and cons of different power-generation methods, and information on worldwide electricity average prices for IT. Cloud computing, discussed in detail in Appendix B, is a significant new technology for green IT. The recent push for "private cloud computing" will have an impact on all of our data centers.

- The Glossary following the appendixes will help you with many terms used in green IT.

This book was written to enable you to go directly to a chapter or section of interest and begin reading without having first read all the previous chapters. The intent is to make the content of each chapter as independently intelligible as possible.

Green IT is and will continue to be an interesting and hot topic worldwide. Enjoy this book. It was a pleasure to write.

—John Lamb

Acknowledgments

Many of the ideas and details presented in the following chapters are based on the green IT projects and green data center installations designed by IBM for its internal and commercial users. Therefore, I would like to thank all those involved with the design of these IBM implementations. In addition, I'd like to thank all the other green IT vendors and organizations who contributed information on green IT, including HP, Dell, Sun, Hitachi, Siemens, PG&E, NiSource, Columbia University, Bryant University, IEEE, ASHRAE, EPA, Emerson/Liebert, SPEC, LEED, The Green Grid, and the University of Colorado.

I would like to thank my management group in IBM's System Engineering, Architecture, & Test (SEA&T) group for their support for this project. This management group includes my direct manager Christin Brown, the SEA&T director Laurie Brickley, and the vice president Damita McDougall. I would also like to thank my former SEA&T manager, Vinny Buscher, for his continued support.

The three reviewers of the book proposal gave some excellent suggestions. Those reviewers were Jody Cefola, IBM Global Technology Services, Site and Facilities Services chief marketing officer for IBM's Big Green initiative; Mike Moran, at the time of the review, a Distinguished Engineer for Content Discovery, IBM Software Group; and Deana Borovich, at the time of the review, the Information Technology architecture manager for the NiSource Energy Utility, headquartered in Merrillville, Indiana.

In addition, I would like to thank the five people who reviewed the book as it moved toward publication readiness. Those five reviewers follow:

- Chris Molloy, IBM Distinguished Engineer, IBM Integrated Technology Delivery, Infrastructure & Resource Management. Chris is involved in all aspects of IBM's Big Green project. He had the wide perspective to review all aspects of green IT technology.

- Wayne Herr, IBM Global Technology Services, Site & Facilities Service Products, CTO. Wayne is the Data Center infrastructure lead on the IBM Green Data Center corporate leadership team. He is also IBM's expert on the data center infrastructure aspects of green IT with emphasis on best practices for energy-efficient cooling.

- Dr. Jean-Michel Rodriguez, Senior IT Architect, Compagnie IBM France, IBM Customer Center PSSC Montpelier. Jean-Michel works with green data centers in Montpelier, France; Beijing, China; and Poughkeepsie, NY. He helped IBM widen its global look at green IT.

- Dave Anderson, Green Architect, IBM Systems & Technology Group, Enterprise Systems Division, IBM Energy Efficiency Initiative. Dave is very much a green architect with an avid interest in all aspects of green IT.

- Jody Cefola, IBM Global Technology Services, Site and Facilities Services chief marketing officer for IBM's Big Green initiative. Jody not only served as a reviewer for the book proposal, but she also brought in her experience in her review of the chapters dealing with the business aspect of green IT.

Green IT requires the collaboration of many groups, so writing this book also required collaborative input from many different groups and individuals. Pirooz (Pete) Joodi, IBM Distinguished Engineer, provided many insights regarding the broad business issues and potential solutions to the green IT issue. Pete's background (a Ph.D. in engineering with a career in IT) is similar to my own, and that was a significant benefit to our collaboration (that is, thinking in engineering terms). Brad Brech, an IBM Distinguished Engineer in the Systems Technology Group, served as our expert on energy management and contributed information on the IBM Systems Director Active Energy Manager (AEM) tool. Ravi Subramaniam, an IBM Software IT Architect, wrote most of Appendix B on cloud computing. Cloud computing, the "ultimate in virtualizing IT systems," will continue to be an important aspect of emerging technology for green IT, and the "cloud" will move from being exclusively in the public Internet domain to the corporate domain. Pam Isom of IBM Global Business Services and lead in the Intelligent Enterprise Archi-tecture project, was especially helpful in her review of how IT architecture impacts green IT. The following IBMers contributed to Chapter 6, "A Most-Significant Step— "Virtualizing" Your IT Systems," on virtualization: Mike Ebbers, Alvin Galea, Michael Schaefer, and Marc Tu Duy Khiem of the IBM team who wrote the IBM Redpaper "The Green Data Center: Steps for the Journey," and Bob Fagan of IBM Boulder who contributed to the VMotion figures and description.

One interesting aspect of green IT is the universal interest among diverse groups of people. Almost everyone is interested in green projects and almost everyone uses a PC with connection to the Internet. Therefore, we see the universal appeal of green IT. I would like to thank all my contacts on this book for their valuable dialogue and suggestions.

Several people helped with the case studies in Chapters 9, 10, and 11. Serkan Sahin of IBM Turkey provided information on the energy-efficiency initiatives for a large data center in Istanbul. Alan Crosswell, associate vice president and chief technologist for Columbia University's Information Technology, along with his Columbia IT colleagues Victoria Hamilton, Lynn Rohrs, and David Millman, provided excellent case study analyses for Columbia University's Green Data Center initiative. Columbia University made for an interesting and important case study for green IT. Not only did the Columbia University case study bring up many of the unique green IT issues within a large research university (for example, each research project likes to have its own servers in its own labs because the funding model works best that way), but the case study also brought up New York City Mayor Michael Bloomberg's 10-year-plan for New York City on reducing carbon emissions by 30 percent based on 2007 levels. The University has committed to that 30 percent reduction, even in the face of greatly increased growth in high perform-ance computing (HPC) requirements fueled by the worldwide research community.

The people at Pearson Education and IBM Press who worked with me on this project deserve a special thank-you for helping complete this project in a relatively short time. The Senior Acquisitions Editor was Katherine Bull (a fellow Notre Dame graduate), and the Development Editor was Kevin Ferguson. Kevin has a significant background in green technology that proved to be a great help. Cindy Teeters was a great help with the paperwork related to the book contract. On the IBM Press side,

I'd like to thank Tara Woodman, Steve Stansel, and Ellice Uffer, who were of great help, especially in helping me navigate through the IBM Press requirements for new books.

Finally, I would like to thank Steve Sams, IBM vice president, Global Site and Facilities Services. Steve is a leader for IBM's Project Big Green on providing green data center technology and innovation for customers. He and his team provided a wealth of information for this book based on their green IT experience and lessons learned.

About the Author

John Lamb is a Senior Technical Staff Member for IBM Global Business Services in Somers, New York. He is an IBM Senior Certified IT Architect, and he holds a B.A. degree from the University of Notre Dame and a Ph.D. in engineering science from the University of California at Berkeley. He is a senior member of the IEEE and ASME engineering societies. He has published more than 50 technical papers and articles and has coauthored four books, including *Lotus Notes® and Domino®5: Scalable Network Design* (McGraw-Hill, 1999) and *IBM WebSphere® and Lotus: Implementing Collaborative Solutions* (Prentice-Hall, 2004).

1

The Importance of Green IT

"As more and more people understand what's at stake, they become a part of the solution, and share both in the challenges and opportunities presented by the climate crises."

—Al Gore on global warming

Information Technology (IT) is at the heart of every successful modern business. Without it, success is impossible. Yet, the pervasive deployment of IT has had significant, unintended side effects, namely as a significant contributor to the economically unsustainable worldwide dependence on fossil fuels. The awareness of these side effects, though somewhat late in coming, has led some successful companies to turn to a sustainable practice known as "IT greening." IT greening is about using IT more efficiently to achieve reductions in energy consumption, and therefore, considering the acquisition of energy-efficient IT solutions. Within this book, you can find details on the environmental impact of IT, including data centers' consumption of fossil fuel-based electric energy. In addition, we examine many case studies, extracting lessons learned and best practices for implementing green IT.

IT is so pervasive that energy efficiency through the implementation of green IT has moved to center stage for many companies in their pursuit of environmentally helpful practices. This book provides details on the importance of implementing green IT; the significant and growing role of IT and data centers in the world's consumption of electric energy and carbon footprint; and especially the case studies for "lessons learned" and the best-practice approaches for implementing green IT.

As I mentioned in the Preface, green IT is an ideal way for most companies to make a significant step in reducing their carbon footprint for several reasons. First, for competitive reasons, most companies already refresh their computer hardware—laptops, desktops, servers, and storage devices—every three to four years. That refresh cycle provides a recurring opportunity to buy increasingly energy-efficient technology, such as virtual servers, virtual networks, and virtual data storage. Such virtualization can easily reduce IT power consumption for the replaced equipment by up to 50 percent. (For examples, refer to the Environmental Protection Agency's [EPA] "Report to Congress on Server and Data Center Energy Efficiency" or the reports by Jonathan Koomey listed in the Bibliography.) A second compelling reason to move to green IT is that virtualization technology enables you to reduce equipment and system management costs for your data center. Data center green technology is based on a solid business case—even before we consider the savings due to reduced energy costs. A third reason for moving to green IT is that all large companies are moving to such implementation improvements (in IT virtualization, cloud computing, and so on). In addition to information on IT virtualization, this book also includes information on new energy-efficient cooling technologies that support IT, and the impact of electric utility-rate case incentives and government incentives and regulations on promoting IT energy efficiency.

Green IT has many different aspects. In this book, we use the terms **green IT**, **green computing**, and **green data centers**. Green IT—as used here—is the most comprehensive because it includes all computing, inside and outside the data center. The emphasis of our discussion is on the business aspects of green IT, so the focus is on what to do, rather than the details of how to do it. However, several chapters, especially the case studies, do give details on how to implement green IT, using best practices based on recent experience and lessons learned through dealing with many companies and organizations throughout the world.

In the following chapters, we look at the benefits and roadblocks in moving to green IT, including the following:

1. Organizational issues in addressing the problem (for example, CIO doesn't pay the electricity bill).
2. The future of regulations as external factors for change.
3. Overall motivation for executives to move to green IT.
4. Evaluation of product end of life and asset disposal, procurement policies, and supply-chain issues (solutions to avoid climate impact, and such).

Executives have one significant aspect of motivation to move to green IT that is not covered in any depth in this book, and that is the area of corporate social responsibility. A growing body of evidence shows that companies can do well by doing good. In fact, books have been written about this corporate motivation for going green. (See the reference to *Green to Gold* in the Bibliography.) The Internet's ubiquitous connectivity has created new relationships among businesses, customers, employees, and partners. People now have access to massive amounts of information and opinions about products and company practices. This information is available in every part of the globe, every minute of every day. Collaboration over the Internet is taking place during a time of increased visibility of corporate actions, a time when customers' perceptions of companies—and their consequent purchasing behaviors—are fundamentally changing. Thus, having your company become part of the **green wave** (to use a term used in the *Green to Gold* book) should be an additional motivation (besides the standard business case) for companies to pursue green IT.

Although this book emphasizes the business aspects, rather than the technical aspects, of green IT, several chapters give technical details, including the case study chapters (Chapters 9, 10, and 11). I'm an engineer by training, and I'm fascinated by the technical aspects of green IT. The energy used for green IT and green data centers is electricity, so I would like to give a brief review of the familiar electricity concepts and relationship of volts, amps, and watts, which are fundamental in our quest to reduce energy used for green IT. The relationship between volts, amps, and watts is this: watts = volts × amps. A watt is the measure of electrical power. Energy is power over a unit of time. We pay for electricity in terms of energy used with a measure of kilowatt hours or KWH. One kilo watt hour (KWH) of electrical energy is the energy used by having 10 one-hundred-watt light bulbs on for one hour. In the New York City area, one KWH costs about 20 cents, whereas in West Virginia, a KWH costs only about 5 cents. The big difference in cost is due to the big difference in generation costs. With the high cost of electricity, the region of the country is becoming a significant factor in deciding where to locate a new data center.

Besides the cost per KWH, another aspect of basic electricity to consider for your data center is the voltage level. In the United States, we typically have two voltages to use in our homes, offices, and data centers: 110 volts or 220 volts. The actual volts can fluctuate somewhat during the day (as you can discover using a simple voltmeter), and electrical engineers often give the two voltages available as 120V or 208V. If you have an electric range, an electric clothes dryer, or a large electric air conditioner in your home, they'll be connected to the higher 208V service. The reason is that they need more power; using a higher voltage gives more power and also saves energy. Higher voltage saves energy because the formula for electric losses due to transmission over a wire is $I^2 R$, where I represents amps, and R is the fixed resistance of the wire. Because watts = volts × amps, we can double the power (watts) by doubling the volts or doubling the amps. However, doubling the amps would increase the losses by four times. Thus, to transmit electricity over long distances, the practice is to increase the voltage as much as possible. In high-tension towers, the voltage is often as high as 120,000 volts, and even in the power lines outside our houses, the voltage is often 4,000 volts. That voltage drops to 110V for use in our houses to reduce danger of electrocution. As noted, 220V power is used only for electric ranges, clothes dryers, and so on, although in Europe, the base power is 220V. One easy way to reduce energy transmission losses at data centers is to use 220V (208V) service. Higher input voltage results in more-efficient operation. Most servers (just like our laptops or hair dryers) are capable of either 110V or 220V service. Older data centers often have 110V power sources for servers, but switching to 220V (208V) would provide significant savings. This change in voltage at data centers to reduce energy use is mentioned in several places throughout the book.

The Growing Significance of Green IT and Green Data Centers

Much of the emphasis in the following chapters is on data centers because they almost always represent the starting point for green IT initiatives for companies. Data centers—the facilities that primarily contain electronic equipment used for data processing, data storage, and communications networking—have become common and essential to the functioning of business, communications, academic, and governmental systems. Data centers have been growing and expanding quickly as our economy continues to shift from paper-based to digital information management. The U.S. EPA's 2007 "Report to Congress on Server and Data Center Energy Efficiency" estimated that the energy use of the nation's servers and data centers doubled from 2000 to 2006 to approximately 61 billion KWH. Under current efficiency trends, national energy consumption by servers and data centers could nearly double again by 2011 to more than 100 billion KWH, representing a $7.4 billion annual electricity cost.

Data centers are found in nearly every sector of the economy, including financial services, media, high-tech, universities, and government institutions. Dramatic server growth at data centers is indicated by well-known web services such as Google, Amazon, and eBay. Estimates indicate that Google maintains more than 450,000 servers, arranged in racks located in clusters in cities around the world. Google has major data centers in California, Virginia, Georgia, and Ireland, and new facilities in Oregon and Belgium. In 2009, Google is planning to open one of its first sites in the upper Midwest in Council Bluffs, Iowa, close to abundant wind power resources for fulfilling green energy objectives and proximate to fiber optic communications links. For additional information on the positioning of new data centers close to abundant renewable electric power sources, see Appendix C, "Comparison of Different Power-Generation Methods." Amazon.com and eBay also have thousands of servers. It is estimated that the Second Life Internet-based virtual world launched in 2003 has more than 9,000 servers. Even with these large numbers of current servers, IBM consultants estimates that in the next decade, server shipments will grow by six times and data storage by an amazing 69-fold.

Green energy-efficient data centers can help us reduce greenhouse gases—which, in turn, can help reduce global warming. The recent UN and White House sessions on climate change emphasize the environmental importance of green projects. Although the extent of the global warming danger might continue to be open to debate, implementing green data centers presents a significant opportunity for all of us to help reduce greenhouse gasses.

In many instances—such as building alternative energy sources by implementing solar panels, or wind turbines—going green has not been economical and can be justified only by government or energy utility rebates. Yet implementing green data centers can be quite financially rewarding—especially when you go first after the low-hanging fruit. As I've indicated throughout this book, going to green IT is a win/win for all parties involved. Energy expenditures for IT keep increasing. Figures mentioned previously bear repeating. According to the research firm IDC: By 2010, for every $1 spent on hardware, 70 cents will be spent on power and cooling, and by 2012, for every $1 spent on hardware, $1 will be spent on power and cooling. Green IT has generated significant customer interest throughout the world. Much of the interest comes from the financial return on green data center investment.

Here is a general definition of a green data center: A repository for the storage, management, and dissemination of data in which the mechanical, lighting, electrical, and computer systems are designed for maximum energy efficiency and minimum environmental impact. The construction and operation of a green data center involve use of advanced technologies and strategies. The strategies and goals include the following:

- Minimizing the footprints of the buildings
- Using low-emission building materials, carpets, and paints
- Creating sustainable landscaping
- Initiating waste recycling
- Installing catalytic converters on backup generators
- Using alternative energy technologies such as **photovoltaics** (PVs) and fuel cells
- Increasing the efficiency of heat pumps, variable speed fans, and free-cooling technology

However, in the following chapters, we concentrate on the ways data centers can become more energy efficient by first exploring the low-hanging fruit. The basic technologies that we should first examine for existing data centers range from the use of efficient cooling towers and variable speed blowers to the use of energy-efficient IT systems, such as virtual servers, blade centers, and virtual data storage. Server consolidation—although initially undertaken to save server hardware capital—is also an excellent way to reduce server energy use. A step way beyond server consolidation is data center consolidation—also done to reduce facility and personnel resource cost; however, a significant side effect is reduced data center energy use. Most data centers have already started to employ newer IT technology such as virtual servers or server consolidation, so this book first explores the technologies that have already started to be employed at your data center for capital cost-saving—and discuss the ways this same technology can significantly reduce energy use. The experiences described in the case studies presented in later chapters are a way to leverage those lessons learned for your data center.

Many consultant reports indicate that data centers are at a "tipping point." Some well-publicized issues supplying adequate electrical power to data centers include Canary Wharf in London and the area south of 14th Street in New York City. In 2006, the financial institutions at Canary Wharf were told that the power infrastructure could not supply power for additional servers at their data centers. In recent years, financial organizations have been adding significant server power, often with racks of blade servers. The racks of blade servers can greatly increase the power required per square foot in the data center. Each blade server requires about the same energy as larger, older servers, and the data center needs similar levels of electricity to cope with the heat generated. Canary Wharf didn't have the power infrastructure to support the increased demands. A similar limit of the power structure occurred during 2008 for data centers south of 14th Street in Manhattan. Power restrictions to data centers based on inadequate power infrastructure is only a part of the problem. Data center floor space has also become a significant concern for data centers, especially in large cities. Often, a company runs out of data center floor space with no easy capability to expand.

The green IT techniques described in later chapters (such as server and data storage virtualization, and server consolidation), in addition to cutting power requirements by 50 percent, also reduce data center floor space requirements. Using virtual server techniques to replace ten stand-alone physical servers with one large physical box that includes ten virtual servers can easily reduce the data center floor space required by 80 percent. Practicing green IT promotes a "win-win" situation for all aspects of your data center: electric-power reduction, server cost, data center floor space, and management of the physical boxes.

Although building and certifying a green data center or other facility can often be expensive upfront, substantial long-term cost savings can be realized on operations and maintenance. The green data center technologies described later can all be based on the typical business case, where a significant **return on investment** (ROI) would be required before proceeding with a project. Of course, there are also significant nonfinancial returns to consider—because green facilities (including green data centers) offer employees a healthy, comfortable work environment. In addition, we cannot ignore the fact that green facilities enhance relations with local communities.

We are all aware of the growing pressure from environmentalists and, increasingly, the general public for governments to offer green incentives: monetary support for the creation and maintenance of ecologically responsible technologies. Server refresh offers data centers a convenient opportunity to go green, which always makes economic (as well as environmental) sense. IBM estimates that a typical 25,000 SF data center with electrical costs at 12 cents per KWH will cost a company $2.5 million a year in electrical energy costs for IT power and cooling. IBM also estimates that the typical data center can reduce its annual electricity cost by up to 50 percent by going green. Of course, as energy costs continue to climb, so will the savings due to the installation of energy-efficient IT equipment and optimization of data center cooling techniques.

Recent EPA reports stress that the U.S. data center industry is in the midst of a major growth period stimulated by increasing demand for data processing and storage. This demand is driven by several factors, including the following:

- Increase in electronic transactions in financial services, such as online banking and electronic trading
- Growth of Internet communication and entertainment use
- Increase in online shopping and related transactions
- Shift to electronic medical records for healthcare
- Growth in global commerce and services
- Adoption of satellite navigation and electronic shipment tracking in transportation

Other important trends contributing to data center growth in the government sector include the following:

- Use of the Internet to publish government information
- Government regulations requiring digital records retention
- Enhanced disaster recovery requirements
- Emergency, health, and safety services
- Information security and national security
- Digital provision of government services (for example, e-filing of taxes and U.S .Postal Service online tracking)
- High-performance scientific computing

During the past five years, increasing demand for computer resources has led to significant growth in the number of data center servers, along with an estimated doubling in the energy used by these servers and the power and cooling infrastructure that supports them. This increase in energy use has a number of important implications:

- Increased energy costs for business and government
- Increased emissions, including greenhouse gases, from electricity generation

- Increased strain on the existing power grid to meet the increased electricity demand
- Increased capital costs for expansion of data center capacity and construction of new data centers

For these reasons, there has been mounting interest in opportunities for energy efficiency in this sector. To its credit, the Information Technology (IT) industry is actively investigating and developing solutions, such as power-managed servers and adaptive cooling.

The direct energy use of IT and infrastructure equipment is not, however, the only way that data centers affect energy use. The data-processing and communication services provided by data centers can also lead to indirect reductions in energy use in the broader economy, which can exceed the incremental data center energy expenditures in some cases. For instance, e-commerce and telecommuting reduce both freight and passenger transportation energy use. When we use an electronic bookstore such as Amazon.com, that use of e-commerce can save us from driving to the local bookstore, and, hence, save energy. We can attend a "virtual" conference using a web-conferencing service such as Webex or Microsoft® Live Meeting and thus save the energy expenditure of an airline flight to the conference, use of a rental car, and all the other energy use that travel entails.

The pursuit of energy efficiency opportunities in data centers is especially important because of the estimated continued rapid growth of direct energy use in data centers and the resulting impact on both the power grid and U.S. industries.

To repeat the theme: We're all aware of rising energy costs in today's data centers and the growing concerns over global warming and other environmental issues. These problems have made green IT one of the hottest topics in the IT area. But what exactly is green IT and green computing and how does it affect IT infrastructures? This book provides an outline on the concepts, benefits, and business value of green computing, such as the following:

- A definition/analysis of green computing and its benefits
- An overview of green computing solutions
- The business case for going green
- Implementation of an energy management solution
- Why energy efficiency is so important

All Companies Can Take Basic Steps Toward Green IT

According to Gartner research firm, the green wave has only begun to rise. The research company predicts that in 2009, more than one-third of all IT organizations will place environmental concerns among their top six buying criteria. By 2010, Gartner says, three-quarters of companies will use carbon-footprint considerations in calculating their hardware-buying strategy, and by 2011, large enterprises will develop policies requiring their suppliers to prove their green credentials through an auditing process.

Most companies are talking a good game but not actually going green where it counts. According to a survey of 124 IT operations by Forrester Research in May 2007, some 85 percent of respondents said environmental factors are important in planning IT operations. But only one-fourth of survey respondents have actually written green criteria into their company's purchasing processes. Enterprises that have started the green journey, however, have found that reducing total energy requirements can be accomplished through some fairly straightforward improvements that don't take years to implement or to bring return. The following six tasks are applicable to all green IT projects. Chapter 2, "The Basics of Green IT," gives details on the five steps used by IBM to implement green data centers. Those five green data center steps include the virtualize, cooling, and measure tasks in the following list. Also, Chapter 9, "Green IT Case Studies for Energy Utilities," and Chapter 10, "Green IT Case Studies for Universities and a Large Company," give details on the five steps used for case studies.

1. Communicate Green IT Plans and Appoint an Energy Czar

Measuring the current state of affairs, energy wise, is one of the first steps to take. A baseline on which to start measuring the impact of an organization's energy-saving initiatives in the green IT area is needed. Of course, you must also communicate your proposed energy-efficiency initiatives right away. Inform all employees about the plans and goals to save energy via green IT. Besides communicating with your employees, set up an organization to drive the effort. You may start by making one person responsible; give that person a title (like "Energy Czar"). Details on the importance of communication and collaboration for green IT is the subject of Chapter 3, "Collaboration Is Key for Green IT."

2. Consolidate and Virtualize

Consolidating IT operations, and using virtualization to reduce server footprint and energy use, are the most well-recognized and most-often-implemented efficiency strategies of the past few years. Some of the largest technology organizations in the world—including Advanced Micro Devices®, Hewlett-Packard®, Intel®, IBM, and Sun Microsystems®—have recently (2008) completed major data center consolidation projects. The projects also included server consolidation and virtualization. Details on the significance of virtualization for your IT systems in going to green data centers is the subject of Chapter 6, "A Most-Significant Step—'Virtualizing' Your IT Systems."

3. Install Energy-Efficient Cooling Units

In most cases, traditional data center design called for bulky **computer room air conditioners (CRAC)** units that are placed on the perimeter of the floor to move large amounts of air around the data center. However, in-row or supplemental cooling units have been shown to save energy. The in-row units typically enclose a row or two of servers, and the backs of all the servers are pointed into a single "hot" aisle. Heat in the aisle is contained by a roof and end-row doors, allowing cooling to be applied directly to the heat source, rather than trying to cool after the heat is dispersed into the general data center floor. Details on data center cooling strategies for green data centers are given in Chapter 8, "What About Chillers, Cooling Tower Fans, and All That Cooling Equipment Usually Ignored by IT?"

4. Measure and Optimize

In 2009, several groups (including the The Green Grid) are expected to release important deliverables in the form of metrics that businesses can use to measure the power-usage effectiveness of facilities infrastructure equipment. Most businesses can already readily identify areas where infrastructure optimization can achieve increased efficiency by simply monitoring and measuring their existing infrastructure equipment. The EPA is also working to create metrics. About 100 companies have indicated that they will provide raw power data and other information to the EPA for use in developing its new benchmark. The EPA indicated that the results of the benchmark should be available by 2010.

Until widely accepted metrics become available, businesses should make sure that the utility costs associated with their data center operations are broken out separately from those for other corporate facilities. In addition, metering specific equipment racks or types of equipment such as servers can provide valuable insight into which specific consolidation, virtualization, and optimization projects will yield the best ROI going forward. The status of energy-use metrics is the subject of Chapter 7, "The Need for Standard IT Energy-Use Metrics."

5. Implement Efficient Applications and Deduplicate Data

Software and application efficiency can be significant for green IT. The author has had a recent experience where the procedure for creating a data warehouse report was reduced from eight hours to eight minutes merely by changing the Oracle data warehouse search procedure. (For example, don't search the entire database each time when only a much smaller search is required.) During the eight hours required to create the report, the large server was running at near peak capacity. Sure, that type of significant application inefficiency has been created and fixed many times over the history of programming. But what about the cases where a few application efficiencies can make an application run 20 percent faster? That 20 percent more-efficient application can also result in 20 percent lower energy use. The steps required to improve application efficiency by a few percent are often not easy to determine; however, the added incentive of saving energy—while making the application run faster—is a significant plus.

Data-storage efficiency, such as the use of tiered storage, is also significant. **Data deduplication** (often called **intelligent compression** or **single-instance storage**) is a method of reducing storage needs by eliminating redundant data. Only one unique instance of the datum is actually retained on storage media, such as disk or tape. Redundant data are replaced with a pointer to the unique data copy. For example, a typical email system might contain 100 instances of the same one-megabyte (MB) file attachment. If the email platform is backed up or archived, all 100 instances are saved, requiring 100MB storage space. With data deduplication, only one instance of the attachment is actually stored; each subsequent instance is just referenced back to the single saved copy. In this example, a 100MB storage demand can be reduced to only one MB.

Data deduplication offers other benefits. Lower storage space requirements can save money on disk expenditures. The more efficient use of disk space also allows for longer disk-retention periods, which provides better **recovery time objectives** (RTO) for a longer time and reduces the need for tape backups. Data deduplication also reduces the data that must be sent across a WAN for remote backups, replication, and disaster recovery.

Data deduplication uses algorithms to dramatically compress the amount of storage space needed. Many organizations deal with increased scrutiny of electronically stored information because of various regulations; this need to preserve records is driving significant growth in demand for storing large sets of data. Depending on the type of information compressed, deduplication can enable a compression rate of between 3:1 and 10:1, allowing businesses to reduce their need for additional storage equipment and associated tapes and disks. Many businesses are already using the technology. Application efficiency as part of green IT strategy is discussed in Chapter 2.

6. Make Use of Rebates and Incentives

More utility providers offer rebates or other incentives that encourage businesses to update equipment and adopt efficient operational practices that can help reduce peak and total power demands. Companies doing this include Pacific Gas and Electric in San Francisco and Austin Energy in Austin, Texas.

New electric power-generation stations are very expensive, and power companies are more than willing to avoid building new capacity. Thus, the power companies encourage data center efficiency through rebates and other incentives. Also, the organization's facilities team doesn't have to build as much new data center space. The IT organization and engineering groups get new equipment that is smaller, cooler and faster than before—and everyone ends up happy. The roles of government and energy utility rebates and incentives are the subjects of Chapter 4, "The Government's Role—Regulation and EPA Activity," and Chapter 5, "The Magic of 'Incentive'—The Role of Electric Utilities."

What This Book Covers

This book includes the following topics to help you understand green data centers and your potential role in creating and maintaining them:

- The significant role data centers have in the world's consumption of electric energy and carbon footprint.
- How companies are offering services and products to help reduce data center energy use—for example, IBM's Big Green $1 billion annual investment in green data centers.
- How IT employees (for example, corporate CIOs (chief information officers), IT architects, IT specialists, and IT project managers) can help drive the implementation of green data centers.
- Case studies of organizations implementing green data centers.
- Details on the best ways to measure data center energy use and report to your executives. Because "You can't manage what you can't measure," the first step is to start the measurement process and understand the need to continually improve your measurement process. This is necessary to better quantify the savings due to your energy initiatives.
- Study of the different ways to measure server utilization and look at trends. You need to answer the question: How has customer server virtualization increased server CPU utilization?
- Continuing follow-up on the literature on green data centers because technology is progressing at a fast pace. The U.S. EPA is key to following the U.S. government recommendations and incentives for data center energy efficiency.
- Survey of emerging technology for server and storage enhancement to reduce data center energy use. This includes the following:
  - **Information Lifecycle Management** (ILM), overall storage management, tiered storage
  - Server virtualization enhancements such as PowerVM®, VMware enhancements, and such
  - Active energy management
  - Enhanced cooling technology
- Analysis of emerging technology for server and storage enhancement to reduce data center energy use.

2

The Basics of Green IT

"Success depends upon previous preparation, and
without such preparation there is sure to be failure."

—Confucius

There are many benefits but also many challenges in moving to green
IT, including organizational issues (for example, the CIO doesn't pay the
electricity bill), government regulations and incentives, and effective
solutions to avoid climate impact, such as product end of life and asset
disposal. This chapter gives an overview of the different ways companies
are moving to green IT. Included in the overview are proven best practices for green IT, such as data center consolidation, server consolidation,
virtual servers, virtual storage, flexible test systems using virtual
resources, and so on. As with any IT project, planning for green IT, both
for the near term and for the long term, is essential for success.

Environmental and energy-conservation issues have taken center stage
in the global business arena in recent years. The reality of rising energy
costs and their impact on international affairs—coupled with the
increased concern over the global warming climate crisis and other environmental issues—have shifted the social and economic consciousness of
the business community. Fortunately, green computing solutions exist
today that address many of these concerns while providing the good

business practices of decreasing operating expenses and boosting profitability. Here are the significant discussion points:

- Organizational issues in going to green IT
- Regulations as factors for change
- Motivation for executives to move to green data centers
- Issues of product end of life and asset disposal, procurement policies, and such
- The basic steps required for green IT
- The role of software, applications, and process workload for green IT
- Laptops and other distributed and mobile equipment as an important part of green IT
- The need for energy measurement and management
- Resources to get the latest information on green IT

Green data centers can be built from scratch, or they can be modified traditional data centers. Currently, there is no demarcation point as to when a data center becomes green. There are some simple metrics like **Power Usage Effectiveness** (PUE) and **Data Center Infrastructure Efficiency** (DCiE) for energy efficient data centers, but these metrics don't cover the entire scope of the data center. We can postulate that a five-passenger automobile is energy efficient if it gets at least 30 miles per gallon on the highway. We can have similar criteria for what makes a bus, light truck, or large 18-wheeler energy efficient—or, even better, a "green" bus or truck. Efforts are underway to establish metrics for energy-efficient or "green" servers. The work to establish standard server and data-storage energy use metrics is discussed in detail in Chapter 7, "The Need for Standard IT Energy-Use Metrics." Establishing energy use efficiency for a server or data-storage device is considerably more complicated than for an air conditioner. A large data center creates an immensely complicated environment to place on an energy-efficiency scale.

We know that when we consolidate server and data-storage resources to reduce server equipment cost, server management cost, and data center space, we also significantly reduce energy use. Thus, the starting point for a green data center is to optimize (for example, use the minimum) the amount of equipment (and hence floor space) needed through projects such as data center consolidation, server consolidation, virtual servers, virtual storage, flexible test systems using virtual resources, and so on. Typically, servers and data storage devices at a data center are "refreshed" on a four- to five-year cycle. That's similar to the typical three-year refresh cycle on your corporate desktop computer or corporate laptop. The thinking is that computer technology is moving so fast that to keep our productivity up, our companies should provide new laptops every three years—or so. That provides a great opportunity for establishing green data centers—because chances are many of the devices at your data centers are about to go through a refresh cycle. The new servers should be procured with an energy-efficiency policy in mind. In addition, the replacement servers need to be recycled in an environmentally friendly way.

This chapter gives details on the benefits and problems in moving to green IT.

Organizational Issues in Addressing the Problem

Organization is one of the first issues to address for green IT. The organization issue usually starts with who manages and controls the IT power bill. Often, the CIO doesn't pay the electricity bill, and the power cost for a data center is allocated to the different groups in the building based on square footage. That's a good deal for the data center group, but it doesn't provide motivation to reduce energy use in the data center. We know that the cost of powering and cooling the data center and communications closets is escalating. In early 2008, Gartner correctly predicted that by 2009, power and cooling costs would be second only to salaries in many IT budgets. This issue on the IT power bill does not try to solve the climate change problems. It is focused directly on the energy conservation solutions now available and their impact on the enterprise bottom line. The Uptime Institute is a research-based academic group founded to serve data center owners/operators and senior facilities engineers across the U.S., searching for leading practices for data center facilities and infrastructure systems design, engineering, and operations.

The organization measures the energy waste in data centers resulting from power supply, distribution, and cooling. According to Institute data gathered from the 85 large-scale corporate members in its network, it takes 2.5 watts at the building's electricity meter to deliver 1.0 watt to the compute load. So, where are the other 1.5 watts going? According to an Institute white paper, many solutions that can improve energy efficiency by 25 percent to 50 percent are technically feasible today with little or no new capital expense. The problem is that performance measures for data center staff are related to uptime and software integration/enhancement projects: There is no sizeable upside for their professional careers in data center energy efficiency. That's because the largest stakeholders on energy efficiency, the CFO and the CIO, aren't usually part of the strategic conversation. For example, although fluid cooling rather than air conditioning reduces cooling requirements by approximately 60 percent to 70 percent, most CIOs are not ready to spend their operations budget on the investment; to them, it just doesn't seem as critical as other budget items related to business applications growth.

The Future of Regulations as External Factors for Change

Looking to the IT department for leadership on sustainability gives you a splendid opportunity to study the "spinal cord" of the organization. After all, the biggest product and business process innovations need to be affected by—or directly affect—the IT infrastructure. The urgency and the critical need to analyze energy spending today are driven by the utility industry's move toward demand-based pricing. This is discussed in more detail in Chapter 5, "The Magic of 'Incentive'—The Role of Electric Utilities," on the role of electric utilities.

Overall Motivation for Executives to Move to Green Data Centers

A study commissioned by chip maker AMD in 2007 found that data center servers and related infrastructure worldwide doubled their energy consumption between 2000 and 2005. In the United States alone, data centers required five billion watts of electricity, equivalent to the output of five 1,000 MW power plants. This level of energy consumption makes data centers among the most significant contributors to global carbon dioxide emissions and, therefore, to global warming. About two percent of global carbon emissions are due to the direct effects of IT usage, especially data centers.

Under current efficiency trends, data center energy consumption may nearly double by 2011. That is, if no action is taken to "green" data centers by making them more energy efficient, their peak power consumption can increase from seven gigawatts today to 12 gigawatts globally. Thus, it is important for IT managers worldwide to consider seriously how to make their data centers green by making them more energy efficient.

Energy costs represent the second largest line item associated with data center operations today, consuming more than ten percent of a typical enterprise's IT budget—a number that many experts predict will rise quickly in just a few years. And make no mistake: These fast-rising costs are not just the concern of those far-away, energy-guzzling Americans. Indian data center managers should be equally concerned, if not more so. Indeed, energy is said to cost 39 percent more in India than in China—and even more if compared to costs in the United States. As energy costs continue to rise and power grid capacity is pushed to the brink, energy provisioning and consumption are emerging as critical concerns for today's CIOs, IT administrators, and facility managers. Experts say the problem needs immediate attention worldwide, especially in hot economies like those of China, India, and Brazil.

Product End of Life, Asset Disposal, Procurement Policies, Supply-Chain Issues

Green IT can give a company a great strategic advantage, making the IT department competitive in today's economy. A nimble IT department can mean a shorter time to market, faster product cycles, and closer communication with your customer base. The IT department can provide the facilities to store knowledge and disseminates it, properly versioned, to all the right parties. Service Oriented Architecture (SOA) and business process redefinition are a part of that more responsive IT department.

Many freight forwarders are working together in industry consortia to accomplish greater efficiency, and supply-chain management leaders are contributing their expertise and their pilot budgets. But most experts agree that ocean shipping and cross-border ground transport have a decade of work to do before they are as efficient as the freight forwarders. Driving the forces for cooperation among competitors in the freight forwarding industry are reduced delivery costs for all of us. There is also another dimension and driving cost: global warming. Stagnation anywhere is a big waste of resources. How much does it save a shipper to turn around his cargo in port eight hours faster? He might know the dollar amount down to the penny, but there is a CO_2 emissions savings per hour saved as well. FedEx planes warming their engines, waiting for documentation, are burning fuel. So are trucks running their engines as they wait in line to cross borders while custom officials thumb through paperwork.

So far, we have discussed only the service end of the business. The true cost of transportation includes the paper production, delivery, storage in more paper boxes and binders, incineration, and landfill of old documents. That's the big picture as we hop onto the 21st-century Silk Road. Product end of life is becoming a significant factor in green IT. Cisco® and most IT manufacturers have processes to reduce the environmental impacts associated with IT products throughout their entire life-cycle, from product development, manufacturing, use, service, and eventual product end of life. This is described at this Cisco Web site: http://www.cisco.com/web/ordering/ciscocapital/refurbished/green_it.html.

Important Steps for Green IT

In moving to green IT, first set up the measurement and monitoring process. It is important to first "baseline" the energy use at your data centers. The mantra in implementing green IT and green data centers is "You can't manage what you can't measure."

As we've seen, data centers provide a huge opportunity for saving energy. Data centers consume more energy per square foot than any other part of an office building. But they're part of an information and services supply chain that begins with raw materials and ends with the disposal of waste. The chain includes people, the space they occupy, and the cars they drive. Along the way, the chain increasingly gobbles energy and spews out greenhouse gases.

The IT department is in a unique position to change that. The place to start is with the data center. Energy consumption in the data center is predominantly from two loads: servers and cooling. Figure 2.1 shows the process used by IBM for creating energy-efficient green data centers. This is a general five-step process that IBM has continued to refine for data centers. The green data center tasks of measuring, cooling, and virtualizing are included in the green IT steps described in Chapter 1, "The Importance of Green IT."

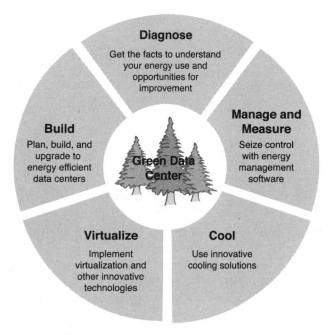

Source: IBM Big Green Team

Figure 2.1   IBM Big Green approach to data center energy efficiency

Five-Step Process Used for Data Center Energy Efficiency

As indicated in Figure 2.1, the five-step process is to diagnose, manage and measure, use energy-efficient cooling, virtualize, and build new or upgrade facilities when feasible.

Diagnose the Opportunities and Problems

This step is to perform a data-center energy-efficiency assessment. Many data center energy consultants bring in tools such as Mobile Measurement Technology (MMT) to look at "hot spots" in the data center and areas where cold and hot air mix too early and thereby waste energy. The assessment should include a list of unused IT equipment that can be turned off. In addition, the diagnostic phase can help encourage organizations to retire unused software applications and focus on adopting more effective software that requires fewer CPU cycles. A typical x86 server consumes between 30 percent and 40 percent of its maximum power when idle. IT organizations should turn off servers that don't appear to be performing tasks. If anyone complains, organizations should look into whether the little-used application can be virtualized. Check with your electric utility. Some utilities such as PG&E offer free energy audits.

Manage and Measure

Many hardware products have built-in power management features that are never used. Most major vendors have been implementing such features for quite some time. These features include the capability of the CPU to optimize power by dynamically switching among multiple performance states. The CPU drops its input voltage and frequency based on how many instructions are run on the chip itself. These types of features can save organizations up to 20 percent on server power consumption.

Several companies offer green testing and measurement tools for the data center. In 2008, Ixia released the IxGreen, which measures the amount of power required to run components in the data center at various performance levels. Miercom, a network product test center, announced a Certified Green testing program. The Miercom program tests products to challenge networking equipment suppliers to design power-efficient network infrastructure. Cisco switches were the first to receive the certification.

Cool

Many data centers might use hot aisle or cold aisle configurations to improve cooling efficiency, but they can also make some small adjustments. Simple **blanking panels** can be installed in server racks that have empty slots. That's a great way to make sure the cold air in the cold aisle doesn't start mixing with the hot air in the hot aisle any sooner than it needs to. Organizations should also seal cable cutouts to minimize airflow bypasses. Data organizations should consider air handlers and chillers that use efficient technologies, such as variable frequency drives that adjust how fast the air-conditioning system's motors run when cooling needs dip.

Virtualize

Virtualization continues to be one of the hottest green data center topics. Vendors have said current server utilization rates typically hover between 5 percent and 15 percent. Direct-attached storage utilization sits between 20 percent and 40 percent, with network storage between 60 percent and 80 percent. Virtualization can increase hardware utilization by five to 20 times and allows organizations to reduce the number of power-consuming servers. Such figures show why virtualization has become a significant topic at all computer conferences. For example, at the Interop 2008 conference, keynote speakers predicted that next-generation data centers will take virtualization far beyond servers in a bid to expedite application delivery. Data center consolidation and the shift from virtualization at the server to implementing it throughout the network for accelerated application delivery were threads running through several 2008 Interop keynotes and conference sessions.

Build

Going green is easiest if you build a new data center. First, you make a calculation of your server and other IT requirements for the foreseeable future. Next, you plan a data center for modularity in both its IT elements and its power and cooling. Then you use data center modeling and thermal assessment tools and software—available from vendors such as APC, IBM, HP, and Sun—to design the data center. The next step is to procure green from the beginning, which partly means to buy the latest equipment and technologies, such as blade servers and virtualization.

After you have the equipment, you integrate it into high-density modular compute racks, virtualize servers and storage, put in consolidated power supply, choose from a range of modern cooling solutions, and, finally, run, monitor, and manage the data center dynamics using sensors that feed real-time compute, power, and cooling data into modern single-view management software that dynamically allocates resources.

Over the next five years, the proliferation of 10 gigabit Ethernet will enable a migration of IT to the new data center technology and better delivery of applications. Also, we should see a complete move to virtualization at the server, as well as the router, the storage network, and the switches—basically throughout all network components. In that process, new issues will arise, including how to ensure security and compliance. An overview of an energy-efficiency strategy for data center facilities is shown in Figure 2.2.

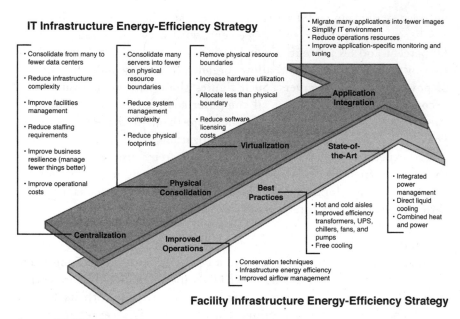

Source: IBM Big Green Team

Figure 2.2   An energy-efficiency strategy for facility infrastructures

Software/Applications/Process Workload– Often-Overlooked Areas for Green IT

Our discussion on green IT has focused on IT equipment and facilities requirements. This includes the significant energy-efficiency topics such as virtualization to improve server efficiency, or to power off unused equipment. However, the software that uses the IT equipment can also be a significant opportunity for saving energy. Applications require CPU cycles to execute the millions of instructions needed to complete transactions and units of work. Storage devices for source code, executables, and the information used and produced as the applications execute all consume energy and facilities space, and produce e-waste. Although it might not be immediately obvious, you can take actions to make your applications greener, reducing both the energy and resources required to keep your business running.

Here are some ways to start:

- Replace paper forms with e-forms in business processes.
- Increase automation to achieve more with less environmental impact.
- Model and then automate processes and workflows to gain end-to-end process visibility.
- Take advantage of SOA to dynamically allocate and optimize workloads across servers and applications.
- Leverage charge-back accounting for services consumed.
- Address environmental regulatory requirements.

There are two important areas for optimizing workloads. First, the business workload is defined by the business process activities your organization performs daily. This business workload is represented by the multiple business processes that utilize people and consume energy for each process execution. Understanding your business processes as well as the location of critical and expensive steps in their sequencing enables you to redesign and automate your processes or activities with a focus on reducing energy consumption. The second focus of workload optimization is the applications and systems that support the business processes. The hundreds or thousands of software applications that run every day to support your business or organization indirectly have a carbon footprint associated with them. Applications utilize resources and, therefore, drive energy consumption and CO_2 emissions. For additional details on how software and business process can contribute to green IT, use this URL: http://www.306.ibm.com/software/solutions/green/.

Green IT Is More Than Data Centers— Your Laptop Is Included

Although servers and data centers are the focus of this book, it is important to remember that green IT also includes your laptop. When traveling with a laptop, we always need to be concerned about battery life. So, we happily configure the power management functions to power off the screen after 15 minutes and let the laptop go to "sleep" mode after 30 minutes of inactivity. Our motivation is to conserve the battery when we're not plugged in. However, use of sleep mode is a good green computing practice. Universities, often on the forefront of concern for the environment, frequently have a green computing section on their Web sites. (Just Google "green computing at universities," and you'll see the hits.) The following sections include some relevant information on green computing for desktop PCs and laptops at the University of Colorado (CU) taken from their Web site: http://ecenter.colorado.edu/energy/projects/green_computing.html. This CU Web site is periodically updated, so the following information is a "snapshot in time." This type of Web site provides a good lead-in to the importance of collaboration—in this case, collaboration among the university's IT groups, students, faculty, and so on. Collaboration for green IT is discussed Chapter 3, "Collaboration Is Key for Green IT." CU also has an IT site for computer efficiency: http://www.colorado.edu/its/energy/.

The growing use of computers on campus has caused a dramatic increase in energy consumption, putting negative pressure on CU's budget and the environment. Each year, more and more computers are purchased and put to use. Over the last fifteen years, computers have transformed the academic and administrative landscape at the University of Colorado. In 2008, there were more than 18,000 computers on campus. Personal computer (PC) operation alone might directly account for nearly $550,000 per year in University energy costs. Computers generate heat and require additional cooling, which adds to energy costs. Thus, when the cooling requirement is added, the overall energy cost of PCs at CU is more likely approximately $700,000 per year. But it's not just the number of computers that is driving energy consumption upward: The way we use computers also adds to the increasing energy burden. Research reveals that most personal desktop computers are not used most of the time they are running, and many PCs nationwide are needlessly left on continuously. Every time we leave on computers or lights, we waste electricity. As we must constantly remind ourselves, these fuels emit pollutants, sulfur, and carbon dioxide into the air. These emissions can cause respiratory disease, smog, acid rain, and global climate change.

Here's another challenge: Meeting computer cooling needs in summer (and winter) often compromises the efficient use of building cooling and heating systems by requiring colder fan discharge temperatures. In the summer, these temperatures might satisfy computer lab cooling needs while overcooling other spaces. Given CU's commitment to energy conservation and the environmental stewardship, the University must address the issue of responsible computer use. By adopting conserving practices, the University can save $300,000 to $400,000 annually.

How Much Energy Does Your Laptop Computer System Use?

A typical desktop PC system is composed of the computer itself (the CPU or the "box"), a monitor, and printer. Your CPU might require approximately 100 watts of electrical power. Add 50 watts to 150 watts for a 15–17-inch monitor, proportionately more for larger monitors. The power requirements of conventional laser printers can be as high as 100 watts or more when printing, though much less when idling in a sleep mode. Ink-jet printers use as little as 12 watts while printing and 5 watts while idling.

How a user operates the computer also factors into energy costs. First, let's take the worst-case scenario: continuous operation. Assuming you operate a 200-watt PC system day and night every day, direct annual electrical costs would be more than $125 (at $0.075/KWH). In contrast, if you operate your system only during normal business hours, say 40 hours per week, the direct annual energy cost will be about $30— plus, of course, the cost of providing additional cooling.

Considering the tremendous benefits of computer use, neither of the preceding cost figures might seem like much, but think of what happens when these costs are multiplied by the many thousands of computers in use at, say, CU. The energy waste dollars add up quickly.

Energy-Efficient Desktop and Laptop Computing

Following are some tested suggestions for you to reduce your computer energy consumption by 80 percent or more, while still retaining most or all productivity and other benefits of your computer system, including network connectivity.

Screen Savers Save No Energy

If screen-saver images appear on your monitor for more than five minutes, you are wasting energy! Screen-saver programs might save the phosphors in your monitor screen, but this is not actually a concern with newer monitors, especially LCD screens. And screen savers do not save any energy. A screen saver that displays moving images causes your monitor to consume as much electricity as it does when in active use.

These screen-saver programs also involve system interaction with your CPU that results in additional energy consumption. A blank screen saver is slightly better, but even that reduces monitor energy consumption by only a few percent.

Enable Power Management Features

Thanks to the U.S. Environment Protection Agency (EPA), personal computer systems purchased today can be easy on energy. You can program these Energy Star computers and monitors to power-down automatically to a low power state when they are not being used. You can achieve these efficiency gains without any sacrifice in computing performance.

The EPA estimates that providing all computers in the United States with sleep mode reduces their energy use by 60 percent to 70 percent—and ultimately saves enough electricity each year to power Vermont, New Hampshire, and Maine; cut electric bills by $2 billion; and reduce carbon-dioxide emissions by the equivalent of five million cars.

How can we achieve such impressive savings? Follow these simple steps to access computer and monitor power management features for Macintosh and Windows®.

Macintosh: From any application, select the Apple menu. Select System Preferences, (OS X) or Control Panels (OS 9) and then click Energy Saver.

Windows: Point your cursor at the desktop background and right-click. From the pop-up menu, choose Properties. Go to the Screen Saver page; in the lower-right corner near the ENERGY STAR® logo, click the Settings button. This brings up another dialog box from which you choose power management settings.

The University of Colorado gives recommended settings of 20 minutes for monitor sleep and 30 minutes for system sleep. Remember that to save energy with your monitor's built-in power management system, your monitor must go to sleep (shut itself down). As a comparison, IBM recommends that employees use a setting of 15 minutes of inactivity to power-off the monitor and 30 minutes of inactivity for system sleep mode.

"When Not in Use, Turn Off the Juice"

This is the most basic energy conservation strategy for any type of equipment. Consider the following:

- Turn off your computer and peripherals when they are not in use.

- Don't run computers continuously unless they are in use continuously.

- Always turn off your computer at night and on weekends.

- Look for ways to reduce the amount of time your computer is on without adversely affecting your productivity.

Turning your equipment on and off will not harm it.

You Can Turn Off Your Computer!

The common misconception that a computer's life is shortened by turning it on and off has led some to leave their computers on all the time. Others are reluctant to switch their computers on and off a couple times during their workday, despite using this equipment for only a fraction of that time. Desktop computers are designed to protect the internal circuitry from power damage through on and off switching. Turning PC equipment off at night or on and off a few times a day will not appreciably affect its useful life. Electronic equipment life is a function of operating hours and heat; both these factors are reduced when equipment is switched off. Modern hard drives are designed and tested to operate reliably for thousands of on and off cycles.

Thus, you *can* turn off your computer (and monitor and printer)! The inconvenience of waiting a minute or two for a computer to reboot or a peripheral to come online might be trivial compared to the energy savings achieved by keeping computer equipment off when it's not in use.

Some Specific Suggestions

Unless you require immediate access to e-mail or other Internet services, break the habit of turning on all your computer equipment as soon as you enter the office each day. If practical, informally group your computer activities and try to do them once or twice a day, leaving the computer off at other times.

- Avoid using the switch on a power strip to turn on all your equipment.

- If you use a laser printer, don't turn on your printer until you are ready to print.

- Turn off your entire computer system (CPU, monitor, and printer), or at least your monitor and printer, when you go to lunch or will be out of the office for a meeting or an errand.
- As for computer servers that must be on to serve network functions, explore ways to turn them off at night.
- If monitors are not needed for servers to operate, keep server monitors off. If you need server monitors during the day, at least turn them off at night and on weekends.

Although the preceding energy-saving suggestions are appropriate for many campus PC users, some of the suggestions might be inappropriate for certain computer applications or work situations. When in doubt, discuss possible energy conservation measures with your colleagues, supervisor, or computer lab director to determine which steps you can take without harming productivity. An energy conservation program will not work without your help. Be an energy educator and gently remind your coworkers and colleagues to save energy by changing their computer habits.

Other Considerations for Going Green on the Client Side

Much ongoing green technology coverage and debate focuses on energy efficiency and environmental responsibility in the data center. But there's plenty that can be done on the client side at customer sites, too. Many best practices can improve a customer's green profile on the desktop. Among the topics to consider are the role of power management software utilities, evolving power supply design and battery considerations, display technologies, and the latest multicore microprocessors. Of course, you can use handy sources of information for green best practices and certification information, such as the Federal Energy Star program and Electronic Product Environmental Assessment Tool (EPEAT). The motivation to go green also provides additional momentum for moving to thin client and desktop virtualization options.

Data Center Energy-Efficiency Considerations

As discussed previously, both IT equipment and cooling consume most of the power in a data center. As server power consumption has increased, so has heat dissipation in the data center, requiring increases in cooling capacity. Most IT spokesmen believe that to sustain greening, there will be increasing adoption of virtualization, consolidation, automation, and standardization. Virtualization is universally accepted as a key to necessary cost-savings, despite the complex data center environment. Companies with server or storage virtualization deployments face low data center spending. Also, standardizing on a single layer of infrastructure software that supports all major storage and server hardware platforms can protect information and applications, enhance data center service levels, improve storage and server utilization, and drive down operational costs.

Figure 2.3 gives an overview of all the data center energy-efficiency considerations for green IT.

Data Center Talking Points

Integrated Infrastructure

- Industry-leading integration of IT equipment and building management systems (BMS) to automatically optimize to varying IT equipment configurations and building loads
- Provides for future integration with IBM Systems Management software products and allows development of additional energy-efficiency software programming, data mining, and analysis
- Backup and recovery offering
- Virtualization offerings
- 3D billing with energy rider

Electrical

- Utility capacity, reliability, and robustness (reliability)
- Dual feeds to distribution panels for IT loads
- Monitoring of branch circuits at PDU/RDC level
- ARC flash assessment
- 6, 10, 15 mwh 3 phases (modularity, flexibility)
- High density zones
- 480V equipment (flexibility, energy)
- Catcher bus maintenance (reliability) (design TBD)
- High-efficiency static double-conversion UPS (energy)
- Timestamps—faults are recorded at same time/waveform capture (reliability)
- PLC building control system (efficiency/reliability)
- Double-ended substations (reliability)
- Note: No mention of amount of space or power density (intentional)

Architectural

- Experiential customer interface (customer facing)
- State-of-the-art building technology
- LEED silver or gold
- Viewing area/visitor center displays
- Base build (not a retrofit)
- Reflective roof (energy)

Mechanical

- Variable speed CRAC and chillers (energy)
- Removal of CRAC filters after start-up (energy)
- Elevated temperature and humidity criteria (energy)
- Rainwater harvesting and reuse (green)
- Provisions for direct water-cooled equipment (flexibility)
- VESDA air sampling fire detection system (no false alarms)
- Flex-head sprinkler assemblies (flexibility)
- Chilled water storage +1m gal condenser water (resiliency)
- Water-side economizing
- Under floor static air pressure controls (resiliency)
- 360 degree design for chilled water allows for zone maintenance

Source: IBM Big Green Team

Figure 2.3   Data center energy-efficiency considerations

You Can't Manage What You Can't Measure

One of the first steps needed in any IT project is to measure the current status of energy use. That baseline will be a guideline as to the improvements to be made. A major problem in this area is that buildings have been typically equipped with one electric meter for the entire building. If the building is almost all data center, the measurement problem is not so bad. However, if the data center is only a small portion of the building, measurement of the current energy use in your data center is a significant first issue you need to consider.

To assist in this measuring task, server manufacturers are starting to provide devices in the server itself that can be monitored. For example, IBM has recently made significant enhancements to a tool for measuring and managing energy use in servers and other IT equipment. The tool is IBM Active Energy Manager™ (AEM), an extension of the IBM Director already used by many companies. AEM has hooks to Tivoli® for energy management. It is a significant step forward in energy management for looking at the actual energy use of each server. With this type of tool, you can measure energy-saving results when, for example, you virtualize ten stand-alone Windows servers onto a big server using PowerVM or a similar virtualization system. You can also measure the efficiency advantages of using the steps toward grid computing, such as Partition Mobility. Additional details on the AEM tool for IT energy measurement and management are in Appendix A, "Green IT Checklist and Recommendations." The Web site for the latest information on the Active Energy Manager tool is http://www-03.ibm.com/systems/management/director/extensions/actengmrg.html.

Tools for IT Energy Measurement, Monitoring, and Management

This AEM tool and similar tools provide solutions to help companies monitor energy consumption to allow better utilization of available energy resources. The application software enables customers to trend actual energy consumption and corresponding thermal loading of IT systems running in their environment with their applications. Such monitoring helps companies do the following:

- Allocate less power and cooling infrastructure to servers.
- Lower power usage on select servers.
- Plan for the future by viewing trends of power usage over time.
- Determine power usage for all components of a rack.

To better understand energy usage across your data center:

- Identify energy usage.
- Measure cooling costs accurately.
- Monitor IT costs across components.
- Manage by department and user.

AEM software allows IT managers to control—even set caps on—their energy use for servers, storage, and networking, as well as the air conditioning and power management systems that keep the data center running. The software supports monitoring of devices that are connected to select "smart" power strips used to provide power to multiple devices, including IBM and non-IBM servers and storage systems, as well as energy-monitoring support using select wireless devices that might extend beyond traditional data center walls.

Another server manufacturer providing a tool for measuring and managing energy use in servers and other IT equipment is HP's Insight Control. Insight Control allows management of HP ProLiant and BladeSystem infrastructure systems. Management functions include power measurement and power capping. The HP Insight Control and IBM AEM software can also be used with equipment from facility management providers. For example, the software can retrieve temperature and power information from companies such as SynapSense Corporation's wireless sensors, which can be located virtually anywhere in the data center. The software can also receive alerts and events related to power and cooling equipment through interaction with equipment from a wide variety of cooling vendors and building management system providers. The alerts can notify IT administrators about issues with facilities equipment, such as overheating, low battery power on uninterruptible power supply batteries, or other conditions.

Other Ways to Save Energy in the Data Center

As mentioned previously, Gartner Inc. predicts that the cost of supplying energy to a server over its three-year lifetime will soon exceed the server's acquisition cost. At a Gartner Data Center Conference in 2008, these energy-efficient methods were included in a larger list that included the typical technologies such as virtualization:

- **Consider blade servers:** As mentioned previously in this chapter, many IT vendors (such as HP) have evangelized the virtues of blades and virtualizations. In general, organizations should consolidate servers, storage, and networks wherever possible. They should replace rack-mounted servers with blade servers because of shared resources such as power, fans, networking, and storage. Blades require between 10 percent and 25 percent less power and cooling for the same computing capacity. Organizations should also consolidate storage by using tiered storage for different workloads.

- **Use high-efficiency IT equipment power supplies:** A lot of manufacturers are starting to manufacture equipment that can get better than 80-percent efficiency. IT organizations that improve the energy efficiency of their power supply units can raise the efficiency of their entire energy delivery infrastructure. This could lower a data center's power and cooling needs by 15 percent.

- **Use a high-efficiency Uninterruptible Power Supply (UPS):** UPS efficiency can range from 80 percent to 95 percent. If you were only 80-percent efficient, maybe with an older UPS system, and you replace that with a newer UPS system that's getting 95-percent efficiency, there's tremendous gain to be had. You might want to consider replacement if you run a system that was built in the '80s or '90s. Efficiency losses in a data center's UPS represent about 5 percent to 12 percent of all the energy consumed in data centers. Manufacturer specifications can differ widely from measured results because of differences in loading conditions and test procedures. There might also be differences between efficiencies measured under reference conditions and under in-use conditions in data centers. Newer measuring technologies are now being developed to estimate how much energy you can be save by improving UPS efficiency, developing standardized testing protocols, and proposing efficiency metrics for use by the marketplace in comparing units for purchase.

- **Adopt power distribution at 208 volts or 230 volts for servers:**
  Using high-voltage power cords such as 208 volts or 230 volts instead of standard 120-volt power distribution can push server power efficiency from 82 percent to 84 percent or 85 percent. All you have to do is make sure, when deploying your servers and deploying your power distribution into your racks, to use the high-voltage power distribution capability and the capability the servers actually have. Keep the voltage as high as possible while feeding to the server.

Resources to Get the Latest Information on Green IT

In the age of the Internet. many Web sites provide the latest information on green IT. The following list of some of the author's favorites provides a segue to Chapter 3 on the need for collaboration for green IT. Chapter 3 provides additional information on the role of several of the organizations given in the list (for example, The Green Grid, ASHRAE, The Uptime Institute, and so on):

- **The Green Grid—Industry Group Focused on Data Center Energy Efficiency**

  http://www.thegreengrid.org/home

  The Green Grid, founded in 2007, has a mission to further data center energy-efficiency initiatives. The Green Grid consists of IT equipment and component manufacturers, manufacturers of facility support equipment, and data center operators and designers.

- **ASHRAE—American Society of Heating, Refrigerating, and Air Conditioning Engineers**

  http://www.ashrae.org/

  The ASHRAE engineering society was established in 1894 and has always been involved in the design of efficient plumbing to heat and cool buildings and data centers. It is one of the "Grand-Daddy" engineering groups involved in energy efficiency for data centers. The group publishes a set of documents and manuals that provide cooling strategies for data centers. My association with ASHRAE goes back to the mid-seventies, when I regularly attended ASHRAE conferences and also presented papers on energy conservation during the energy crisis of the late 1970s.

- **The Uptime Institute—Organization of Data Center Operators**

  http://uptimeinstitute.org/

  The Uptime Institute, mentioned previously in this book, is a consortium of data center operators that focuses on tools and strategies to maintain the serviceability and reliability of data centers. It sets various data center performance levels through the tier system, which dictates equipment redundancy and data center environment criteria to maintain a specified level of system availability. Uptime has been adding energy optimization as another critical criterion for data center operation and reliability and one that needs to be factored in when considering data center reliability and availability.

- **EPA/DOE—Environmental Protection Agency/Department of Energy**

  http://www.energy.gov/

  Department of Energy (DOE) laboratories such as Lawrence Berkeley National Labs and Pacific Northwest National Labs are cooperating in development of research and best practices for green IT. Government agencies like the Environmental Protection Agency (EPA) are leading the effort to standardize metrics to measure energy consumption. Organizations are taking on the responsibilities that they can deliver on—not worrying about turf.

- **EU Code of Conduct—European Union Code of Conduct**

  http://re.jrc.ec.europa.eu/energyefficiency/html/standby_initiative_data%20centers.htm

  The European Code of Conduct for data centers was published in 2008 ahead of the Energy Star Rating for Data Centers and is a great piece of work to identify and quantify improvements to a data center.

- **AFCOM—Association for Computer Operations Management**

  http://www.afcom.com/

  AFCOM provides education and resources for data center managers. It devotes a portion of its efforts to assisting data center managers to identify energy-efficiency activities.

- **Alliance to Save Energy**

  http://www.ase.org/

  The Alliance to Save Energy (ASE) promotes energy efficiency world-wide. It was founded in 1977 and consists of members from both government and industry. The ASE stresses that energy efficiency is the quickest, cheapest, and cleanest way to extend our world's energy supplies.

- **Energy Utilities—Web Site for PG&E Energy Savings and Rebates**

  http://www.pge.com/mybusiness/energysavingsrebates/

  This energy utility in California has many program areas related to energy saving, including the following:

  - Energy Analyzers & Audits
  - Rebates and Incentives
  - Solar Energy
  - Demand Response Programs
  - Self-Generation Incentive Program

- **Software and Green IT**

  http://www-306.ibm.com/software/solutions/green/

  Applications require CPU cycles to execute the millions of instructions required to complete transactions and units of work. Storage devices for source code, executables, and the information used and produced as the applications execute all consume energy and facilities space. They also produce e-waste. Although it might not be immediately obvious, you can take actions to make your applications greener, reducing both the energy and resources required to keep your business running.

- **Grove Associates Blog on Green IT**

  http://www.grovesgreenit.typepad.com/

  Blogs on green IT are popular. Grove Associates has an informative blog. Major green-related categories discussed in the daily blogs include the following:

  - Corporate data center energy efficiency
  - Corporate sustainability
  - Green data centers

Chapter Summary and Conclusions

You can reach the following conclusions from the discussion on green IT:

- The huge expenditure of electrical power on IT has reached the point where it has attracted both government and environmental attention.
- The projection for additional IT applications will only exacerbate the situation if current inadequate and wasteful technology trends continue unchanged.
- Virtualization is the most-promising technology, addressing both the issues of IT resource utilization and facilities space, power, and cooling utilization.
- Solutions and processes address the situation from end to end: at the server end through power management features, and at the data center end through integrated IT facilities modular solutions.

These conclusions should excite anyone in the IT industry, as the ways to save energy in IT are pervasive enough that everyone can have a part in improving a company's IT energy efficiency.

3

Collaboration Is Key for Green IT

"The recent focus on energy efficient computing has forced tech giants in Silicon Valley to collaborate more than ever before."

—Consulting Firm Grove Associates, October 2007

To meet the challenge for effective green IT, collaboration is a must. Green data center technology covers a broad spectrum, from efficient cooling towers and variable speed blowers to the use of energy-efficient IT systems, such as virtual servers, blade centers, and virtual data storage. Significant contributors to the collaboration team include IT technology vendors, data center design businesses, infrastructure technology providers, energy utilities, and governments. This chapter includes descriptions on how to help make this collaboration happen. A key starting point is to have an executive champion for implementing a green data center. Chapter 5, "The Magic of 'Incentive'—The Role of Electric Utilities," covers in detail this position on energy utilities and organization. Energy utilities have additional interest in implementing green IT because they can use their experience to help establish rate-case incentives on green computing technology for their customers.

In the previous chapter, the last section ("Resources to Get the Latest Information on Green IT") included some of the many groups that are involved in green IT. The following sections give additional information on how many of these groups are collaborating.

IT Technology Vendors

There is evidence that the continued focus on energy-efficient computing has forced tech giants in Silicon Valley and other areas to collaborate more than ever before. This collaboration should result in a better range of energy-efficient products (hardware and software), as well as faster product turnaround. Companies are collaborating by discussing what works and what doesn't work, instead of everybody having to reinvent the wheel individually.

For example, competitors like HP, IBM, and Sun are sitting at the same table to work out green standards with The Green Grid. Department of Energy (DOE) laboratories such as Lawrence Berkeley National Labs and Pacific Northwest National Labs are cooperating in development of research and best practices for green IT. Government agencies like the Environmental Protection Agency (EPA) are leading the effort to standardize metrics to measure energy consumption. Organizations are taking on the responsibilities that they can deliver on—not worrying about turf.

Data Center Design and Build Businesses

Several industry groups focus on data center energy efficiency. The Green Grid is the most recently formed group, founded in 2007. Its primary mission is to further data center energy-efficiency initiatives. The Green Grid is composed of IT equipment and component (power supplies, microprocessors, and such) manufacturers, manufacturers of facility support equipment (CRACs, UPS, rack level cooling devices, and others), and data center operators and designers. The group seeks to drive the development of metrics that provide a meaningful measure of data center energy utilization and performance, drive the development of standard protocols to facilitate collection, sharing, and reporting of power and thermal data from IT and facilities equipment, and design and operating strategies that promote optimal data center energy use. The Green Grid has published a collection of white papers on data center metrics and data management. See http://www.thegreengrid.org/home for additional information on The Green Grid.

Also, the American Society of Heating, Refrigerating, and Air Conditioning Engineers (ASHRAE) has had a data center subcommittee in operation for many years. The group publishes a set of documents and manuals that provide data centers with cooling strategies that optimize cooling delivery, data center temperature, and humidity profiles, and maximize the cooling delivered per unit of energy applied. Please see http://www.ashrae.org/ for additional information on ASHRAE.

The Uptime Institute consortium of data center operators focuses on tools and strategies to maintain the serviceability and reliability of data centers. The Institute sets various data center performance levels through the tier system, which dictates equipment redundancy and data center environment criteria to maintain a specified level of system availability. Uptime has been adding energy optimization, as well as other critical criteria for data center operation and reliability, which needs to be factored in when considering data center reliability and availability. Please see http://uptimeinstitute.org/ for additional information on the Uptime Institute.

Another group involved in data center and energy-efficiency activities is the Association for Computer Operations Management (AFCOM), which provides education and resources for data center managers. It devotes a portion of its efforts to assisting data center managers to identify energy-efficiency activities. Please see http://www.afcom.com/ for additional information on AFCOM.

Many other groups are associated with energy-efficiency activities. One active group is the Alliance to Save Energy (ASE). The ASE mission: "The Alliance to Save Energy promotes energy efficiency worldwide to achieve a healthier economy, a cleaner environment, and greater energy security. Energy efficiency is the quickest, cheapest, cleanest way to extend our world's energy supplies." See http://www.ase.org/ for additional information on ASE. In addition to the groups discussed previously in this section, ASE collaborates with the following organizations:

- **ITherm:** An international conference for scientific and engineering exploration of thermal, thermo mechanical, and emerging technology issues associated with electronic devices, packages, and systems (www.itherm.com).

- **Efficient Power Supplies:** A Web site created by EPRI Solutions, Inc., and Ecos Consulting to encourage a global discussion of energy-efficient power supplies (www.efficientpowersupplies.org).

- **Consortium for Energy Efficient Thermal Management:** A collaboration of Georgia Institute of Technology and the University of Maryland to conduct "research on thermal and energy management of electronics and telecommunications infrastructure" (http://www.me.gatech.edu/CEETHERM/).

- **7x24 Exchange:** An association facilitating the exchange of information for "...those who design, build, use, and maintain mission-critical enterprise information infrastructures....7x24 Exchange's goal is to improve the end-to-end reliability by promoting dialogue among these groups" (http://www.7x24exchange.org/index.html).

Collaboration of Building Energy Management and IT Energy Management

Beyond the familiar challenge of establishing energy-efficient data centers lies a huge opportunity scarcely tapped by IT: the green possibilities of the building itself. Growth is driving global trends in resource depletion, air and water pollution, energy consumption, and climate change. A third of U.S. energy consumption comes from commercial buildings. Businesses are automating those buildings to reduce costs and emissions. Will IT lead, or follow, the coming change? IT can have a green impact on a company's energy and emissions: Start with the data center; manage desktop energy use; and enable mobility.

IT departments operate in an environment surrounded by sophisticated data acquisition, analyses, and networking systems of which IT itself is largely unaware. Building automation systems (BAS) are the brains of commercial and industrial buildings that control their own environments. The benefits of building automation—energy savings, improved occupant comfort, added security and safety, and reduced maintenance costs—are all at the top of the list for conservation-minded building owners.

Building automation systems, such as lighting and temperature controls, are common in larger facilities. Energy management systems (EMS) go further, centralizing the control of lighting, heating, ventilating, and air conditioning with the goal of reducing the energy those systems consume. Almost every campus (corporate, medical, or academic) has an EMS, as do 40 percent of the Fortune 100. Manufacturers have adopted automation for efficiency, and those industrial systems are now being leveraged to reduce energy consumption.

Groups of forward-looking vendors have begun to think about how the EMS and IT worlds should converge. The concepts center around removing the long-standing wall between building networks and IT (tenant) networks. Mixed into this dialogue are other low-profile systems common in most buildings, such as security, air quality, and life safety. Cisco has approached the building controls industry with the notion that information is the "fourth utility" after electricity, gas, and water. Cisco has proposed moving EMS to the IP network, not only for efficiency, but also for the information synergies involved. Business information has a strategic and tactical value, and information about the building's performance is no different.

Protocols, however, are among the stumbling blocks. Building systems operate on largely special-purpose open systems (such as BACnet or LonWorks), and a few proprietary systems remain popular. Today, both types of systems can talk to the IP network through gateways. Within the last few years, the building-control industry has discovered XML. Middleware applications gather information and normalize it for consumption by ERP, accounting, and other enterprise applications.

Energy Utilities

This topic is covered in more detail in Chapter 5 (and specific case studies are analyzed in Chapter 9, "Green IT Case Studies for Energy Utilities"). Electric utilities provide interesting case studies because they can provide incentives for their customers to move to green IT. For example, the Pacific Gas and Electric Co. (PG&E) has worked with several IT vendors to consolidate its servers, and the company has developed new ways to measure and reduce heat in data centers. They announced this initiative in 2007 at a conference in New York City, where companies such as American Power Conversion Corp. (APC), Eaton Corp., General Electric Consumer & Industrial, IBM, and others gathered to discuss green computing and power-saving initiatives.

Before embarking on its server consolidation efforts, PG&E teamed with IBM Research to develop a tool to measure the three-dimensional temperature distributions in its data centers. IBM used its new Mobile Measurement Technology (MMT) to survey the relevant physical parameters of PG&E data centers and visualize (via 3-D images) hot spots, air leakage, and other inefficiencies. The data was then used to build customized thermal and energy models to help mitigate hot spots and rectify imbalances within the data center.

PG&E was the first company to offer incentives for power-saving technologies, encouraging customers to get rid of underutilized computing and data storage equipment through virtualization. In addition, the company recently spearheaded a coalition of utilities to discuss and coordinate energy-efficiency programs for the high-tech sector, focusing on data centers.

The online business tools offered by Pacific Gas and Electric Company provide companies with help to make their data centers more efficient. The tools include the following:

- Business Tools Features
- Energy Usage
- Billing History
- Rate Comparison Tools
- Energy Outage and Restoration Status
- Billing Details
- Account Aggregation

Check with your electric utility on energy audits. Some utilities such as PG&E offer free energy audits. Here's the PG&E Web site on the free audit: http://www.pge.com/mybusiness/energysavingsrebates/analyzer/.

Of course, after your free audit, you might be eligible for rebates for your green IT initiatives. For an example, see http://www.pge.com/mybusiness/energysavingsrebates/rebatesincentives/.

Governments

This topic was mentioned at the end of Chapter 2, "The Basics of Green IT," and is covered in more detail in Chapter 4, "The Government's Role—Regulation and EPA Activity." With all the recent publicity on the growth of energy use by Enterprise Level IT equipment, the 2008 quantity of energy use—about 2 percent of 2008 global energy use; and the expected double-digit increases in data center energy growth for the next five years (Koomey 2007, 2008)—various governments around the world are taking action to encourage data center operators to improve their energy performance of their data centers. If we look at all IT energy use (including the energy used for all our laptops), the percent of global energy use is approaching 10 percent.

Current government initiatives include the following:

- **US EPA ENERGY STAR data center rating system:** As mentioned previously, US EPA has an ENERGY STAR building program. It is currently working on a data center rating system. It released a draft document for comments, for which companies provided input by 2/22/08. Its initial proposal appears to be focused on a variation of the PUE. Comments have been made on the rating system proposal, suggesting that the rating system consider the percent of equipment that utilizes virtualization technology and power management and measuring technology (like AEM), as well as facilities with thermal and space planning and regular review of thermal profiling (for example, via MMT, tile flow, and so on). Beginning in March 2008, the EPA began soliciting data centers to test the rating system. IBM intends to have one or two data centers participate in the testing.

- **DOE Save Energy Now Data Center initiative:** Also, as mentioned previously, the DOE is partnering with the Lawrence Berkeley National Lab to develop a model that characterizes the power use and thermal profile of the data center. The software tool will collect specific energy-use data for the data center, calculate the DCIE metric, create estimated energy-use breakouts by system, and prepare a list of applicable energy-saving actions. Concurrently, it is preparing a data center energy assessment program, based on the LBNL best practices checklists, which can be used by energy service providers to assess data center energy use and recommend specific energy-savings actions.

- **EU Code of Conduct for data centers:** The European Code of Conduct for data centers was published in 2008. The EU CoC is an excellent publication to help improve energy efficiency in data centers. Thus, the EU CoC was published before the EPA's ratings for data centers.

- **Other geographies:** Australia is beginning to talk about initiating a data center energy-efficiency effort and has contacted IBM representatives about participating in such a program.

Overall, industry information on system power demands, utilization, and opportunities for energy-efficiency improvements in data centers have made it clear that there are significant worldwide opportunities to reduce energy usage in data centers. In turn, they are promoting energy-efficiency programs to encourage public and private entities to capture those opportunities.

Collaboration Within Your Own Company

As discussed previously, green IT collaboration includes governments, IT vendors, electric utilities, and many other groups. However, collaboration is also needed among the different departments in your company. The Uptime Institute recommends that every data center look at the following five issues for both short- and long-term energy savings:

- Server consolidation, configuration, virtualization
- Enabling "power-save" features on servers
- Turning off "dead" servers (no longer in use but running)
- Pruning "bloatware" (the application efficiency issue)
- Improving the site infrastructure energy-efficiency ratio

Typically, data centers can improve energy savings by 25 percent to 50 percent over a two-year period just by tackling each of these challenges in a cross-discipline way. The Institute has developed a multifunctional team methodology known as Integrated Critical Environment (ICE) to provide both the business and technical rigor required. A tried-and-true method not on the preceding list is to send an e-mail to all users announcing server shutdown for maintenance for a 24-hour period. Active server users rebel instantly with reasons why their servers can't be shut down. If no angry responses result, shut them off indefinitely and then disconnect the servers. This frees up space, energy, and manpower.

In reexamining, retrofitting, and redesigning data centers, mitigating business risks are as important as energy savings. Such considerations are at the nerve center of every company, large or small. Active participation, support, and collaboration are required from five key individuals across the organization: representatives from the offices of the CFO, CIO, real estate and facilities, data center IT, and facilities managers, and the technical teams who deal with applications and IT solutions for your company.

Universities Collaborate

Universities are in a unique position to collaborate on green IT. The case study on Columbia University in Chapter 10, "Green IT Case Studies for Universities and a Large Company," gives an excellent example on how Columbia is collaborating on green IT—within the university, with other universities, with New York State organizations, and with New York City. Columbia's Business School's Green Club has already indicated its enthusiasm to collaborate in the green IT exercise. This can help lay the foundation for Columbia's plans to submit the green data center results to Educause, NYSERNet, NYSgrid, the Center for IT Leadership, the Ivy Plus consortium, and the Common Solutions Group as a real-world case study. Columbia University anticipates good attendance at the Open House Workshop at the conclusion of the project. The vice president and chief information officer, the assistant vice president for Environmental Stewardship, and the E-Science Task Force have all endorsed this proposal. The opportunity to rigorously measure recommended best practices and technological innovations in a real-world environment, validated by the scrutiny incorporated from the beginning via the three potential user groups, can have a far-reaching impact within and beyond Columbia. The Columbia green IT collaboration also includes New York City and Mayor Michael Bloomberg's ten-year plan for New York City on reducing carbon emissions by 30 percent based on 2007 levels. Columbia University has committed to that 30 percent reduction even in the face of greatly increased growth in High Performance Computing (HPC) requirements fueled by the worldwide research community.

In the past several years, HPC has been growing at every research university, government research laboratory, and high-tech industry in New York State, nationally and internationally. HPC is a cornerstone of scientific research disciplines, many of which had previously used little or no computing resources. Researchers are now performing simulations, analyzing experimental data from sources such as the Large Hadron Collider at CERN, genetic sequencers, scanning-tunneling electron microscopes, econometric and population data, and so on. These applications have led to an explosion of computing clusters now being deployed throughout Columbia, as well as in peer research institutions and New York State's biotechnology, nanotechnology, financial, and other industries; this increase frequently requires construction of new server rooms, putting pressure on space in existing data centers and leading to increased demand for energy. Without this research, New York State cannot compete in an increasingly high-tech, computationally intensive world.

The Green Grid Collaboration Agreements

The Green Grid (mentioned at the beginning of this chapter and at the end of Chapter 2) represents an excellent example of organizations collaborating for energy efficiency. The Green Grid is a global consortium dedicated to advancing energy efficiency in data centers and business computing ecosystems. In 2008, The Green Grid announced Memorandums of Understanding (MOUs) with the U.S. Environmental Protection Agency (EPA) and the Storage Networking Industry Association (SNIA). The Green Grid's agreement with the EPA will first promote energy efficiency in EPA computer facilities and then broadly share results to impact change within both other governmental agencies and the private sector. The alliance with SNIA, formally announced by SNIA in mid-2008, is designed to further networked storage best practices for energy efficiency.

The Green Grid's MOU with the EPA and SNIA highlight the organization's continuing efforts and progress in working with government agencies and key industry players to define and promote the adoption of standards, processes, measurements, and technologies for energy efficiency in the data center.

The Green Grid's collaboration with the EPA will accelerate the adoption of best practices for energy efficiency in existing computer and server rooms throughout the EPA. As an initial step, The Green Grid and the EPA will identify an existing small EPA computer or server room as a target for an energy-efficiency showcase and execute a public project demonstrating the feasibility, approach, and benefits of optimization. The results, best practices, and real-world takeaways from this project will be shared with other governmental agencies, industry stakeholders, and the private sector. As announced by The Green Grid, this "…agreement between the EPA and The Green Grid will build further collaboration between the private and public sectors, and to set an example by improving energy efficiency in federal government computer facilities. The Green Grid will play a key role in this project by providing a team of technical experts who will perform the assessment and direct strategies and techniques for maximizing energy efficiency."

SNIA also announced a formal alliance with The Green Grid. The Green Grid will work with SNIA and its Green Storage Initiative to develop and promote standards, measurement methods, processes, and technologies to improve data center energy efficiencies. SNIA will use its expertise in networked storage and membership (more than 400 member companies and 7,000 individual members) to work with The Green Grid on best storage practices for achieving more-efficient storage infrastructures, including more-efficient storage networking technologies.

SNIA strongly believes that addressing the challenges associated with energy efficiency and green computing will require collaboration across all IT areas, including the storage industry. SNIA believes that The Green Grid is a key industry organization for improving energy efficiency within data centers and business computing ecosystems. Through its Green Storage Initiative—dedicated to applying the technical and educational expertise of the storage industry to develop and find more energy-efficient solutions in the data center—SNIA is committed to work with The Green Grid to develop best practices and education for the industry.

Collaboration and Carbon Trading

Carbon trading, although still ramping up, is an interesting area of collaboration between companies in the green space. Governments usually have the role of regulating carbon emissions through systems such as cap and trade. In a cap and trade system, the regulatory body sets a limit or cap on the amount of pollutant a company can emit. Companies are issued emission permits and are required to hold an equivalent number of allowances (or credits), which represent the right to emit a specific amount. The total of allowances and credits cannot exceed the cap (the total emissions). Companies that need to increase emissions can buy credits from companies that pollute less. A purchase of credits is the trade. Chapter 4 goes into more detail on carbon trading as a way for organizations to collaborate in reducing the total amount of greenhouse gases.

IT Vendors and Collaboration

In April 2008, IBM announced new energy-management software, an expansion of its energy certificates program, and an energy benchmark to help clients establish energy-efficiency goals, optimize for energy efficiency, and measure and verify its green IT progress across the enterprise. The offerings for energy measurement included IBM Active Energy Manager software to measure power usage of key elements of the data center, from IT systems to chilling and air-conditioning units; an expansion of IBM's Energy Certificates program to 34 countries; and an online energy assessment benchmark.

Since launching Project Big Green in May 2007, IBM has already helped more than 2,000 clients implement green initiatives that have helped to reduce cost and environmental impact. Additionally, IBM has recycled more than one billion pounds of IT equipment removed from clients' data centers. "Clients today are looking for ways to measure their green IT projects and have positive business results that can be documented and verified," says Rich Lechner, vice president, Enterprise Systems, IBM. "Today's announcements, which are based on IBM's experience with thousands of clients, help them do just this as they transform to a new enterprise data center."

Energy Manager Software

IBM Systems Director Active Energy Manager™ (AEM) tracks energy consumption in data centers and helps customers monitor power usage and make adjustments to improve efficiency and reduce costs. The new software enables IT managers to control—even set caps on—their energy use for servers, storage, and networking, as well as the air-conditioning and power management systems that keep the data center running. The software supports monitoring of devices that connect to select smart power strips that provide power to multiple devices.

Additionally, the software can be used with equipment from facility management providers. For example, the software can retrieve temperature and power information using SynapSense Corporation's wireless sensors, which can be located virtually anywhere in the data center. It can also receive alerts and events related to power and cooling equipment through interaction with Liebert SiteScan from Emerson Network Power. The alerts can notify IT administrators about issues with facilities equipment, such as overheating, low battery power on uninterruptible power supply batteries, or other conditions that might keep IT equipment in a data center from running properly.

Global Significance of Energy-Efficiency Certificate Program

To help clients benchmark and improve the efficiency of their IT operations and reduce their environmental impact, IBM and Neuwing Energy have expanded the Energy-Efficiency Certificate (EEC) program to reach customers in 34 countries. This program enables clients to measure their energy usage while earning energy-efficiency certificates for reducing the energy used to run their data centers. The certificates earned—based on energy-use reduction verified by a certified third-party—provide a way for businesses to attain a certified measurement of their energy use reduction, a key emerging business metric. The certificates can be traded for cash on the growing energy-efficiency certificate market or otherwise retained to demonstrate reductions in energy use and associated CO_2 emissions.

In addition to the United States, Canada, and Mexico, clients in the following countries can now apply for energy-efficiency certificates associated with improvement in IT: Ireland, UK, France, Germany, Italy, Spain, Belgium, Netherlands, Denmark, Portugal, Luxembourg, UAE, Saudi Arabia, Kuwait, Bahrain, Oman, Qatar, Egypt, Jordan, Pakistan, India, China, Singapore, Malaysia, Indonesia, South Korea, Thailand, Australia, New Zealand, Philippines, and Japan.

"Establishing a worldwide energy certificates program with the help of IBM is important to clients around the globe who are dramatically improving the efficiency of their infrastructures to meet their environmental responsibility goals as opposed to simply buying renewable energy certificates," said Matthew Rosenblum, CEO and president, Neuwing Energy. "This program gives clients the incentive to become more efficient at the source and helps reduce energy costs at the same time. We have already seen dramatic results from both utilities and Fortune 500 companies as they start to understand how productive this program is in keeping economic expansion growing while reducing energy costs."

IBM has applied for EEC to document energy savings in its data center in Southbury, Connecticut. A data center thermal assessment was completed in late 2007 using the Mobile Measurement Tool. The assessment identified air flow modifications that allow the Southbury data center to turn off 18 computer room air-conditioning systems while maintaining current data center operations. The pending energy-efficiency certificates are expected to document a total of 1,600 megawatt hours of reduced electricity use annually.

Al Gore and Green Collaboration

Green collaboration covers a wide spectrum. In April 2008, the California firm of Kleiner Perkins Caufield & Byers (KPCB) and Generation Investment Management announced a collaboration to find, fund, and accelerate green business, technology, and policy. The firm also announced that Nobel Prize winner and former Vice President Al Gore had joined KPCB as a partner. KPCB will co-locate their European operations at Generation's offices in London.

Gore stated that the alliance would bring together world-class business talent to focus on solving the climate crisis. He emphasized that, together, KPCB and Generation have a working understanding of this urgent, multidimensional challenge and are resolved to help business and government leaders accelerate the development of sustainable solutions. The collaborating groups said the alliance represents "a landmark alignment of resources to effect global change to protect the environment. It combines the research expertise of both organizations with a track record of successful investments in public and private companies, from early stage to large capitalization business. It aligns the convening power of Mr. Gore, the KPCB Greentech Innovation Network, and the Generation Advisory Board toward a common goal. In addition, KPCB's presence in Asia and the United States, combined with Generation's presence in the United States, Europe, and Australia, will support global-scale solutions."

Gore also announced that as part of the agreement between the two firms, 100 percent of his salary as a partner at KPCB will be donated directly to the Alliance for Climate Protection—the nonpartisan foundation he chairs that focuses on accelerating policy solutions to the climate crisis. So, collaboration in the green space, including green IT, will continue to be far-reaching.

Al Gore's July 2008 Bold Plan to Save the Planet

In July 2008, Al Gore announced an initiative to save the planet. The plan was so bold that the July 18, 2008 issue of *Time* magazine ran an article titled "Gore's Bold, Unrealistic Plan to Save the Planet." Gore challenged America to generate 100 percent of our electricity from sources that do not lead to global warming—and to do it within ten years.

Speaking in Washington on July 17, 2008, Gore called on Americans to completely abandon electricity generated by fossil fuels within ten years and replace them with carbon-free renewables like solar, wind, and geothermal. It is a bold plan, almost to the point of folly. But at the very least, it's one that certainly matches the scale of his rhetoric. "The survival of the United States of America as we know it is at risk," he said. "The future of human civilization is at stake." Gore ended his speech on his plan with a rousing reminder of President John F. Kennedy's challenge to put a man on the moon—a challenge that was met, Gore noted, in less than a decade. He stated, "We must now lift our nation to reach another goal that will change history."

Gore's vision of a completely decarbonized electrical supply within ten years makes discussions toward green computing seem like a piece of cake. However, Gore's bold plan fits very well with the topic of this chapter: We must all collaborate on green IT, and much more collaboration is required to solve the issues of climate change and global greenhouse gas emissions. Gore's emphasis on problems of national security, foreign oil dependency, and high energy prices should get a majority of Americans to support going green.

Although the Kennedy challenge for getting a man on the moon within ten years is an interesting comparison, the climate challenge will be quite different. The difference is largely in the global collaboration required. The moon shot called for focused scientific resources for a single target. Outside Houston and Cape Canaveral, most of us just watched. But decarbonizing our energy supply will require innovation, funding, and sacrifice at every level of society. It will be long and arduous, and even if it works, we won't be rewarded with stirring film of a man on the moon. Nevertheless, we in information technology have an opportunity to almost immediately contribute—to collaborate—in the global effort of going green.

Chapter Summary and Conclusions

From the preceding discussion on collaboration for green IT, the following conclusions can be reached:

- IT vendors have started to offer a significant set of integrated hardware, software, and services offerings to help customers improve their energy-management initiatives.
- Industry organizations are establishing efficiency metrics at the server and data center level to integrate facilities and IT resources.
- The EPA is establishing efficiency metrics at the server level as an extension to its ENERGY STAR workstation metrics.
- Many IT companies are addressing the situation from end to end: at the servers end through power management features, and at the data centers end through integrated IT/facilities modular solutions.
- The required collaboration for green IT is a part of the overall global collaboration required to solve the climate crisis.

Success for global green IT depends on the continued collaboration among groups within your company, among technology vendors, data center design and build businesses, energy utilities, governments, and organizations such as The Green Grid and the Uptime Institute. In short, almost everyone can collaborate on green IT, because almost everyone is a user of IT through PCs, the Internet, cell phones, and so on.

4

The Government's Role—Regulation and EPA Activity

"Just a few short years ago, government's green IT focus centered on recycling print cartridges, but now the focus is on how to be green throughout the entire IT lifecycle."

—EPA CIO Molly O'Neill, March 2008, at Federal Executive Forum

Governments have a significant role in providing motivation for companies to move to green IT. This motivation can be in the form of tax incentives or in the form of regulation. Government agencies such as the U.S. **Environmental Protection Agency (EPA)** continue to have a significant role in advancing energy efficiency in IT equipment and data centers. One of the significant aspects of the information in this chapter is to help convince us of the economic sense of moving to green computing. The environmental and social aspects of reducing energy use become significant added benefits to initiatives that can be sustained based on business cases alone. In addition to the EPA's push for energy efficiency in IT, the government also has a role in regulating carbon emissions through policies such as cap-and-trade systems.

Regulating Greenhouse Gases

By 2008, many countries in Europe had already set regulations to limit carbon emissions. The consensus is that the U.S. Congress will also set similar regulations. The regulations are intended to curb greenhouse gas emissions without putting key U.S. industries at a competitive disadvantage. The regulations in the United States would be similar to those in Europe and would establish a cap-and-trade system, limiting greenhouse gas emissions while allowing companies to buy and sell the right to emit specified amounts of pollution. The United States is viewed globally as a laggard on climate change because, alone among major nations, it chose not to ratify the 180-nation Kyoto treaty. The 1997 accord required advanced nations to reduce carbon emissions below 1990 levels but exempted developing countries, such as China, from reducing greenhouse gas output.

The cap-and-trade system is an administrative approach that controls pollution by providing economic incentives for achieving reductions in the emissions of pollutants. In this system, a central authority (usually a government or international body) sets a limit or cap on the amount of a pollutant that can be emitted. Companies or other groups are issued emission permits and are required to hold an equivalent number of allowances (or credits) that represent the right to emit a specific amount. The total amount of allowances and credits cannot exceed the cap, limiting total emissions to that level. Companies that need to increase their emissions must buy credits from those who pollute less. The transfer of allowances is referred to as a *trade*. In effect, the buyer is paying a charge for polluting, whereas the seller is rewarded for having reduced emissions by more than was required. Thus, in theory, those companies or other groups that can easily reduce emissions most cheaply will do so, achieving the pollution reduction at the lowest possible cost to society.

Active trading programs exist for several pollutants. For greenhouse gases, the largest is the European Union Emission Trading Scheme. In the United States, a national market currently reduces acid rain and several regional markets to reduce nitrous oxide. Markets for other pollutants tend to be smaller and more localized.

Carbon trading is sometimes seen as a better approach than a direct carbon tax or direct regulation. By aiming solely at the cap, trading avoids the consequences and compromises that often accompany taxes and regulations. It can be cheaper and politically preferable for existing industries because the initial allocation of allowances often includes a grandfathering provision where rights are issued in proportion to historical emission levels. In addition, most of the money in the system is spent on environmental activities, and the investment directed at sustainable projects that earn credits in the developing world can contribute to the Millennium Development Goals. However, critics of emissions trading point to problems of complexity, monitoring, and enforcement and sometimes dispute the initial allocation methods and cap.

The overall goal of an emissions-trading plan is to reduce pollutants worldwide. The cap is usually lowered over time—aiming toward a national emissions reduction target. In some systems, a portion of all traded credits must be retired, causing a net reduction in emissions each time a trade occurs. In many cap-and-trade systems, organizations that do not pollute might also participate; thus, environmental groups can purchase and retire allowances or credits and, hence, drive up the price of the remainder according to the law of demand. Corporations can also prematurely retire allowances by donating them to a nonprofit entity, thus becoming eligible for a tax deduction.

Because emissions trading uses markets to determine how to deal with the problem of pollution, it is often touted as an example of effective free-market environmentalism. Although the cap is usually set by a political process, individual companies are free to choose how or if they will reduce their emissions. In theory, firms will choose the least-costly way to comply with the pollution regulation, creating incentives that reduce the cost of achieving a pollution reduction goal.

China, currently the world's largest source of carbon emissions, issued its own 63-page climate change policy in 2007. However, China also asserted that countries that have been heavy polluters since the industrial revolution began should do the most to tackle climate change. China's emissions are still low on a per-person basis, and its leaders, while mindful of the costs of environmental damage, are focused on further development of their still-poor nation.

In the United States, political momentum behind domestic measures to counter climate change is building. But reducing greenhouse gases will impose significant costs on energy-intensive industries such as steel, cement, and chemicals. Many of the foreign rivals of U.S. industries are based in developing countries, such as China or India, that have no current carbon limits. And further international measures to address climate change aren't due until a planned Copenhagen summit in December 2009.

To prevent foreign makers from enjoying an advantage in the U.S. market—and to keep U.S. companies from moving abroad in search of looser regulations—the U.S. Senate bill would require importers to purchase emissions allowances at the border. Supporters say the requirement also would encourage developing countries to enact their own greenhouse gas limits. However, opinions are split on whether the so-called border adjustment is the most-effective way to cushion the competitive blow from new greenhouse gas limits. American Electric Power, one of the nation's largest utilities, is in favor of the border adjustment plan. The American Iron and Steel Institute, on the other hand, favors barring imports from countries whose steel production is dirtier than the United States.

Role of the EPA

Whereas government regulations on carbon emissions are not specific to IT, the EPA has been busy generating government information aimed at improving energy efficiency for IT. The EPA produced a report to the U.S. Congress on August 2, 2007, titled "Report to Congress on Server and Data Center Energy Efficiency—Public Law 109-431." This was part of the EPA's ENERGY STAR program. This section describes the U.S. government's role (mostly through the EPA) in encouraging the implementation of green IT. One significant government role is in the area of incentives, and this chapter describes the different government incentives for establishing green data centers. The information in this section was taken from the August 2007 report previously mentioned.

The EPA has more than a decade of history of advancing energy efficiency in IT equipment as well as commercial buildings, beginning with the first ENERGY STAR specifications for computers established in 1992 and the Green Lights program established in 1991. Through the ENERGY STAR program, the EPA now qualifies a wide array of IT products, including personal computers, imaging equipment, printers, and monitors. The EPA has made particular strides in addressing standby energy and power management for these products, demonstrating that it is possible to encourage rapid development and adoption of energy-efficient technologies and practices. The energy savings from efficiency improvements in these products are currently in the billions of dollars per year (U.S. EPA 2006). The EPA has also developed an innovative commercial building rating system that helps owners and managers assess the energy performance of their buildings and target efficiency improvements.

In January 2006, the EPA convened the first national conference dedicated to examining energy-savings opportunities for enterprise servers and data centers. Representatives from the utility, financial services, healthcare, Internet, and manufacturing sectors attended the conference (http://www.energystar.gov/datacenters). The EPA is now working on the first priority identified in that conference: the development of objective measurements of server energy performance, on which future efficiency criteria would be based.

To develop this report, the EPA convened a study team led by researchers from the Lawrence Berkeley National Laboratory. The study team offered stakeholders multiple opportunities to give input to and review this report, including the following:

- Conducting preliminary calls with key stakeholders to help plan the study

- Holding a public workshop on February 16, 2007 (attended by approximately 130 people) to solicit input on the topic of energy efficiency in servers and data centers

- Following up on workshop attendees' offers of assistance to gather and refine information for the study

- Posting on the ENERGY STAR Web site an open call for interested parties to submit information, as well as a list of data needs

- Posting on the ENERGY STAR Web site a public review draft of this report

- Incorporating into the final version of this report comments on the public review draft from more than 50 organizations and individuals

The EPA's Estimates on Energy Use in Data Centers Through 2011

The energy used by the nation's servers and data centers is significant. It is estimated that this sector consumed about 61 billion kilowatt-hours (KWH) in 2006 (about 2 percent of total U.S. electricity consumption), for a total electricity cost of about $4.5 billion. This estimated level of electricity consumption is more than the electricity consumed by the nation's color televisions and similar to the amount of electricity consumed by approximately 5.8 million average U.S. households (or about five percent of the total U.S. housing stock). Federal servers and data centers alone account for approximately 6 billion KWH (10 percent) of this electricity use, for a total electricity cost of about $450 million annually.

The energy use of the nation's servers and data centers in 2006 is estimated to be more than double the electricity that was consumed for this purpose in 2000. One type of server, the volume server, was responsible for the majority (68 percent) of the electricity consumed by IT equipment in data centers in 2006. The energy used by this type of server more than doubled from 2000 to 2006, the largest increase among different types of servers. The power and cooling infrastructure that supports IT equipment in data centers also uses significant energy, accounting for 50 percent of the total consumption of data centers. Among the different types of data centers, more than one-third (38 percent) of electricity use is attributable to the nation's largest (that is, enterprise-class) and most rapidly growing data centers.

EPA Incentives and Voluntary Programs to Promote Energy Efficiency

To realize the potential benefits from greater energy efficiency in the nation's data centers, a number of market barriers need to be addressed. The adoption of energy-efficient technologies and practices is often impeded by barriers such as higher first cost, lack of knowledge, institutional failures, and perverse incentives, and these issues apply equally to data centers. The barriers that prevent data centers from adopting changes that offer reasonable paybacks are typically not technological but organizational. Three barriers of particular importance for data centers follow:

- **Lack of efficiency definitions:** It is difficult to define energy efficiency for a complex system such as a data center or a server. **Energy efficient** is usually defined based on the delivery of the same or better service output with less energy input, but for servers and data centers, service output is difficult to measure and varies among applications. Data center operators need standard definitions of productivity to purchase energy-efficient equipment, operate it in an optimal way, and design and operate the buildings to house it.

- **Split incentives:** In many data centers, those responsible for purchasing and operating the IT equipment are not the same people who are responsible for the power and cooling infrastructure, who, in turn, typically pay the utility bills. This leads to a split incentive, in which those who control the energy use of the IT equipment (and, therefore, the data center) have little incentive to do so.

- **Risk aversion:** With the increasing importance of digital information, data centers are critical to businesses and government operations. Thus, data center operators are particularly averse to making changes that might increase the risk of down time. Energy efficiency is perceived as a change that, although attractive in principle, is of uncertain value and, therefore, might not be worth the risk.

Such impediments to energy efficiency are not unique to data centers but might be most pronounced in this sector. There is a long history of incentive and informational programs to address barriers like these in other sectors—for example, in government agencies and public and private utilities. Although few current programs specifically target data centers, existing energy policies and programs that promote high-efficiency buildings and equipment—such as product labeling programs, commercial building technical assistance programs, financial incentives, and government procurement—might be applicable to data centers. These programs include the following:

- **Product labeling:** Labels identify products that meet certain specifications for performance, including high-energy performance, based on standard methods for measuring energy efficiency. These labels can make customers aware of the energy costs associated with their purchasing decisions and encourage consumer acceptance and recognition of high-efficiency products. The performance specifications that underlie the labels form clear purchasing guidelines. This, in turn, encourages manufacturers to make increasing numbers of efficient products.

- **Commercial building technical assistance:** The growth of data centers is a relatively recent phenomenon, so best practices for design and operation are only recently developed. Technical assistance programs provide information to facility designers and operators to help them effectively incorporate energy efficiency in the design and operation phases for their facilities. Newer practices in this area include establishment of whole-building energy performance benchmarking. Technical assistance can be provided by government agencies, electric utilities, professional organizations, and industry groups.

- **Financial incentives:** Electric utilities and governments often offer financial incentives to encourage investments in energy-efficiency measures. Financial incentives help buy down the additional cost of more-efficient products when initial product costs are higher than for less-efficient products; help compensate for the increased effort needed to learn about and locate energy-efficient equipment; draw attention to technologies; and legitimize these technologies in the eyes of consumers. The most active utility in the data center sector is Pacific Gas and Electric Company, which offers incentives for server consolidation, among other strategies. (See the PG&E discussion in Chapter 3, "Collaboration Is Key for Green IT," for additional details.)

- **Government procurement:** Federal, state, and local governments spend tens of billions of dollars annually on energy-consuming products, which means that thousands of opportunities exist to reduce government energy use through the purchase of energy-efficient products. Government procurement programs help raise awareness of new-to-market energy-efficient products, increase comfort levels as efficient products are put into use, and reduce costs of manufacture through economies of scale. The federal government is required by law to purchase energy-efficient products unless these products are proven to be not cost-effective. The government has developed energy performance specifications for more than 70 types of products.

EPA has begun to address the energy performance of equipment in data centers by supporting development of energy-performance metrics for servers. In addition, governments and utilities are exploring program mechanisms for promoting improved efficiency.

EPA Recommendations on Ways to Promote Data Center Energy Efficiency

The EPA recommends that a mix of programs and incentives is necessary to achieve a significant portion of the potential savings identified in their report. The EPA believes improvements are both possible and necessary both at the level of the whole facility (system level) and at the level of individual components. Although it is not possible to optimize data center components without considering the system as a whole, it is also true that efficient components are important for achieving an efficient facility. (For instance, efficient servers generate less waste heat, which reduces the burden on the cooling system.) Nevertheless, the greatest efficiency improvements will likely result from a comprehensive approach, given that there are opportunities for improvement in many areas of the IT equipment and infrastructure systems.

Based on a review of a range of incentives and voluntary programs that have been used in other sectors, and considering the unique aspects of the server and data center market, a number of recommendations can be made to pursue improved energy efficiency in the near term. These recommendations include the following:

- **Standardized performance measurement for data centers:** Data center operators need standard metrics to assess and report the energy performance of their facilities. The federal government and industry should work together to develop an objective, credible energy performance rating system for data centers, initially addressing the infrastructure portion but extending, when possible, to include a companion metric for the productivity and work output of IT equipment. These metrics should account for differences in data centers in areas such as computing output and availability requirements.

- **Federal leadership:** The federal government can act as a model in encouraging improved data center efficiency. The government should commit to publicly reporting the energy performance of its data centers when standardized metrics are available; conducting energy-efficiency assessments in all its data centers within two to three years; and implementing all cost-effective operational improvements. Additionally, the Architect of the Capitol should implement the server-related recommendations from the Greening of the Capitol report (Beard 2007).

- **Private-sector challenge:** The federal government should issue a challenge to private-sector chief executive officers (CEOs) to conduct DOE Save Energy Now energy-efficiency assessments, implement improvements, and report energy performance of their data centers. These assessments require protocols and tools that should be jointly developed by government and industry.

- **Information on best practices:** Objective, credible information is needed about the performance of new technologies and about best practices, as well as the effect of both on data center availability. This information can help raise awareness of energy-efficiency issues in this sector and reduce the perceived risk of energy-efficiency improvements in data centers. The government should partner with industry to develop and publish information on field demonstrations and case studies of best practices. This information should be disseminated as part of a campaign to make data center managers aware of the benefits of energy efficiency in addressing power and cooling constraints in data centers.

- **Standardized performance measurement for data center equipment:** Purchasers of data center equipment, such as servers, storage, network equipment, and Uninterruptible Power Supplies (UPSs), need objective, credible energy performance information if they are to purchase efficient products.

- ◆ The federal government should work with industry to develop objective, credible energy performance metrics for this equipment.
- ◆ Using these metrics, the government should also investigate whether development of ENERGY STAR specifications for these product categories would be an effective strategy to complement the whole-facility approaches previously outlined.
- ◆ If ENERGY STAR specifications are developed, federal procurement specifications that build on ENERGY STAR should be implemented.

- ■ **Research and development:** The federal government, in collaboration with industry, universities, electric utilities, and other stakeholders, should initiate a comprehensive research and development (R&D) program to develop technologies and practices for data center energy efficiency. Specific research should be included in the following topics: computing software, IT hardware, power conversion, heat removal, controls and management, and cross-cutting activities.

- ■ **Public and private partnership for energy efficiency in data centers:** The federal government should engage stakeholders to formulate a common initiative (including public policies and private-sector actions) to promote energy efficiency in data centers to continue the dialogue that this report initiates. Logical next steps would include defining priorities for the various strategies outlined in this report, developing timelines, defining roles for the various stakeholders, and identifying gaps and issues that require further assessment.

In addition to these near-term actions, several other actions can also play an important role in saving energy used by servers and data centers:

- ■ **Federal Government:**
  - ◆ Develop a procurement specification for the energy performance of outsourced data centers.
  - ◆ Work with industry to develop better tools, such as life-cycle risk models and total cost of ownership models that incorporate energy costs, for management of energy in data centers.
  - ◆ Separately meter all federally owned data centers with significant energy use.

- Charge data center tenants for energy consumption of IT equipment in government-owned data centers.

- Partner with electric the utilities, the universities, and the data center industry to develop one or more neutral, real-world testing and demonstration centers ("National Center for Data-Center Best Practices") to verify new technologies for reducing energy consumption in data centers.

- Help organize a technology procurement program to bring to market energy-efficient products for data centers.

- Partner with training organizations to develop education and training information and curricula about energy efficiency in data centers.

- Target data centers for efficiency upgrades using **Energy Services Performance Contracts (ESPCs)** and **Utility Energy Service Contracts (UESCs)**.

- Provide technical assistance for demonstration projects of energy efficiency in data centers.

- Conduct demonstration and education projects for fuel cells and other clean, efficient **Distributed Generation (DG)** technologies used for **Combined Heat and Power (CHP)** in data centers.

- Develop a procurement specification to improve the efficiency of high-performance computing facilities.

- **State and Local Governments:**

  - Consider requiring separate utility meters on large data centers, either through utility regulation or building codes.

  - Consider offering financial incentives for clean, efficient technologies used for CHP in high-availability installations (data centers, telecom facilities, and so on).

- **Electric Utilities:**

  - Consider offering incentives for energy-efficient data center facilities and equipment, based on the metrics previously described.

  - Consider partnering with the federal government to develop a neutral, real-world testing and demonstration center to verify new technologies for reducing energy consumption in data centers.

  - Consider partnering with the federal government to develop a technology procurement program for efficient products.

- ♦ Consider offering education and training resources as a component of energy-efficiency programs for data centers.
- ♦ Consider offering financial incentives for clean, efficient DG and CHP in data centers.

■ **Data Center Industry:**

- ♦ Consider partnering with the federal government to develop an objective, credible energy-performance rating system for data centers.
- ♦ Consider partnering with the federal government to develop improved tools, such as energy-aware total cost of ownership models and lifecycle risk models, for management of energy in data centers.
- ♦ Consider partnering with the federal government to develop a neutral, real-world testing and demonstration center to verify new technologies for reducing energy consumption in data centers.

IT Company Support of Government Regulation

Although it's the government's role to create laws and regulations to foster energy efficiency in the IT area, commercial IT companies have been busy producing products and services to help in the measurement, monitoring, and management of IT energy efficiency. Details on IT vendor collaboration efforts in energy efficiency with other IT vendors and with government and nonprofit organizations are discussed in Chapter 3.

Educational Institutions and Government Regulation

Educational institutions (grade school through university) have an important role in working with all levels of the government on green IT. Of course, it's not just the schools collaborating with the government on energy efficiency regulation. Schools have an extremely important role in educating students on energy efficiency concepts and on the role of governments and many other organizations in establishing the best practices guidelines for green IT. Chapter 2, "The Basics of Green IT," describes the green computing guidelines on the Web sites established by the University of Colorado. This provides an excellent example of how universities can foster green IT practices among their IT staff, faculty, and students. Based on my experience, universities are becoming very proactive in promoting overall energy efficiency, which includes green computing because computers are central to all university fields of study.

The case study on Columbia University in Chapter 10, "Green IT Case Studies for Universities and a Large Company," and the collaboration section in Chapter 3, describe how Columbia is working on green IT with federal, state, and city governments. Those sections describe how Columbia plans to rigorously measure recommended government and industry best practices and technological innovations in a real-world environment. The Columbia green IT plan includes working with New York City's government and Mayor Michael Bloomberg's ten-year-plan on reducing carbon emissions by 30 percent based on 2007 levels. Columbia's green IT plan also involves working closely with other research universities, different government agencies, and organizations on high performance computing (HPC).

State and other government agencies don't just work with educational institutions on energy efficiency guidelines, regulations, and incentives, of course. In New York State's Con Edison territory, data centers that can permanently reduce electric demand by at least 20 kilowatts can get help paying for their capital improvement costs with an incentive of $600 per kilowatt from **New York State Energy Research and Development Authority (NYSERDA)**. There is a cap of 65 percent of costs or $1.25 million per facility. NYSERDA is also examining potential incentives for data center procurement and energy management but has not yet finalized any details.

Chapter Summary and Conclusions

The following conclusions can be made from the preceding discussion on government regulation and green IT:

- Governments have become very involved in IT energy use and related environmental regulation. The large amount of electrical power spent on IT has been a significant motivation in attracting both government and environmental attention.
- Industry organizations are establishing efficiency metrics at the server and data center level to integrate facilities and IT resources.
- The EPA is establishing efficiency metrics at the server level as an extension to its ENERGY STAR workstation metrics.

- Many IT companies and governments are addressing the situation from end to end—at the server end through power management features and at the data center end through integrated IT/facilities modular solutions.

Although governments have a vital role in the push to green IT, complete success requires the continued collaboration among many groups including your company, IT technology vendors, data center design and build businesses, energy utilities, governments, and organizations such as The Green Grid and the Uptime Institute. In short, almost everyone can collaborate on green IT, because almost everyone is a user of IT through PCs, the Internet, cell phones, and so forth.

5

The Magic of "Incentive"—The Role of Electric Utilities

"Pacific Gas and Electric Company (PG&E) helped gather the nation's utilities together in order to curtail energy demand in the Information Technology industry. The Utility IT Energy-Efficiency Coalition is comprised of over 24 utilities from across the U.S. and Canada that are primed to address the high tech, data center, and IT infrastructure markets."

—San Francisco News Item, March 2008

Energy corporations, especially electric utilities, have an interesting role in the establishment of green data centers. On one hand, electric utilities are for-profit corporations that make money by selling electricity—so the more electricity they sell, the more profit they make. On the other hand, electric utilities have a significant interest in avoiding having to build new electric power plants to meet peak demand. New power plants are extremely expensive—and the strict emission controls for coal-fired plants greatly add to the expense. New nuclear power plants face even more hurdles—although during 2008, for the first time in 30 years (since the Three Mile Island disaster), the United States has seen requests to build new nuclear power plants.

Most electric utilities in the United States are for-profit. (One exception is the state-run utility in North Dakota.) All are under the control of a **Public Utility Commission** (PUC), and all PUCs are now at least starting to push utilities to establish rate-case incentives for energy conservation. Also, a public relations incentive for energy corporations helps erase their (sometimes undeserved) corporate "bad boy" reputation as lacking environmental concern.

Electric-utility-rate-case incentives work this way. The PUC that has jurisdiction over the electric utility allows (usually encourages) a utility to increase electric rates with the additional revenue due to the increase earmarked as rebates to the utility's customers when it buys energy-efficient equipment (for example, virtual servers for its data centers). The rebate incentives vary widely over the country, with some utilities (for example, California's PG&E in conjunction with the California PUC) on the leading edge. These rebates can go to home owners as well as businesses and cover more exotic energy-saving technology such as solar cells for electric generation on your rooftop. As the global economy evolves from heavy dependence on oil to a mixture of energy alternatives, the marketplace will push for new alternatives in the supply and demand of energy. Electric utilities are in position to have a significant role in motivating companies to move to green IT.

The Significant Role of Electric Utilities and IT Energy Ratings in Green IT

Electric utilities and governments now often offer financial incentives to encourage investments in energy-efficiency measures. As the largest portion of the cost of generating electricity is in plant (capital) expenditures, it is actually good business (as well as good for our planet) if utilities use existing facilities more efficiently while reducing wasteful demand. Providing electricity for energy-efficient equipment—as opposed to planning capacity for inefficient equipment—can be a win-win situation for both electric utilities and their customers. Such financial incentives for commercial and individual energy consumers help buy down the additional cost of more-efficient products (when initial product costs are higher than costs for less-efficient products); help compensate for the increased effort needed to learn about and locate energy-efficient equipment; draw attention to technologies; and legitimize these technologies in the eyes of consumers.

Currently, the most active utility in the data center sector is the Pacific Gas and Electric (PG&E) Company in Northern California, which offers incentives for server consolidation, among other strategies. Corporations in California can receive up to $4 million in incentives for data center energy-efficiency projects such as the migration to virtual servers. Virtualization drives up IT equipment utilization, reduces infrastructure power and cooling demands, and helps organizations meet application performance needs with a flexible and resilient technology that uses much more sustainable than inefficient-adding, low-utilized servers. David F. Anderson, IBM's green architect, has identified virtualization as one of the greenest technologies. "Virtualization is like car pooling or using mass transportation for applications. It has the potential to actually eliminate energy-consuming equipment from the data center while providing equal or better service." (See also earlier mentions of PG&E's pioneering work in Chapter 3, "Collaboration Is Key for Green IT.")

Almost all electric utilities are starting to consider offering incentives for many types of energy-efficient data center facilities and equipment, based on the metrics being developed by the government and corporations dealing with data centers. Electric utilities are starting to partner with the federal government to develop a neutral, real-world testing and demonstration center to verify new technologies for reducing energy consumption in data centers. They are also starting to partner with the federal government to develop a technology procurement program for efficient products and to offer education and training resources as a component of energy-efficiency programs for data centers.

PG&E Led Utility Energy-Efficiency Coalition

Pacific Gas and Electric Company, a subsidiary of PG&E Corporation, is one of the largest combined natural gas and electric utilities in the United States. Based in San Francisco, with 20,000 employees, the company delivers some of the nation's cleanest energy to 15 million people in northern and central California. For more information, visit www.pge.com/about/. In March 2008, the PG&E announced that 24 of the nation's utilities are participating in the PG&E-sponsored Utility Information Technology Energy-Efficiency Coalition to dramatically reduce power usage in data centers and other IT applications.

The Utility IT Energy-Efficiency Coalition is composed of more than 24 utilities from across the United States and Canada that are primed to address the high-tech, data center, and IT infrastructure markets. California utilities are well represented, with Southern California Edison, San Diego Gas and Electric, Sacramento Municipal Utility District, City of Palo Alto, and Los Angeles Department of Water and Power attending the meeting. Utilities from the Pacific Northwest, Texas, New York, and Canada also participated in the two-day event. To the extent possible, the utilities intend to drive toward consistent energy-efficiency program and service offerings, leveraging the support of vendors and service providers to the IT industry. The meeting also featured technology and program briefings, a view of market potential from top industry analysts, and a tour of data centers in Silicon Valley that have implemented leading energy-efficient technologies and management practices.

PG&E founded the Coalition in 2007 and has established a collaborative Web site where member utilities share program documentation, technical resources, and market intelligence. In addition to sponsoring the Coalition, PG&E supports other industry associations such as The Green Grid, and is a board member of the Climate Savers Computing Initiative.

With a large concentration of high-tech companies and data centers located in the San Francisco Bay Area, along with a 30-plus-year history of developing and delivering energy-efficiency programs, PG&E has developed a comprehensive program portfolio to serve this market segment. The portfolio includes customer education and training programs, technical evaluation support, and financial incentives and rebates for customers who adopt energy-efficient technologies and practices.

PG&E's services for this market segment are part of a full suite of customized energy-efficiency products and services the company offers to its customers, including rebates and incentives, energy analyses, demand response programs, and more. Since the inception of these programs in 1976, PG&E customers have achieved significant cumulative life-cycle energy and cost-savings of more than 118 million megawatt hours of electricity and more than $22 billion, avoiding the release of more than 135 million tons of carbon dioxide (CO_2) into the atmosphere.

PG&E Energy-Efficiency Program

The P&E, like other California utilities, must have approval from the **California Public Utilities Commission (CPUC)** for its public programs, and any shareholder incentives or utility performance awards derived from them; for measuring the impact of energy-efficiency and low-income assistance programs; and for verification of program results through bill analysis and installation of monitoring equipment. The reports and regulatory filings found on the PG&E Web site represent a portion of the application, measurement, and verification process.

Example of Energy Utility Rate Case Incentives

Utility companies create their rate case rebates to customers based on proven ways to save electrical energy on IT (usually at the company's data center). In Europe, for several years, consumers and businesses have earned more favorable rates if they use less energy during peak hours. This way of charging for energy has already been adopted in the United States as well. So, during peak air-conditioning and lighting hours, prices go up. According to the PG&E Web site, **Critical Peak Pricing** (CPP) benefits customers on weekdays in the summer season by reducing or shifting energy usage away from the noon to 6 p.m. peak period during 12 or fewer CPP events. In exchange for this, customers receive a discount on all part and on-peak usage on all other days of the summer period that starts May 1 and ends October 31.

With the capability to switch data processing over to geographical areas not affected by the peak pricing, data centers can potentially avoid the higher-priced energy—if they are prepared and if they receive enough advance notice to send processing elsewhere. Data centers are used today to help smooth demand by working with electric utilities to go "off the grid" during critical times to avoid brownouts or blackouts. The use of emergency generators, normally diesel fueled units, might not necessarily be a green alternative because the data center's emergency generators might actually produce more carbon emissions than the local utility. Clean cogeneration of electricity can be accomplished today with fuel cells and natural gas, and the use of small nuclear power plants has even been proposed for the future.

With the availability of high-speed networks, data centers can be moved almost anywhere—offshore as well as out of the region. Ideally, multiple data centers enable flexibility for natural or man-made disasters plus the capability to operate to optimize for energy efficiency. The flat world of the 21st century has enabled global corporations to optimize their IT anywhere on the planet it makes business sense. As energy costs become a bigger factor in the costs of operations, optimization will include energy efficiency, performance, and qualities of service.

You might ask, "Are the electric utilities giving money away at the expense of their stockholders?" Most electric rates can be built with a small percentage added on for efficiency rebates. This rewards opportunistic innovators with the overall market, not the shareholder, paying for efficiency improvements. The small tax in the rate primes the innovation pump benefiting society overall by reducing energy consumption.

Using Utility Rebates to Minimize Energy Costs in the Data Center

In the previous sections, we discussed the types of energy-efficiency incentives that energy utilities can give to their customers. Based on a 2008 survey, here are some of the actual incentives in place or planned.

The Incentive for Utilities

In response to customer concerns, utilities look for ways to provide greener power. One way utilities can be green is to reduce power demand in the first place by encouraging greater energy efficiency from their customers. This seems to run counter to a utility's self-interest because profits are normally tied to energy sales. But in a growing number of states, utilities are motivated to promote energy efficiency by **decoupling** and other forms of regulatory reform. Decoupling separates a utility's capability to make money from the amount of electricity that it sells.

Decoupling uses a rate-adjustment mechanism to break the link between a utility's capability to recover agreed-upon fixed costs, including its profit margin, from the actual volume of sales. The basic principle is that if the actual sales are less than what was forecast, there is a slight upward adjustment in rates to compensate the utility. California, the first state to adopt decoupling, discontinued it during deregulation in 1996, but then brought it back in a groundbreaking energy-efficiency campaign that includes $2 billion of approved investments in efficiency from 2006 to 2008. Other states adopting, or in the process of adopting, various forms of decoupling include Oregon (natural gas), Maryland, Idaho, New York, and Minnesota.

Available Incentive Programs

In August 2006, PG&E in California became the first utility to offer rebates to business customers that replace existing computing equipment with new, high-efficiency servers or implement virtualization and server consolidation projects. In 2007, PG&E extended its rebate program to data center disk-storage equipment.

With PG&E's High Tech Energy-Efficiency Incentives program, qualifying customers can earn a rebate of up to $4 million per project site. The program has industry support from many high-technology companies, such as VMware, Intel, HP, Dell, IBM, and Rackable Systems.

For virtualization, incentives are based on the amount of energy-savings achieved through data center consolidation. PG&E customers apply for the rebate before pursuing a virtualization project. PG&E currently offers a flat rebate of $158 per server that is consolidated through the project. In addition to the rebate, the changes customers make are estimated to save them $300 to $600 in annual energy costs for each server that is virtualized. Those savings can almost double when reduced data center cooling costs are also taken into account. **San Diego Gas and Electric** (SDG&E) and Austin Energy have similar programs.

Here's a 2008 snapshot of other utilities currently offering or planning incentives:

- Avista Utilities, the utility serving Spokane, Washington, offers rebates of up to $5,000 per rack for customers implementing a chip-level liquid cooling solution from SprayCool.

- Xcel Energy, a utility with operations in eight states (Colorado, Michigan, Minnesota, New Mexico, North Dakota, South Dakota, Texas, and Wisconsin), offers a custom project program. Business customers can also receive up to $15,000 toward an efficiency study to identify savings.

- Austin Energy in Austin, Texas, has data center programs providing rebates on various efficiency measures, including server virtualization and efficient cooling practices.

- In Con Edison territory, data centers that can permanently reduce electric demand by at least 20 kilowatts can get help paying for their capital improvement costs with an incentive of $600 per kilowatt from **New York State Energy Research and Development Authority** (NYSERDA). There is a cap of 65 percent of costs or $1.25 million per facility. NYSERDA is also examining potential incentives for data center procurement and energy management but has not yet finalized any details.

Tips on qualifying for incentives and maximizing the advantage you get from them follow:

1. **Find available programs:** The first step is to contact your electrical utility or state energy-efficiency program to determine what energy-efficiency incentives might be available for IT consolidation or data center energy-efficiency improvement projects. You can also check the **Database of State Incentives for Renewables & Efficiency** (DSIRE). This comprehensive source includes information on state, local, utility, and federal incentives that promote renewable energy and energy efficiency. Be aware that most incentive programs have detailed application procedures and require project prenotification. So, the next step, after finding an organization offering a rebate or incentive, is to contact it to learn about its requirements.

2. **Assess energy usage:** Many organizations see only a monthly power bill of their total consumption. Consequently, those in charge rarely see the impact of their equipment decisions and cannot prove their changes saved energy. To participate in a rebate program, you need to determine the power usage for the total data center or the systems or hardware you target to improve. Specific measurements might include chillers, air handling units (HVAC), and IT equipment such as servers and storage arrays. Measurement methods depend on your facility's power monitoring capabilities and the recommendations of the utility or state energy-efficiency team. The best measurements include both peak and seasonal events to better comprehend the energy provisioning required.

3. **Take advantage of project design and energy-efficiency teams:** Many energy-efficiency groups can provide project support to help maximize energy-efficiency gains, cost-savings, and incentives. Partnering with your utility can help ensure you meet all the program requirements.

4. **Calculate energy savings:** You probably need to provide direct measurements of your power usage before and after your project is implemented or perform other required calculations of the energy-savings benefits. Your utility or efficiency program can help you with this requirement.

5. **Submit incentive or rebate payment application:** Programs generally require proof that changes have been done and energy is being saved. You can reap additional goodwill benefits from your project by publicizing your energy-efficiency efforts.

Power Company Incentives for Companies to Go Green

Companies in every industry—from nonprofits to consumer goods—are paying much closer attention to their power bills, as the amount spent on data center power has doubled in the past six years. The CFO is getting the bills, and IT is the biggest user of energy, as data centers can use up to 100 times more energy per square foot than normal office buildings. IT execs are happy that their conservation efforts have a social good, but they measure their progress in dollars saved. However, IT execs would be wise to keep an eye on more than the economics of energy-efficient computing. Energy consumption is huge—U.S. data centers consume as much power in a year as is generated by five power plants—and governmental policy makers are taking notice and considering more regulation. A group of government and industry leaders is trying to set a clear standard for what constitutes a green computer, a mark that IT execs might find themselves held to. Global warming concerns have begun to spark a public opinion swing. This can result in either a backlash against big data centers or a PR win for companies that can position themselves as green. IT vendors are responding to the call for energy conservation, making energy efficiency central to their sales pitches and touting ecofriendly policies such as **carbon-neutral computing**.

A Gartner poll in 2008 showed that more than 69 percent of data centers are constrained for power, cooling, and space. Yet, energy-efficient servers are available from all the major vendors. For example, Sun's CoolThreads technology is said to make servers more efficient by a factor of five. Efficient processors from IBM, AMD, and Intel have made their way into the mainstream, so your favorite server is now available in green, with efforts to continue to improve energy efficiency an ongoing commitment. Key measurements to determine the greenness of a server are performance per watt or logical images/watt. Benchmarks for both idle and load conditions are frequently touted by server vendors. Ideally, purchase decisions on energy efficiency should be made with a consideration of server use. Energy-aware servers will become commonplace as vendors offer the ability to throttle back and turn off servers when they are not needed. Running servers at 100% all the time is like driving a car at top speed just because you can. Using the performance you need rather than what the machine is capable of will use much less energy.

The payoff of efficient servers is twofold. Servers that consume less energy also throw off less heat, requiring less energy for cooling. Today's computer-room air conditioners (CRACs) have variable-speed fans and can adjust dynamically to their data center environments. Alternative cooling approaches, including ice storage and geothermal energy, accept the heat and focus directly on reducing the cost of cooling the data center. Reducing cooling loads gets the attention of utilities because their summer peak demand periods are caused by air conditioning. Pacific Gas and Electric Company is offering $1,000 rebates to customers who buy efficient servers that generate less heat.

Utilities also offer incentive programs for virtualization, which reduce the number of physical servers required. Virtualization is not new, but vendors are strongly promoting it now that energy costs are of concern. Virtualization, the representation of physical resources with logical ones, has also matured and can simplify IT while saving costs. As emphasized throughout this book, virtualization is one of the most effective tools for more cost-effective, greener computing. By dividing each server into multiple virtual machines that run different applications, companies can increase their server-utilization rates and shrink their sprawling farms. Virtualization can also extend to the network and storage, again eliminating energy-drawing equipment from the data center, while more efficiently utilizing the remaining equipment. Virtualization is so energy-friendly that PG&E offers rebates of $300 to $600 for each server that companies eliminate using Sun or VMware virtualization products, with a maximum rebate of $4 million or 50% of the project's cost, whichever is less. Virtualization is also a key technology in qualifying for Energy-Efficiency Certificates, issued by Neuwing Energy ventures.

The actual rebate for a smaller company might, of course, be far more modest and might not drive a virtualization project's return on investment. For example, Swinerton Construction estimated it would get a $3,200 rebate from PG&E when it implemented VMware virtual machines, but it ended up with only $800 after PG&E completed complicated calculations for power use. Still, the project saved the company more than $140,000 in 2008, if you subtract the cost of servers it hasn't had to buy, as well as more than $50,000 saved on power and cooling.

Energy-Efficiency Ratings for IT

Electric utilities need to base their rebates on proven, measurable ways to save energy in the data center. Tools such as IBM's Active Energy Manager can monitor and manage the use of energy in the data center. Guidelines such as EPEAT tool are starting to provide those energy ratings for the data center. EPEAT and other IT energy-efficiency rating schemes are discussed next.

As discussed in Chapter 4, "The Government's Role—Regulation and EPA Activity," in the summer of 2008, the EPA was required to report to Congress national estimates for energy consumption by data centers, along with recommendations for reducing its energy consumption. That is one of several ways lawmakers are looking to soften the environmental impact of computing. The use of voluntary guidelines is only a start on the road to our environmental revolution. However, two forthcoming guidelines embraced by U.S. regulators, combined with tough laws from the European Union on hazardous materials, could go a long way toward forcing green computing onto businesses.

Let's start with the **Electronic Product Environmental Assessment Tool (EPEAT)**. Bush's directive to use EPEAT for government buying guarantees that these standards will get some traction. But businesses will likely find them useful when they need an effective argument for buying green. EPEAT was developed over the past three years by 100 stakeholders, including electronics manufacturers, with funding from an EPA grant. These standards cover only PCs and monitors today but will likely be extended to servers, routers, printers, and maybe even cell phones.

The standards dictate 23 required criteria and 28 optional criteria for IT vendors covering eight broad categories, including energy conservation, recycling or disposal, packaging, and reduction or elimination of dangerous materials such as PVC, mercury, and lead. Some 350 products from 14 vendors are EPEAT-compliant, though none at the highest gold rating. EPEAT's energy-consumption criteria are based on the EPA's ENERGY STAR requirements for PCs, and the sensitive-material criteria require companies to meet the European Union's tough standards for limiting the hazardous chemicals and components used to make them.

The ENERGY STAR ratings on PCs are just like those on refrigerators and washing machines. The PC ratings were enhanced in July 2008, when the EPA issued new, more demanding specs for energy efficiency of PCs and high-end CAD/CAM workstations. PC energy-savings can make a difference to companies. For example, Union Bank of California expects to reduce its energy costs 10 percent to 12 percent annually just by buying more energy-efficient PCs. The EPA has also developed tests to compare energy consumption of different servers and is expected to make those methods available at the beginning of 2009.

Among the strictest regulations on the computer industry are the European Union's Restriction of Hazardous Substances directive, or ROHS. Introduced in 2007, the directive, which covers hardware sold in the EU, restricts the use of six toxic substances, including lead and mercury. China and India are expected to adopt versions of ROHS within the next year. The EU has two other significant green-tech rules: the Waste Electrical and Electronic Equipment regulations, which require sellers to take back any product they sell for recycling; and Registration, Evaluation, and Authorization of Chemicals, which aims to improve the management and risk assessment of dangerous chemicals.

The United States has no federal computer-recycling mandate, but California's Electronic Waste Recycling Act is a cradle-to-grave program aimed at reducing hazardous substances in electronic products sold in that state. It includes a recycling fee of $6 to $10 paid by buyers of PCs and monitors. Other states are likely to follow. Also, the European ROHS standards are slowly becoming de facto requirements, as the United States makes them part of the EPEAT standards and vendors look to standardize products worldwide. "There's a global marketplace for IT, so when there are new regulations by the EU, we all benefit," says Andrew Fanara, the EPA's ENERGY STAR products team leader.

Electronic Product Environmental Assessment Tool (EPEAT)

EPEAT was created through an **Institute of Electrical and Electronics Engineers** (IEEE) council. EPEAT was created because companies and government agencies wanted to put green criteria in IT requests for proposals. EPEAT got a huge boost on January 24, 2007, when President Bush signed an executive order requiring that 95 percent of electronic products procured by federal agencies meet EPEAT standards as long as there's a standard for that product.

The United Nations estimates that 20 million to 50 million tons of computer gear and cell phones worldwide are dumped into landfills each year. It's the fastest-growing segment of waste, says Greenpeace legislative director Rick Hind. At most, 12 percent of PCs and cell phones are recycled, he says: The rest leech chemicals such as mercury and PVC into the environment. "The good news is that computer companies are talking about greenness, touting green programs," Hind adds. CIOs will keep setting IT strategy against their bottom lines, but they're sure to face more questions about whether they can meet environmental goals at the same time. Here's a practical guide to what's happening in green computing, and why IT people should care.

Energy Ratings for Data Centers

Energy consumed by data centers in the United States and worldwide doubled from 2000 to 2005, according to Jonathan Koomey, a consulting professor at Stanford University and staff scientist at Lawrence Berkeley National Lab. Data center servers, air conditioning, and networking equipment sucked up 1.2 percent of U.S. power in 2005. The biggest reason for the power surge: double the number of low-end servers, Koomey says. As a result, some companies are chasing cheaper data center power. Google is building a data center on Oregon's Columbia River to tap hydroelectric power, while Microsoft builds nearby in Washington for the same reason. Financial services company HSBC is building a data center near Niagara Falls. Some such efforts are hardly green, however. Wyoming is trying to lure data centers with the promise of cheap power from coal-fired plants.

But chasing cheap power isn't practical for most companies. For Lehman Brothers, proximity to New York City was crucial because automated trading programs can't spare the milliseconds it takes for data to travel to upstate New York and back, though a remote data center could work for certain batch jobs. At lighting products company Osram Sylvania, the data center isn't so time-sensitive, but the company will not consider the hassle of building a remote center to lower power costs. For these companies, green computing means staying put and cutting costs.

IT Vendors Help Lead the Charge

It's not reasonable to recommend that a customer use energy-efficient technology if we don't use it already in our own IT operations. Specialists in IT at IBM are always talking about first "eating our own cooking." In the field of green IT, from all the articles on the subject, it's clear that IT vendors are also applying green standards to their own operations. There are lots of reasons for this practice: new revenue opportunities, governmental regulations, fear of a customer backlash, or just the desire to act like good corporate citizens. It's also good PR: Vendors are trying to make the case that a key difference between us and our competitors is that we are more concerned about the environment. That competition and PR will continue to help push green computing.

Examples of IT companies practicing what they preach abound. In January 2008, Salesforce.com announced an initiative to "offset its carbon footprint"—that is, compensate for the 19,700 tons of carbon emissions created by everything from its data centers consumption to employee travel. That effort includes a partnership with Native Energy, a Native American-owned company involved in renewable energy projects, with $126,000 invested in five projects to develop alternative energy sources, including windmill and methane farms. Sun created a Sun Eco office a year ago to oversee all the company's green programs, including telecommuting as well as core products such as low-power servers. Sun is touting its Project Blackbox—a data center in a shipping container—as not just portable but also 20 percent more energy efficient than today's data centers.

Cisco also pulled most of its green initiatives under one umbrella, the Eco Board. Its efforts include using its own high-end videoconferencing and other IP tools to cut company travel by 20 percent a year—2 million miles—which the company estimates will lower its CO2 emissions by 10 percent, or 72,000 tons. Cisco also is working with the cities of San Francisco, Seoul, and Amsterdam to find ways to reduce CO2 through broadband and other networking technologies that support telework.

In February 2008, Dell launched "Plant a Tree for Me," through which consumers pay an extra $2 for a laptop or $6 for a desktop to plant trees aimed at offsetting the equivalent computer emissions. It launched www.dell.com/earth to tout its green policies. HP says it has offered recycling since 1987, and today lets consumers send back equipment from HP or competitors. It keeps products such as old Digital Equipment VAX and AlphaServer machines available for parts, for instance. HP set a goal in 2004 to take back 1 billion pounds of product for recycling by 2007 and made its target.

Reuse, Recycle, and Relax

The three "Rs"—Reuse, Recycle, and Relax—have become the mantra for the environmentally conscious. For many IT vendors, recycling those old servers replaced by new virtual servers has become a significant part of the green data center process. Reusing and recycling is a big part of the overall green revolution. A few years ago, the old PCs and other IT equipment at IBM were often sent to third-world countries. That doesn't happen anymore, and companies such as IBM pride themselves on recycling more than 95 percent of the material in old servers and other IT equipment. More than 99.9 percent of the parts in today's mainframes are recyclable.

Recycling PCs, servers, and other IT equipment has never been a huge priority for U.S. businesses. Servers are designed with the total product life cycle in mind. But some companies are finding a new motivation: security. With today's rising concerns about identity theft and data breaches, companies need to know there's no sensitive data left on machines before they're trashed or recycled. That concern led Union Bank of California to more secure disposal that also proved to be greener. The bank hires a company called Intechra that erases data from drives and removes asset tags and other forms of corporate identification and then refurbishes this equipment for resale or grinds them up to recycle the material. None of it goes into a landfill. Union Bank pays $20 to $30 per PC for disposal and gets back 50 percent to 60 percent of any resale value, which is $200 to $300 on high-end notebooks and $50 on desktop PCs. Without this erasure process and resale, the bank states that they'd have to have an internal team scrub the old systems. IBM has a facility of more 300,000 square feet in Endicott, New York, devoted to recycling of IT equipment. There, IT equipment disk drives are ground up and precious metals recovered as part of the normal end-of-life processes.

Telecommuting

IT can directly help reduce greenhouse gases if this reduction enables workers to telecommute. For instance, since 2001, the federal government has required agencies to have a formal policy to let eligible workers telecommute, but many have been slow to act, often because managers aren't sure how to deal with remote reports. At Sun, 14,219 employees work from home two days a week, and 2,800 work from home three to five days a week. Some use drop-in centers closer to home that save an average of 90 minutes in commute time. About 40 percent of employees use the telecommuting program to some extent. That saves 6,660 office seats, cutting Sun's real estate costs by $63 million in the last fiscal year. Reduced commuting by Sun workers resulted in an estimated drop of 29,000 tons of CO_2 emissions. Gartner estimates that 12.6 million U.S. workers were telecommuters in 2007 for more than eight hours a week. Gartner believes that number will have increased just 3 percent in 2008. Not exactly on pace to save the planet! The slow adoption of this type of energy-saving process is often the reality of corporate green initiatives.

Companies will, however, push telecommuting if it helps them to retain employees or cut office expenses. IBM has promoted telecommuting and has had mobile employees for more than a decade. Many of IBM's employees work from home or wherever they are with today's easy-to-use and secure access to IBM's secure intranet and the Internet. With wireless cards in laptops, the need for an office is gone. This changes the need for employee commuting. With the higher cost of fuel, many employees welcome the option to telecommute.

A reduction in car emissions is good PR, but it won't drive many business decisions. Green computing is on the radar screens of CIOs, but, as previously mentioned, it's not primarily motivated by eco-friendliness. The primary motivation is more likely technology's cost. The good news for Mother Earth is that a lot of money-saving, eco-friendly steps are just waiting for IT execs to take.

Where's It All Heading?

The last three chapters on the need for collaboration, the government's role, and the magic of incentive (rebates for efficient technology, ratings for new equipment, and such) are all closely related. We all need to be in this together; we need the federal government involved in all aspects of the environmental crisis; and incentives along with energy-efficiency ratings will all help us on the road to green IT. It's also good to be continually reminded that green IT is probably the best win-win direction for all companies to take in the direction of becoming environmentally friendly. In the author's experience, going green using technology such as virtual servers, virtual storage, and energy management provides an excellent business case without even considering energy-savings. That's because IT technology is already being refreshed every three or four years, and combining ten stand-alone physical servers into one physical server using server virtualization immediately reduces the capital cost for new servers by 50 percent or more. It also simplifies your IT, making it more sustainable and easier to refresh. The 50 percent additional ongoing energy saving due to server virtualization is just "gravy." The detailed virtues of IT virtualization are given in the next chapter.

6

A Most-Significant Step—"Virtualizing" Your IT Systems

"Virtualization can increase hardware utilization by five to 20 times and allows organizations to reduce the number of power-consuming servers."

—Gartner Data Center Conference
November 2007

The most-significant step most companies can make in their quest for green IT is in IT virtualization, as briefly mentioned in previous chapters. This chapter describes the significant concepts of virtual servers and virtual data storage for energy-efficient data centers. The descriptions include VMware and other server virtualization considerations. In addition, the virtual IT world of the future, via grid computing and cloud computing, is discussed. Although the use of grid computing and cloud computing in your company's data center for mainstream computing might be in the future, some steps toward that technology for mainstream computing within your company are here now. Server clusters via VMware's VMotion and IBM's PowerVM partition mobility are here now and used in many company data centers. Both of those technologies are described in this chapter.

Based on my experience with data centers for more than ten years, I believe the most important reason to use virtualization is for IT flexibility. The cost- and energy-savings due to consolidating hardware and software are also significant benefits and nicely complement the flexibility benefits.

There are many aspects to IT virtualization. This chapter structure covers the rational, server virtualization, storage virtualization, client virtualization, grid and cloud concepts, cluster architecture for virtual systems, and conclusions.

Over the past 30 or more years, data centers have gone from housing exclusively large mainframe computers to housing hundreds of smaller servers running versions of the Windows operating system or Unix® or Linux® operating systems. Often the smaller servers were originally distributed throughout the company, with small Windows servers available for each department in a company. During the past few years, for reasons of support, security, and more-efficient operations, most of these distributed servers have moved back to the central data center. The advent of ubiquitous high-speed networks has eliminated the need for a server in the same building. These days, network access even to our homes through high-speed networks such as DSL and cable allows network performance from our homes or distributed offices to the central data center to be about equivalent to performance when your office is in the same building as the data center. The Internet was and remains the most-significant driving force behind the availability of high-speed networks everywhere in the world—including to homes in most of the developed world. When we access a Web site from our home, from the airport with a wireless connection, or from the countryside using a PDA or an air card with our laptop, we have a high-speed connection to a server in some data center. If the Web site is a popular site such as Google, the connection might be routed to any one of many large data centers.

When the distributed servers that had been in office buildings were moved in the past ten years to centralized data centers, operations and maintenance became greatly simplified. With a company server at a centralized data center, you could now call the help desk on Sunday morning and find out why you had no access, and central operations could have a technician "reboot" the server if it had gone down. So, the centralized data center provides many advantages—especially with high-speed networks that eliminate network performance concerns. However, with the rapid growth in servers used in business, entertainment, and communications, the typical data center grew from dozens of separate physical servers to hundreds of servers, and sometimes to thousands. Purchasing, operating, and maintaining hundreds of separate physical servers became expensive. The innovative solution was to consolidate perhaps ten of the separate servers into one bigger physical server, but make it appear as if there were still ten separate servers. Each of the ten virtual servers could retain its own server name, its own Internet address (IP address) and appear—even to web developers—to be a separate physical machine (as it had been before becoming a virtual server). Costs go way down because one large physical box is much less expensive to buy than ten smaller physical boxes. Also, it's significantly less expensive to maintain and operate ("take care of") one big server than ten smaller servers. The analogy might be exaggerated—but it's a bit like taking care of one big house rather than ten separate smaller houses.

In simple terms, server virtualization offers a way to help consolidate a large number of individual small machines on one larger server, easing manageability and more efficiently using system resources by allowing them to be prioritized and allocated to the workloads needing them most at any given point in time. Thus, you can reduce the need to over-provision for individual workload spikes.

In general, virtualization at the data center is applied broadly—not just to server virtualization. It provides the capability to simulate the availability of hardware that might not be present in a sufficient amount—or at all! Virtualization uses the available physical resources as a shared pool to emulate missing physical resources. Virtualization is capable of fine control over how and to what extent a physical resource is used by a specific virtual machine or server. Thus, we have the concept of virtual computer memory (which is not real memory but appears to be real) and virtual data storage.

This chapter gives details on virtualization technologies at the data center and explains how those technologies are usually the first and most-important step we can take in creating energy-efficient and green data centers.

The Concepts of Consolidation and Virtualization

In Chapter 2, "The Basics of Green IT," Figure 2.2, shows an overall strategy for moving to a green data center. The IT infrastructure energy-efficiency strategy consists of centralizing data centers, consolidating IT resources at those data centers, virtualizing the physical IT resources, and integrating applications. Server consolidation and server virtualization both reduce energy use by reducing the number of physical servers, but they use different methods. Server virtualization enables you to keep all your servers, but they become virtual servers when many physical servers share the same physical machine. The diagrams and descriptions of the concepts of consolidation and virtualization were based on the descriptions in the IBM red paper, "The

Green Data Center: Steps for the Journey." (See the Bibliography for author Mike Ebbers for additional information.) These diagrams and descriptions should clarify the difference and some of the pros and cons of the two methods: consolidation and virtualization.

Consolidation: A Key in Energy Efficiency

A common server consolidation example that I've seen with many projects over the past few years is the consolidation of e-mail servers. As discussed at the beginning of this chapter, for reasons of cost reduction and server management efficiency, there are significant advantages to moving servers to a central data center. As part of the distributed computing architecture where smaller servers were distributed throughout the company, we had e-mail servers that were distributed, often one for each corporate facility with often only a couple hundred users for each server. When the e-mail servers were centralized, dozens of smaller servers could be consolidated onto one or two large mail servers. This was more than consolidating the physical servers onto one large physical server; the large centralized e-mail servers only had one copy of the e-mail application. So, server consolidation refers to both consolidating physical servers and consolidating the application.

Figure 6.1 illustrates this idea of consolidation and the energy efficiencies to be gained. Let's assume we have four systems, each running two applications (APP). Also, each machine consumes 2 kW power, 8 kW in total. However, as is often the case for small x86 servers, they are utilized at only 10 percent. If we can consolidate these eight applications to a single, more powerful server and run their operation at a utilization of 70 percent with a power usage of 4 kW, this single server can operate more energy efficiently. In addition, if we perform a simple power management technique of switching off the previous four systems, the result is a total power consumption of 4 kW and a 70 percent utilized system.

It's important to note that a decrease in overall power consumption is not the only factor. Hand-in-hand with the power reduction goes the same amount of heat load reduction and another add-on for the infrastructure. This double reduction is the reason why consolidation is an enormous lever to moving to a green data center.

However, a particular drawback of consolidation is that none of systems 1 through 4 is allowed to be down during the time that the respective applications are moving to the consolidated system. So, during that migration time, higher demands on resources might occur temporarily.

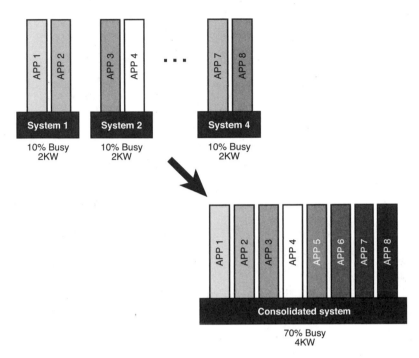

Figure 6.1 Consolidation of applications from under-utilized servers to a single, more-efficient server

Virtualization: The Greenest of Technologies

An alternate method to consolidation is virtualization, the concept of dealing with abstract systems. As discussed at the beginning of this chapter, virtualization allows consolidation of physical servers without requiring application consolidation. So, as discussed earlier, with server virtualization we can take ten servers with completely different applications and consolidate them onto one large physical server, where each of the ten stand-alone servers can retain their server name, IP address, and so on. The virtual servers still look to users as if they are separate physical servers, but through virtualization, we can dramatically reduce the amount of IT equipment needed in a data center.

Virtualization eliminates the physical bonds that applications have to servers, storage, or networking equipment. A dedicated server for each application is inefficient and results in low utilization. Virtualization enables "car pooling" of applications on servers. The physical car (server) might be fixed, but the riders (applications) can change, be diverse (size and type), and come and go as needed.

The example in Figure 6.1 shows how specific applications were moved to another system with a better energy footprint. In the simple case illustrated, we assume all systems are running at the same operating system level. However, what if the applications require different operating system levels or even completely different operating systems? That is where virtualization comes into play.

The term "virtualization" is widely used and has several definitions:

- Can create logical instances of a computer system consisting of CPU, memory, and I/O capabilities
- Can be put together from other virtual components
- Can consist of a virtual CPU or virtual memory and disk
- Can be a virtual network between a virtual computer and the outside world

To have real work done by a virtual system, the virtual system must run on a real system. Obviously, additional intelligence is required to do this. There are pure software solutions, or a system's firmware might offer virtualization features, or such features might be hardwired into the system. Many of the current processor architectures have virtualization features integrated, which can be taken advantage of by software solutions such as the IBM System z® and p machines. In the field, various other solutions are available, such as VMware Server, VMware ESX, Microsoft Virtual Server, and Xen.

To continue with our example, using virtualization gives a slightly different picture, as shown in Figure 6.2. Instead of moving the applications to the consolidated server, we now virtualize the existing systems 1 through 4 on our consolidation target. The effect is clear: Not only is the application moving, but also its complete operating environment has moved with it. Taking a closer look, we find other attractive features, as follows:

- Consider the three separate systems. To communicate, they require a network infrastructure such as NICs, cables, and switches. If our virtualization system supports network virtualization, this infrastructure is no longer needed. The virtualized systems can communicate using the virtualization system's capabilities, often transferring in-memory data at enormous speed. Performance and energy efficiency increase because the network components are dropped. Once again, this method reduces the need for site and facilities resources.

- Each of the separate systems has its own storage system, namely disks. The virtualized systems can now share the disks available to the virtualization system. By virtualizing its storage, the virtualization system can provide optimal disk capacity—in terms of energy efficiency—to the virtualized systems.

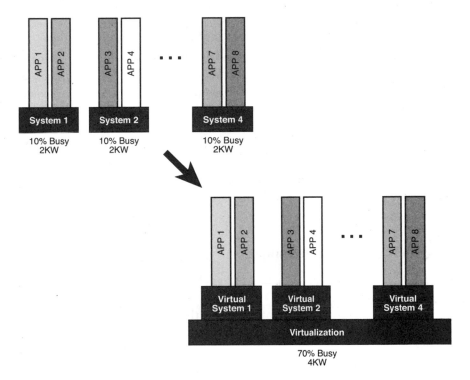

Figure 6.2 Virtualization enables us to consolidate systems, keep the same server names, and so on.

Server Virtualization

This section discusses the techniques that are available for server virtualization, the most attractive approach to consolidation. In many cases, it is the easiest and most-effective way to transfer workload from inefficient, underutilized systems to efficient, well-utilized equipment.

Partitioning

Partitioning is sometimes confused with virtualization, but the partitioning feature is really a tool that supports virtualization. Partitioning is the capability of a computer system to connect its pool of resources (CPU, memory, and I/O) together to form a single instance of a working computer or **logical partition** (LPAR). Many of these LPARs can be defined on a single machine, if resources are available. Of course, other restrictions apply, such as the total number of LPARs a machine can support. The power supplied to the existing physical computer system is now used for all these logical systems, yet these logical systems operate completely independently from one another. LPARs have been available on the IBM System z since the late 1980s and on System p® since approximately 2000. Although the System z and System p partitioning features differ in their technical implementations, both provide a way to divide up a physical system into several independent logical systems.

Other Virtualization Techniques

Many virtualization techniques are available, in addition to partitioning. Popular in the market are the VMware products, Xen and Microsoft Virtual Server. Also, hardware manufacturers extend their products to support virtualization.

VMware ESX Server and Microsoft Virtual Server come with a hypervisor that is transparent to the virtual machine's operating system. These products fall into the full virtualization category. Their advantage is their transparency to the virtualized system. An application stack bound to a certain operating system can easily be virtualized, if the operating system is supported by the product.

VMware offers a technology for moving servers called VMotion. By completely virtualizing servers, storage, and networking, an entire running virtual machine can be moved instantaneously from one server to another. VMware's

VMFS cluster file system allows both the source and the target server to access the virtual machine files concurrently. The memory and execution state of a virtual machine can then be transmitted over a high-speed network. The network is also virtualized by VMware ESX, so the virtual machine retains its network identity and connections, ensuring a seamless migration process. IBM's System p Live Partition Mobility offers a similar concept.

Xen uses either the paravirtualization approach (as the POWER™ architecture does) or full virtualization. In the partial approach (paravirtualization), virtualized operating systems should be virtual-aware. Xen, for example, requires virtual Linux systems to run a modified Linux kernel. Such an approach establishes restrictions to the usable operating systems. However, although they are hypervisor-aware, different operating systems with their application stacks can be active on one machine. In the full approach, the hardware, such as Intel's Vanderpool or AMD's Pacifica technology, must be virtual-aware. In this case, running unmodified guests on top of the Xen hypervisor is possible, gaining the speed of the hardware.

Another technique is operating system level virtualization. One operating system on a machine is capable of making virtual instances of itself available as a virtual system. Solaris containers (or zones) are an example of this technique. In contrast to the other techniques, all virtualized systems run on the same operating system level, which is the only operating system the machine provides. This can become a limiting restriction, especially when consolidating different server generations. Often the application stack is heavily dependent on the particular operating system. We reach a dead end when we want to consolidate servers running different operating systems such as Windows and Linux.

Storage Virtualization

Computer systems are not the only candidates for virtualizing; storage can be virtualized, too. This section describes IBM SAN Volume Controller, which provides a virtual pool of storage consisting of SAN-attached physical storage devices.

IBM SAN Volume Controller

The **SAN Volume Controller** (SVC) is a hardware device that brings storage devices in a SAN together in a virtual pool. This makes your storage appear as one logical device to manage. To the connected computers, SVC offers virtual disks as ordinary SCSI devices. On the SAN side, SVC integrates various storage subsystems, even multivendor, and takes care of the correct block mapping between the SAN devices and the virtual disks for the computers. Figure 6.3 illustrates how it works.

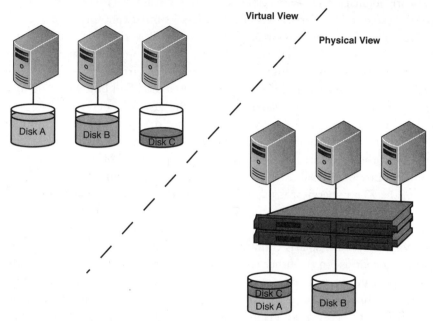

Figure 6.3 Storage virtualization: virtual view and physical view

The following points make the SVC an attractive tool for an energy-efficient storage strategy:

- Data migration from older to newer, more efficient systems can happen transparently.
- Tiered storage enables you to use media with a smaller energy footprint while the SVC cache improves its performance.
- Consolidation of the system's individual storage devices to virtual storage has the same effect—increasing storage utilization—as is shown for server virtualization.

Storage virtualization requires more effort than server virtualization, often requiring us to rethink the existing storage landscape. During consolidation, large amounts of data must be moved from the old systems to the consolidated storage system. This can become a long task that requires detailed planning. However, when done, the effect can be enormous because now storage can be assigned to systems in the most flexible way.

Virtual Tapes

Tapes are the cheapest medium on which to store data. They offer the largest storage volume at the lowest cost, which is the reason that they are the optimal backup medium. Tapes have a long latency compared to disks. This is not always a benefit. Currently, data centers are faced with a time limitation for backing up and probably restoring their data because the time frames for backups shrink, while the amount of data to back up expands. For this reason, many sites prefer large disk-based backup systems instead of tapes.

Tape virtualization might be a solution to this problem. A virtual tape server behaves just like a tape library, but a very fast one. This is made possible with internal disk arrays and a migration strategy to export to and import from real tape libraries.

Client Virtualization

A great potential in energy savings is client, or desktop, virtualization. Various studies have estimated energy savings of more than 60 percent by using client virtualization. In a typical workplace, installed PCs show very low average usage rates. Except when launching an application, an office PC spends most of its time waiting for the user to press a key or click a mouse. However, the PC continues to need a considerable amount of energy to operate, heats up its surrounding environment, and produces noise. Desktop virtualization can dramatically improve the situation.

The underlying principal of client virtualization is to replace the office workstation with a box having a much smaller energy footprint. The needed computing power is moved into the data center. Today's virtualization techniques make this approach even more attractive. The concept of client virtualization—often called thin-client computing—is not a new concept and goes back at least 15 years. In fact, thin-client computing where the server does all the processing is similar in concept to the terminals we used to connect to the mainframe before the advent of the PC.

The benefits of client virtualization are many, and not only to the energy balance. Software deployment in an office environment, for example, can become difficult if each desktop machine contains many different types and versions of software. Client virtualization where the clients all run applications on a central server solves the software problem.

As we've discussed, a thin client is a computer (client) in client-server architecture networks, which depends primarily on the central server for processing activities. In contrast, a thick or fat client does as much processing as possible and passes only data required for communications and archival storage to the server. A thin client is often a network computer without a hard disk drive. Here are some benefits and risks:

- **Benefits:** The significant benefits of client virtualization and the use of thin clients are the low cost of ownership (including lower energy use), security, and reliability. Boot image control is much simpler when only thin clients are used—typically a single boot image can accommodate a very wide range of user needs, and be managed centrally. Thin client technology can be a significant benefit—for example, to support help desks where everyone at the help desk needs to access the same server applications.

- **Risks:** The major risks to moving to thin client technology include the loss of flexibility when moving from a thick client. Our laptops are thick clients and give us the flexibility to use them anywhere, with or without a network connection. Also, a server that supports thin clients must have a higher level of performance since it does all of the processing for the thin clients. Thick clients also have advantages in multimedia-rich applications that would be bandwidth intensive if fully served. But the major risk moving to thin clients is loss of flexibility. On some operating systems (such as Microsoft Windows), software products are designed for personal computers that have their own local resources. Trying to run this software in a thin client environment can be difficult.

In general, virtualization, including client virtualization, will significantly reduce total cost of ownership (TCO) and energy consumption. In the case of a desktop PC, Gartner projects that if IT were to virtualize the graphical user interface of all PC applications and manage the software centrally, indirect IT costs would be cut in half. For IT, that represents a considerable amount of savings, as cutting indirect costs in half cuts PC TCO by about one third.

If thin-client computing and client virtualization in general have all those significant benefits, then why aren't all desktops thin clients in the workplace? It's about personalization of the client, since that's been the norm for many years. However, IT vendors are in the process of changing that. The IBM Virtual Client Solution, for example, can take a full-featured desktop OS such as Windows XP and run it on a virtual server. Under this new approach to thin-client computing, users can retain all the PC experience lost with simple graphical user interface (GUI) virtualization, and the IT team can gain the savings brought about through centralized PC management.

A Further Look at Reasons for Creating Virtual Servers

Consider this basic scenario. You're in charge of procuring additional server capacity at your company's data center. You have two identical servers, each running different Windows applications for your company. The first server—let's call it Server A—is lightly used, reaching a peak of only 5 percent of its CPU capacity and using only 5 percent of its internal hard disk. The second server—let's call it Server B—uses all of its CPU (averaging 95 percent CPU utilization) and has basically run out of hard disk capacity. (That is, the hard disk is 95 percent full.) So, you have a real problem with Server B. However, if you consider Server A and Server B together, on average the combined servers use only 50 percent of their CPU capacity and 50 percent of their hard disk capacity. If the two servers were actually virtual servers on a large physical server, the problem would be immediately solved because each server could be quickly allocated with the resource each needs. In newer virtual server technologies—for example, Unix Logical Partitions (LPARS) with micropartitioning—each virtual server can dynamically (instantaneously) increase the number of CPUs available by utilizing the CPUs currently not in use by other virtual servers on the large physical machine. This idea is that each virtual server gets the resource required based on the virtual server's immediate need.

Figure 6.4 shows typical server utilization for stand-alone servers (that is, *no* virtualization). The multimillion dollar mainframes are typically utilized on a 24/7 basis at least partly because of the large financial investment. Mainframe "batch" processes such as running daily, weekly, and monthly corporate summary reports are typically CPU-intensive and are run at night and on the weekends. The small department Windows server (labeled "Intel-based" in the diagram) is not typically used at night or on the weekends. Creating virtual servers of those Intel-based servers not only allows much better and easier sharing of resources for a mix of lightly and heavily used servers (as in the Server A/Server B preceding example), but also tends to spread out the utilization over 24 hours on the large physical server that houses the virtual servers.

Server Virtualization—the Reason

Current Asset Utilization (Stand-Alone Servers)

	Peak-Hour Utilization	Prime-Shift Utilization	24-Hour Period Utilization
•Mainframes	•85-100%	•70%	•60%
•UNIX	•50-70%	•10-15%	•<10%
•Intel-based	•30%	•5-10%	•2-5%
•Storage	•N/A	•N/A	•52%

Source: IBM Scorpion White Paper: Simplifying the Corporate IT Infrastructure, 2000

Source: IBM White Paper

Figure 6.4 Server virtualization—the reason

The Ultimate in Server and Data Storage Virtualization

Grid computing is a major evolutionary step that virtualizes an IT infrastructure. It's defined by the Global Grid Forum (www.gridforum.org) as distributed computing over a network of heterogeneous resources across domain boundaries and enabled by open standards. Although the industry has used server cluster technology and distributed computing over networks for nearly two decades, these technologies cannot in themselves constitute grid computing. What makes grid computing different is the use of open source middleware to virtualize resources across domains. See Appendix B, "Green IT and Cloud Computing," for details.

Cloud Computing—The Exciting Future

Cloud computing is a new (circa late 2007) label for the subset of grid computing that includes utility computing and other approaches to the use of shared computing resources. Cloud computing is an alternative to having local servers or personal devices handling users' applications. Essentially, it is an idea that the technological capabilities should "hover" over everything and be available whenever a user wants. See Appendix B for details.

Cluster Architecture for Virtual Servers

As discussed previously in this chapter, there are now many IT vendors with virtual servers and other virtual systems. Also briefly discussed was VMware's technology for moving servers called VMotion. By completely virtualizing servers, storage, and networking, an entire running virtual machine can be moved instantaneously from one server to another. I've worked with VMotion implementations on projects at data centers, and it does seem to be a step in the direction in support of the grid and cloud computing concepts discussed in this chapter.

VMware Clusters (VMotion)

The entire state of a virtual machine is encapsulated by a set of files stored on shared storage, and VMware's VMFS cluster file system allows both the source and the target VMware ESX server to access these virtual machine files concurrently. The active memory and precise execution state of a virtual machine can then be rapidly transmitted over a high-speed network. Because the network is also virtualized by VMware ESX, the virtual machine retains its network identity and connections, ensuring a seamless migration process. VMotion servers require external shared storage (SAN).

Figures 6.5 and 6.6 show the VMotion concept and four node cluster examples implemented at a large data center outside of Chicago. The concept of using VMotion clusters for all VMware server needs has worked very well and has basically eliminated the previous need to manage and balance the load among difference physical servers used to host VMware virtual servers. Figure 6.5 shows the general VMware cluster (VMotion) concept used at this data center. Figure 6.6 shows one of the two clusters used.

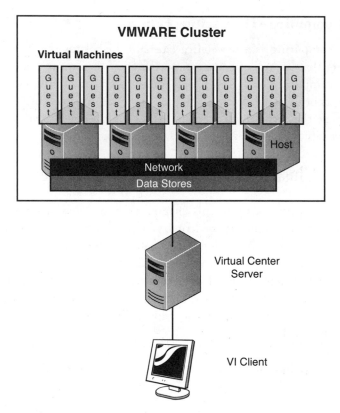

Source: IBM design document

Figure 6.5   VMWare cluster concept

The following list gives the details of the VMWare/VMotion architecture used for the data center:

- **VMware ESX Operating Systems**
- **VMware Virtual SMP:** VM to use up to four physical processors simultaneously.
- **VMware High Availability (HA):** HA for any application running in a virtual machine, regardless of its operating system or underlying hardware configuration.
- **VMware DRS:** Distributed Resource Scheduler monitors utilization across resource pools and allocates available resources among the virtual machines based on predefined rules.

- **VMware VMotion:** The entire state of a virtual machine is encapsulated by a set of files stored on shared storage, and VMware's VMFS cluster file system allows both the source and the target VMware ESX server to access these virtual machine files concurrently.

- **VMware VMFS:** VMFS is a cluster file system that leverages shared storage to allow multiple instances of VMware ESX to read and write to the same storage.

- **VMware Consolidated Backup:** LAN free backup.

- **VMware Update Manager:** Automation of patches and updates.

- **VMware Storage VMotion:** Enable live migration of virtual machine disk files across storage arrays with VMware Storage VMotion.

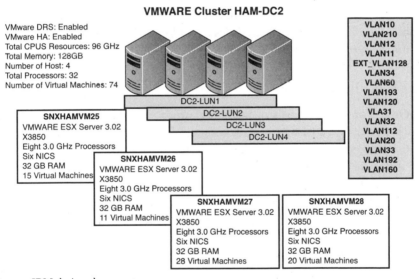

Source: IBM design document

Figure 6.6 VMWare cluster example with four nodes

Blade Servers and Virtualization

Two of the more recent trends in data center optimization are the adoption of blade servers and the deployment of server virtualization. Each of these can bring benefits to business. What's more, combining blade servers with a virtualization strategy can lead to even greater efficiencies for enterprise data centers. This section compares and contrasts the two technologies that are both used for data center simplification and energy savings.

A **blade server** is a chassis housing that contains multiple, modular electronic circuit boards (blades), each of which includes processors, memory, storage, and network connections and can act as a server on its own. The thin blades can be added or removed, depending on needs for capacity, power, cooling, or networking traffic. The products, which are designed for high-density computing, can provide a host of benefits to organizations, including more efficient use of space and energy.

Blade servers provide a broad, modular platform that works well for consolidation as well as building for the future. Blades provide an opportunity for a reduction in complexity by reducing the number of IT components, due to shared components in the architecture. There should be greater manageability, modularity, and flexibility for growth. These all help in reducing **total cost of ownership** (TCO). With blades, you also provide a good modular platform for the future architecture that supports things like I/O, virtualization, and ease of provisioning. Blades should be considered a good hardware counterpart to virtualization software.

The Benefits of Blades

One of the key IT goals of many organizations today is to economize on space, power, and cooling in the data center. In general, blade servers provide a smaller form factor and a better footprint than other types of servers, so organizations can make better use of their data centers. There has definitely been a greater need for this type of technology as energy costs continue to go up. Other benefits of blade servers are more specific to individual manufacturers. For example, some suppliers provide strong management tools. The blade server devices include cutting-edge technology that enables companies and their IT staffs to address fundamental data center challenges, such as cost, change, time, and energy, to achieve better business outcomes. Blade servers are flexible in terms of expansion and management, which is a great benefit for administrators. Blades can also be used in a complete blade system to bring together technologies like virtualization, automation, energy efficiency, and unified management.

Blade servers are available from many vendors, including Hewlett-Packard, IBM, and Sun Microsystems. Sales of blade server technology accelerated in the 2007 to 2008 time period, according to research firm IDC. Overall, blade servers, including x86, Explicit Parallel Instruction Computing (EPIC), and Reduced Instruction Set Computer (RISC) blades, currently account for only a little more than 5 percent of server market revenue (2007 data). However, blade server factory revenue continues to grow rapidly, according to IDC.

Virtualizing Blade Servers?

As we discussed previously in this chapter, server virtualization enables servers to be converted into pools of logical computing resources. Through the use of virtualization software, a single server can be logically divided up into multiple virtual devices. This enables the same hardware device to run multiple operating systems and applications—each independently of the others—as if they were on physically separate devices.

As we also discussed in this chapter, server virtualization offers a host of potential benefits. Virtualization more efficiently employs IT resources to improve asset utilization and simplify management of the data center. It can help improve operational availability by providing flexible resources and software tools that automatically assess when servers need additional resources, and adjust capacity in real time. This alleviates potential bottlenecks and the slowing of systems due to over-provisioning.

Business Continuity–Disaster Recovery

Beyond cost savings, disaster recovery, business continuity, and data recovery are other reasons companies use server virtualization. The same technology is used for virtualizing desktops that go into the data center. Many companies have two physical PCs for one person. Virtualization can eliminate one of those. You can run multiple environments on a single device. Developers, in particular, need multiple environments. Virtualization enables you to take a desktop PC off a person's desk and move it into a data center. There are a lot of manageability benefits to this. The key use cases that are most commonly mentioned for server virtualization are server consolidation, business continuity and disaster recovery, software lab automation, and the desktop scenarios. The two ways to leverage virtualization for desktops include running virtualization on the desktop so that you can have multiple environments on a single system, and running desktop environments on servers accessed via thin clients—what we refer to as **virtual desktop infrastructure**, or VDI. VDI helps organizations by making it easier for them to manage, secure, and protect desktop environments. Developers and call centers are two examples of where businesses have been deploying VDI solutions. Another benefit of server virtualization is increased agility.

Virtualization solutions help make IT environments more flexible by simplifying the management and automation of virtual infrastructures.

HP has been quite vocal on this point. HP indicates that businesses can speed up the deployment of infrastructure components and applications, keep them up and running more efficiently, and adjust infrastructure more quickly when business demands change. Improved quality of service is yet another business benefit. Virtualization products can improve the quality of IT service delivery by aligning IT supply with business demand. Server virtualization can help mitigate business risk if leveraged for business-continuity and disaster-recovery purposes. When combined with the right set of management tools, which varies depending on the environment, virtualization can provide an affordable alternative to maintaining separate duplicate sites for disaster recovery.

Combining Blades and Virtualization

Deploying both blade servers and virtualization can lead to even greater efficiencies in the data center. Physical data center space, power and cooling needs, and costs are all reduced when a virtualization strategy is supported by the use of blade servers. Other benefits include increased server utilization rates and increased reliability, flexibility, and serviceability. Blades and virtualization work well together to provide greater manageability and modularity on both the hardware side and the software side. Both address space-saving issues and consolidation of low utilized servers, and ease of provisioning new servers. They address many of the same issues and are a good hardware and software combination.

Blades and virtualization can be highly complementary strategies. Many users are deploying both at the same time. They work together to provide higher-density computing, giving you a lot more out of your data center blades due to the much smaller form factor and the ability to consolidate multiple workloads on fewer servers. Both also work together to reduce energy consumption costs and conserve data center space. They also make it easier to manage the data center. The combination of blades and virtualization can lead to clear business benefits. These are both technologies that go directly to the return on investment (ROI) and reducing TCO. You get more for what you're spending. Lower TCO comes through reductions in both capital expenses and operating expenses.

Another plus is that server blades and virtualization can help businesses make their data centers more environmentally friendly. For example, there are many cases where corporations would have needed to build a new data center to support growth, had they not implemented a virtualization strategy. By using virtualization, they've avoided the cost of having to build a big, new data center. A typical example is a business that has perhaps 300 servers that it can't bring up because the company doesn't have enough power in its data center. That business needs to economize. It can eliminate the need for most of those 300 additional servers with virtualization and blades. Virtualization with blade servers enables IT administrators to spend less time managing and reorganizing the data center. The time-savings alone gives staff the opportunity to explore new ways to help the company grow from an IT perspective. Based on experience, the time it takes an administrator to bring up a new server in a data center is substantial. In a virtualized environment, the administrator can bring up a new server from his desk in a matter of minutes. IT staff can invest in more productive uses of its time.

Both blades and virtualization are strong enabling technologies for the level of advanced management that can move us closer to dynamic IT or utility computing. They offer the ability to pick the computing resources, the network resources, and the storage resources needed for each project.

Impacts of Server Virtualization on Data Storage

An 2008 ESG Research survey of virtual server users reveals some interesting storage technology and implementation trends. **The Enterprise Strategy Group** (ESG) is an IT analyst and consulting firm focused on information storage, security, and management (http://www.esginc.com). This section references that ESG survey and relates it to some of the case studies given in Chapter 9, "Green IT Case Studies for Energy Utilities, " Chapter 10, "Green IT Case Studies for Universities and a Large Company," and Chapter 11, "Worldwide Green IT Case Studies." The survey stated that it is well known that virtualization is one of the hottest trends in IT. But the survey was intended to show how virtual servers impact end users' storage strategies. Virtual servers have unique requirements in the areas of performance and data protection, and users are just beginning to implement storage technologies and products that enable them to maximize the benefits of server virtualization.

Infrastructure Options and Plans

Although one of the primary benefits of server virtualization is consolidation of resources, the implementation of virtual servers often leads to significant increases in storage capacity. More than half (54 percent) of the virtual-server adopters have experienced a net growth in capacity, whereas only 7 percent reported a net decrease. ESG analysts believe those organizations reporting no change in capacity, or a decrease in capacity, might have benefited from storage consolidation or other infrastructure initiatives as part of their virtualization deployment and might simply be in the early stages of implementation and have not yet reached the tipping point where they experience a net increase in storage capacity. However, the overall conclusion is that server virtualization typically increases capacity requirements.

Together with performance and management demands, the increased storage capacity requirements have a profound effect on how users design their underlying storage infrastructures (for example, DAS, NAS, Fibre Channel SAN, or iSCSI SAN). And in this context, it's important to note that the vast majority (72 percent) of users are sharing storage resources between virtualized and nonvirtualized (physical) servers. Overall, there is a clear trend toward networked storage architectures (Fibre Channel SAN, iSCSI SAN, and NAS), as opposed to DAS. For example, 86 percent of the ESG survey respondents use networked storage, whereas only 14 percent are still relying exclusively on DAS.

As might be expected, Fibre Channel SANs are preferred by larger organizations, whereas DAS is often the preferred architecture for SMBs. Surprisingly, however, adoption rates for iSCSI in virtual server environments are about the same across all sizes of organizations (as is the case for NAS). In any case, the trend toward networked storage in virtual server environments is clear: Today, approximately 60 percent of users' virtual server capacity is networked, and that percentage is expected to increase to 74 percent over the next 24 months. The most commonly cited benefits include better mobility of virtual machines across physical servers (66 percent of survey respondents), easier and more cost-effective disaster recovery, increased uptime and availability, more-efficient upgrades of physical servers, and high-availability storage of multiple copies of virtual machine images (54 percent).

Storage Management Issues

Virtual servers force users to address storage management and data-protection issues such as backup, remote replication, capacity planning, and information security in new ways. But of all the concerns about implementing virtual server environments, performance comes out on top, although collectively, storage management issues are also of great concern.

Data Protection

It's not surprising that end users expect server virtualization and consolidation to reduce the total number of backup licenses they have to purchase. (Almost a quarter of the survey respondents reported that they reduce the number of backup licenses after deploying virtual servers.) To that end, a variety of vendors eliminate the need to have backup agents on every virtual machine. And in a related survey finding, 17 percent of the users have changed their backup software as a direct result of implementing server virtualization.

Disaster Recovery

Improving disaster recovery is one of the driving forces behind the combination of server virtualization and networked storage. In the ESG survey, 26 percent of the virtual server users said they replicate virtual machines to a remote disaster-recovery site, and another 39 percent plan to do so. One of the advantages of server virtualization is that it enables users to replicate many servers to relatively inexpensive virtual machines rather than to physical servers, which significantly reduces the primary barrier to disaster recovery: high costs. In addition, disaster recovery with virtual machines can be less costly than with physical servers because the process can, in many cases, be managed by the virtualization software.

A primary driving force behind remote replication in the context of server virtualization is end users' desire to reduce their **recovery time objectives** (RTO). For example, 85 percent of the survey respondents agree that replicating virtual machine images for disaster recovery enables their organizations to lower their RTO.

Server and Storage Virtualization

Although server virtualization and storage virtualization are usually viewed separately by IT organizations, the clear trend is toward a merging of the two technologies. The primary benefits of server virtualization include lower costs, improved resource utilization, nondisruptive upgrades, and increased availability—all of which are fundamentally enabled by decoupling servers, applications, and data from specific physical assets. Storage virtualization takes those same benefits and extends them to the underlying storage domain. Just as using networked storage for virtual machines instead of DAS means that there is no single point of failure at a disk system level that can bring down many virtual machines at once, storage virtualization adds yet another layer of protection against failures—extending full hardware independence from the server domain to the storage domain.

Chapter Summary and Conclusions

The following conclusions are from this chapter's discussion on virtualization and green IT:

- Virtualization is the most-promising technology to address both the issues of IT resource utilization and facilities space, power, and cooling utilization.
- Many IT companies address the situation from end to end—at the server end through power management features, and at the data center ends through integrated IT/facilities' modular solutions.
- IT virtualization includes server virtualization, storage virtualization, client virtualization, virtualization using cluster architecture, and virtualization of blade servers.
- The ultimate objective and benefit of virtualization is the significant IT flexibility it brings corporate users. IT virtualization can benefit data protection, business continuity, and disaster recovery.

7

The Need for Standard
IT Energy-Use Metrics

"If you can't measure it, you can't manage it"

—Quotation attributed to many, including W. E. Deming and Peter Drucker

As mentioned earlier, to measure green IT, we must have standards as to what constitutes green IT. The standards are IT energy-use metrics. This chapter explores the status and future for IT energy-use metrics. In addition to measurements for IT energy use, this chapter also discusses the Leadership in Energy and Environmental Design (LEED) Green Building Rating System, developed by the U.S. Green Building Council (USGBC). LEED provides a suite of standards for environmentally sustainable construction. LEED does not relate directly to green data centers, but rather to the overall building. LEED's applicability to green IT is discussed in the LEED section of this chapter.

Another metric for green IT is the **Electronic Product Environmental Assessment Tool** (EPEAT). EPEAT got a big boost in January 2007, when President Bush signed an executive order requiring that 95 percent of electronic products procured by federal agencies meet EPEAT standards, if there's a standard for that product. First, however, let's look at some standards and metrics specifically developed for measuring IT and data center energy efficiency, such as SPEC marks and the metrics being developed by the EPA. The EPA is pushing for metrics for all aspects of data center use, and the EPA metrics should be the guideline for green data centers.

The Standard Performance Evaluation Corporation (SPEC) benchmark information has been used for years to compare servers from a power aspect. In the author's experience, companies are very interested in SPEC marks when comparing new servers. Customers use the SPEC marks to compare relative power. Here's the SPEC home page: http://www.spec.org/.

In 2008, SPEC started a benchmark to compare the power consumed by a server with its performance—a metric designed to aid users in boosting data center efficiency. Following is information on SPEC and the server energy-efficiency metrics being developed by SPEC.

SPEC

SPEC is a nonprofit corporation formed to establish, maintain, and endorse a standardized set of relevant benchmarks that can be applied to the newest generation of high-performance computers. SPEC develops benchmark suites and also reviews and publishes submitted results from member organizations and other benchmark licensees.

SPEC Metrics for Virtual Servers

SPEC formed a new subcommittee to develop standard methods of comparing virtualization performance for data center servers. The group investigates the use of heterogeneous workloads that are spread across multiple virtual machines on a single server, and the methods and metrics used by the benchmark will be defined as part of the working group's efforts.

SPEC Server Power and Performance Examples

SPECpower_ssj2008 is the first industry-standard SPEC benchmark that evaluates the power and performance characteristics of volume server class computers. The initial benchmark addresses the performance of server-side Java™, and additional workloads are planned. Figures 7.1 through 7.4 show power measurement results for four different servers.

One of the significant aspects of looking at server electric power consumed versus server processing power produced is the server power used when the server is idle (that is, doing nothing). A typical server uses 40 percent to 50 percent (or more) of its maximum power consumption when it is doing nothing. The SPEC power and performance examples given here for a variety of servers by different manufacturers indicate this high power use, even when the server is doing nothing. To look at power consumed when the server is doing nothing, take a look at the Active Idle row in Figures 7.1 through 7.4. For example, in Figure 7.1, the server at 100 percent load uses 260 watts, while in idle, the server still uses 187 watts (72 percent of the power at 100 percent load). Figure 7.2 shows the server using 143 watts at idle versus 244 watts at 100 percent load or still 59 percent of the maximum power use when the server is not doing anything.

The server power tools discussed in Appendix A, "Green IT Checklist and Recommendations," also indicate significant server power use at idle. One of the advantages of server virtualization discussed in Chapter 6, "A Most-Significant Step—'Virtualizing' Your IT Systems," is that server idle time is reduced on a physical box if the box is configured to house six to ten virtual servers. The virtual servers on a physical server can be chosen so that idle time will be minimized. Also, manufacturers are starting to enable servers to optionally go to sleep mode at night or on weekends when not in use. This is similar to the options most of us have for our laptops where we can choose to have the monitor power go off after 15 minutes of idle time or the CPU go to "sleep" mode after 30 minutes of idle time. These power options were not previously available on servers, mostly because energy conservation was not a significant concern for manufacturers. Our options for laptop power options were primarily there to automatically conserve the limited battery power we have when mobile. For laptops, energy conservation was just an automatic side effect.

Server Sleep Mode

In August 2008, Intel announced a new power-saving technology called Remote Wake that lets outfitted computers doze in a power-saving mode until an appropriate message is received over the Internet, either via a VoIP call or another messaging medium. Although the Wake on LAN® protocol has been around for some years, allowing computers with the right Ethernet card and software to monitor a network even while sleeping, Remote Wake goes far beyond that.

Remote Wake needs to maintain a persistent network connection with a central server to function as Intel intends, as most computers in homes are behind **Network Address Translation (NAT)** gateways that prevent direct access. It's possible that a combination of UPnP (Universal Plug and Play) and Remote Wake are required to leave an external port on the Internet-facing side of the gateway active, so it can route traffic to the snoozing system. Intel and its partners state that you can use Remote Wake to let a computer sleep unless there's a download needed, or a user wants to access files (like media to stream) from a home computer, or a call is incoming via VoIP. Remaining in a standby instead of active state can reduce usage by hundreds of watts a day for a computer that's normally left on in a full-power mode with its monitor off.

Standby modes need to be made more efficient, too. The standby modes of all home electronics, including televisions, toaster ovens with electronic displays, and transformers for DC conversion consume hundreds of terawatt hours per year, equivalent to the output of hundreds of power plants. Standby power can't be eliminated entirely, of course, but newer equipment and smarter engineering can drop standby power use by 90 percent or more.

SPECpower_ssj2008

Copyright© 2007 Standard Performance Evaluation Corporation

Fujitsu Siemens Computers PRIMERGY RX300 S3 (Intel Xeon L5335)			SPECpower_ssj2008 = 446 overall ssj_ops/watt	
Test Sponsor:	Fujitsu Siemens Computers	SPEC License #: 22	Hardware Availability:	Sep-2007
Tested By:	Fujitsu Siemens Computers	Test Location: Paderborn, Germany	Software Availability:	Nov-2007
System Source:	Single Supplier	Test Date: Nov 26, 2007	Publication:	Dec 11, 2007

Benchmark Results Summary

Target Load	Actual Load	ssj_ops	Average Power (W)	Performance to Power Ratio
100%	99.1%	201,689	260	776
90%	89.9%	183,027	256	716
80%	80.3%	163,381	250	653
70%	70.8%	144,116	245	588
60%	60.0%	122,114	238	513
50%	49.8%	101,408	231	439
40%	40.1%	81,694	224	365
30%	29.7%	60,513	215	281
20%	20.2%	41,040	207	198
10%	9.9%	20,240	197	103
Active Idle		0	187	0
Σ ssj_ops / Σ power =				446

© 2009 Standard Performance Evaluation Corporation (SPEC), reprinted with permission.

Figure 7.1   SPEC power and performance for Fujitsu-Siemens RX300 S3

SPECpower_ssj2008

Copyright© 2008 Standard Performance Evaluation Corporation

Dell Inc. PowerEdge 1950 III (Intel Xeon E5440)				SPECpower_ssj2008 = 712 overall ssj_ops/watt	
Test Sponsor:	Dell Inc.	SPEC License #:	55	Hardware Availability:	Mar-2008
Tested By:	Dell Inc.	Test Location:	Round Rock, TX, USA	Software Availability:	Oct-2007
System Source:	Single Supplier	Test Date:	Feb 7, 2008	Publication:	Feb 27, 2008

Benchmark Results Summary

Performance			Power	Performance to Power Ratio
Target Load	Actual Load	ssj_ops	Average Power (W)	
100%	99.0%	284,028	244	1,164
90%	89.8%	257,533	239	1,077
80%	80.2%	230,234	233	988
70%	70.3%	201,611	226	892
60%	60.2%	172,604	218	793
50%	50.3%	144,236	208	695
40%	40.4%	115,928	196	592
30%	29.7%	85,343	183	467
20%	20.0%	57,402	170	337
10%	10.1%	29,070	156	187
	Active Idle	0	143	0
		Σ ssj_ops / Σ power =		712

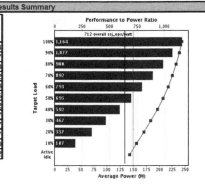

© 2009 Standard Performance Evaluation Corporation (SPEC), reprinted with permission.

Figure 7.2 SPEC power and performance for Dell PowerEdge 1950 III

SPECpower_ssj2008

Copyright© 2008 Standard Performance Evaluation Corporation

Hewlett-Packard Company Proliant DL160 G5 (3.0 GHz, Intel Xeon processor E5450)				SPECpower_ssj2008 = 698 overall ssj_ops/watt	
Test Sponsor:	Hewlett-Packard Company	SPEC License #:	3	Hardware Availability:	Jan-2008
Tested By:	Hewlett-Packard Company	Test Location:	Houston, TX, USA	Software Availability:	Dec-2007
System Source:	Single Supplier	Test Date:	Dec 5, 2007	Publication:	Dec 11, 2007

Benchmark Results Summary

Performance			Power	Performance to Power Ratio
Target Load	Actual Load	ssj_ops	Average Power (W)	
100%	99.2%	308,022	269	1,144
90%	90.2%	280,134	264	1,063
80%	80.0%	248,304	256	971
70%	69.9%	217,096	247	877
60%	60.1%	186,594	238	785
50%	49.6%	154,075	227	680
40%	39.9%	123,805	215	575
30%	29.9%	92,944	203	459
20%	20.1%	62,364	189	330
10%	10.0%	31,049	174	178
	Active Idle	0	160	0
		Σ ssj_ops / Σ power =		698

© 2009 Standard Performance Evaluation Corporation (SPEC), reprinted with permission.

Figure 7.3 SPEC power and performance for HP Proliant DL 160 G5

SPECpower_ssj2008

spec

Copyright© 2008 Standard Performance Evaluation Corporation

Super Micro Computer, Inc. Supermicro 6025B-TR+ (Intel Xeon processor E5345)			SPECpower_ssj2008 = 435 overall ssj_ops/watt	
Test Sponsor:	Intel Corp.	SPEC License #:	13	Hardware Availability:	Nov-2007
Tested By:	Intel Corp.	Test Location:	Hillsboro, Oregon, USA	Software Availability:	Nov-2007
System Source:	Single Supplier	Test Date:	Jan 11, 2008	Publication:	Feb 13, 2008

Benchmark Results Summary

Performance			Power			Performance to Power Ratio
Target Load	Actual Load	ssj_ops	Average Power (W)	Performance to Power Ratio		
100%	99.8%	245,571	334	736		
90%	90.1%	221,834	327	678		
80%	79.7%	196,271	318	617		
70%	69.9%	171,959	309	557		
60%	59.9%	147,354	298	495		
50%	50.1%	123,290	286	431		
40%	40.1%	98,593	273	361		
30%	29.7%	73,019	260	281		
20%	20.2%	49,825	248	201		
10%	10.1%	24,746	234	106		
Active Idle		0	219	0		
Σ ssj_ops / Σ power =				435		

Figure 7.4 SPEC power and performance for Intel Supermicro 6025B-TR+

EPA Metrics

As discussed in Chapter 4, "The Government's Role—Regulation and EPA Activity," the U.S. Environmental Protection Agency (EPA) has more than a decade of history in advancing energy efficiency in IT equipment as well as commercial buildings, beginning with the first ENERGY STAR specifications for computers established in 1992. Through the ENERGY STAR program, the EPA now qualifies a wide array of IT products, including personal computers, imaging equipment, printers, and monitors. In 2008, the EPA created a draft of ENERGY STAR specifications for enterprise computer servers. SPEC created feedback on the EPA's draft specifications. This feedback is mentioned here to again indicate the significant collaboration among many organizations on green IT.

SPEC's Feedback on EPA's First Draft of the ENERGY STAR for Servers Specification

This feedback on the EPA's first draft of the ENERGY STAR for Servers Specification was given in March 2008. The feedback was in the form of a formal letter. It covered areas, such as metrics for server idle state and server idle power, and discussed reporting requirements. Because SPEC has been working with server power metrics for many years, their experience and feedback to the EPA will significantly enhance the EPA's server metrics.

LEED Green Building Rating System

The Leadership in Energy and Environmental Design (LEED) Green Building Rating System, developed by the U.S. Green Building Council (USGBC), provides a certification program for developing high-performance, sustainable buildings. LEED does not directly address the aspect of a rating system for green data centers or green IT. However, there has been activity within LEED to add data centers.

Since its inception in 2000, LEED has grown to encompass more than 18,000 projects in 50 U.S. states and 91 countries covering 4.1 billion square feet (381 square kilometers) of development area. The hallmark of LEED is that it is an open and transparent process where the technical criteria proposed by the LEED committees are publicly reviewed for approval by the more than 19,000 membership organizations that currently constitute the USGBC.

Individuals recognized for their knowledge of the LEED rating system are permitted to use the LEED Accredited Professional (AP) acronym after their name, indicating they have passed the accreditation exam given by the USGBC.

History

LEED began its development in 1994, spearheaded by Natural Resources Defense Council (NRDC) senior scientist Robert K. Watson, who, as founding chairman of the LEED Steering Committee until 2006, led a broad-based consensus process that included nonprofit organizations, government agencies, architects, engineers, developers, builders, product manufacturers, and other industry leaders. Early LEED committee members also included USGBC cofounder Mike Italiano, architects Bill Reed and Sandy Mendler, builder Gerard Heiber, and engineer Richard Bourne. As interest in LEED grew, in 1996, engineers Tom Paladino and Lynn Barker cochaired the newly formed LEED technical committee.

From 1994 to 2006, LEED grew from one standard for new construction to a comprehensive system of six interrelated standards covering all aspects of the development and construction process. LEED also has grown from

Six volunteers on one committee to more than 200 volunteers on nearly 20 committees and three dozen professional staff.

LEED was created to accomplish the following:

- Define "green building" by establishing a common standard of measurement
- Promote integrated, whole-building design practices
- Recognize environmental leadership in the building industry
- Stimulate green competition
- Raise consumer awareness of green building benefits
- Transform the building market

Green Building Council members, representing every sector of the building industry, developed and continue to refine LEED. The rating system addresses the following six major areas:

- Sustainable sites
- Water efficiency
- Energy and atmosphere
- Materials and resources
- Indoor environmental quality
- Innovation and design process

Benefits and Disadvantages

The move toward LEED and green building practices has been driven greatly by the tremendous benefits that are a direct result of implementing a green approach. Green buildings use key resources more efficiently when compared to conventional buildings that are simply built to code. LEED creates healthier work and living environments, contributes to higher productivity and improved employee health and comfort. The USGBC has also compiled a long list of benefits of implementing a LEED strategy, which ranges from improving air and water quality to reducing solid waste. The fundamental reduction in relative environmental impacts and all the economic and occupant benefits go a long way for making a case for green building. It is also important to note that these benefits are reaped by anyone who comes into contact with the project, which includes owners, designers, occupants, and society as a whole.

These benefits do not come without a cost, however. Currently within the industry, green buildings cost more to both design and construct when compared to conventional buildings. These increased costs typically represent initial upfront costs, which are incurred at the start of the project. However, these initial cost increases can be minimized by the economic gains associated with constructing a LEED-certified green building. These economic gains can take the form of anything from productivity gains to decreased life-cycle operating costs. Studies have suggested that an initial up front investment of 2 percent can yield more than ten times the initial investment over the life cycle of the building. From this perspective, there is no initial cost. In fact, the initial cost is actually an investment.

Although the deployment of the LEED Standard has raised awareness of green building practices, its scoring system is skewed toward the ongoing use of fossil fuels. More than half of the available points in the standard support efficient use of fossil fuels, whereas only a handful are awarded for the use of sustainable energy sources. Further, the USGBC has stated support for the 2030 Challenge, an effort that has set a goal of efficient fossil fuel use by 2030. Despite its broad acceptance, mounting scientific evidence suggests that a more aggressive program of sustainable energy deployment is required to protect the climate than that promoted by the LEED Standard and the USGBC.

Certification

Different LEED versions have varied scoring systems based on a set of required prerequisites and a variety of credits in the six major categories previously listed. In LEED v2.2, for new construction and major renovations for commercial buildings, there are 69 possible points, and buildings can qualify for four levels of certification:

- **Certified:** 26–32 points
- **Silver:** 33 –38 points
- **Gold:** 39–51 points
- **Platinum:** 52–69 points

LEED certification is obtained after submitting an application documenting compliance with the requirements of the rating system, as well as paying registration and certification fees. Certification is granted solely by the Green Building Council responsible for issuing the LEED system used on the project.

Recently the application process for new construction certification has been streamlined electronically, via a set of active PDFs that automate the process of filing the documentation.

LEED Versions

Different versions of the rating system are available for specific project types:

- **LEED for New Construction:** New construction and major renovations (the most commonly applied-for LEED certification).
- **LEED for Existing Buildings:** Existing buildings seeking LEED certification.
- **LEED for Commercial Interiors:** Commercial interior fitouts by tenants.
- **LEED for Core and Shell:** Core-and-shell projects (total building minus tenant fitouts).
- **LEED for Homes:** Homes.
- **LEED for Neighborhood Development:** Neighborhood development.
- **LEED for Schools:** Recognizes the unique nature of the design and construction of K–12 schools.
- **LEED for Retail:** Consists of two rating systems. One is based on New Construction and Major Renovations version 2.2. The other track is based on LEED for Commercial Interiors version 2.0.

LEED has evolved since its original inception in 1998 to more accurately represent and incorporate emerging green building technologies. LEED-NC 1.0 was a pilot version. These projects helped inform the USGBC of the requirements for such a rating system, and this knowledge was incorporated into LEED-NC 2.0. The present version of LEED for new construction is LEED-NC v2.2. LEED also forms the basis for other sustainability rating systems such as the EPA's Labs21.

LEED is a popular guide for green building in the United States, and it is developed and continuously modified by workers in the green building industry. Some criticism suggests that although the LEED rating system is sensitive to local environmental conditions, its checklist system does not vary enough by the local environmental conditions. For instance, a building in Maine would receive the same credit as a building in Arizona for water conservation, although the principle is more important in the latter case. Another complaint is that its certification costs require money that could be used to make the building in question even more sustainable. Many critics have noted that compliance and certification costs have grown faster than staff support from the USGBC.

In 2003, the Canada Green Building Council received permission to create its own version of LEED based upon LEED-NC 2.0. This document is called LEED Canada-NC v1.0.

Green Building Council Rating Systems

Table 7.1 shows building rating systems for different countries (source: World Green Building Council www.worldgbc.org):

Australia: Green Star
Canada: LEED Canada-NC 1.0™
Japan: Comprehensive Assessment System for Building Environmental Efficiency (CASBEE)
United Kingdom: BREEAM
United States: LEED Green Building Rating System™

Table 7.1 The World Green Building Council Members (as of 2007), along with the rating system

Country	Rating System / Education	Status
Australia	Green Star	Launched 2003. 25 projects. 800 accredited professionals.
Canada	LEED Canada	Launched 2003. 25 projects. 1,650 accredited professionals.
India	LEED India	LEED India NC launched January 2007; LEED launched in 2003. 17 accredited professionals.

continued

Table 7.1 continued

Country	Rating System / Education	Status
Japan	CASBEE	Launched 2003. 510 accredited professionals.
Mexico	LEED	Not launched; using U.S. LEED.
New Zealand	Green Star NZ	Launched December 2006. Training begins April 2007.
Taiwan	EEWH	Launched 1999.
United Arab Emirates	Under development	Launched 2006.
United Kingdom	BREEAM	Launched 1990. 1,197 licensed assessors.
United States	LEED	Launched 2000 thru 2007 (various sections NC to schools). 35,575 accredited professionals.

LEED and Carbon Trading

It is expected that LEED-NC 3.0 will include a requirement for a carbon footprint (carbon building print) and a significant reduction of GHG (greenhouse gases) beyond a baseline level. The reduction in carbon dioxide must be measured based on the direct and indirect carbon dioxide and equivalent reductions. These include emissions related to the consumption of grid delivered electricity, onsite combustion of fossil fuels, and fugitive refrigerant emissions.

The efforts to quantify emission and reductions in emissions will be to monetize the climate change externality in the same way that a Kyoto Clean Development Project (carbon project) does. One green building project in the world monetized the reductions that act as the main precedent for this type of project: the ITC Hotel Sonar Bangla Sheraton & Towers Kolkata, India.

Professional Accreditation

Green building professionals can become LEED-accredited through the LEED Accredited Professional Exam. This accreditation enables an individual to facilitate the rating of buildings with the various LEED systems. Professional accreditation is administered by the Green Building Certification Institute.

Although LEED is the leading rating system throughout the world for building energy efficiency, the more-specialized rating system required for green IT will come from organizations such as the U.S. EPA working with other government organizations worldwide, professional organizations (for example, the next section of IEEE's EPEAT), electric utilities, IT vendors, and so on.

The Green Grid Data Center Power-Efficiency Metrics: PUE and DCiE

The Green Grid consortium of IT professionals seeks to dramatically raise the energy efficiency of data centers through a series of short-term and long-term best practices and recommendations, which are crucial to the establishment of metric standards. The Green Grid Web site is at http://www.thegreengrid.org/home.

This section describes the very important energy-efficiency metrics for data centers produced by The Green Grid. The first white paper published by The Green Grid in February 2007 was called "Green Grid Metrics: Describing Data Center Power Efficiency." In that paper, The Green Grid proposed the use of **Power Usage Effectiveness** (PUE) and its reciprocal, **Data Center Efficiency** (DCE) metrics, which enable data center operators to quickly estimate the energy efficiency of its data centers, compare the results against other data centers, and determine if any energy-efficiency improvements need to be made. Since then, PUE has received broad adoption in the industry, but DCE has had limited success due to the misconception of what data center efficiency really means. A 2008 white paper from The Green Grid reaffirmed use of PUE, but redefined its reciprocal as data center *infrastructure* efficiency (DCiE). This refinement will avoid much of the confusion around DCE and will now be called DCiE.

In the long term, The Green Grid is developing metrics to measure data center productivity as well as efficiency metrics for all major power-consuming subsystems in the data center. To promote these metrics and drive greater data center energy efficiency for organizations around the world, The Green Grid will publish future white papers that provide detailed guidance on using these metrics. The Green Grid will also continue to collaborate with organizations such as the EPA, DOE, GIPC, ASHRAE, and SNIA to further its mission of advancing data center energy efficiency worldwide.

Short-Term Green Grid Approach

The Green Grid recognizes the importance of establishing metrics for data center efficiency and offers guidance on technologies that claim to improve performance per watt. Ideally, these metrics and processes can help determine if the existing data center can be optimized before a new data center is needed. The two metrics currently in use are PUE and DCiE.

The PUE is defined as follows:

PUE = Total Facility Power / IT Equipment Power

and its reciprocal, the DCiE, is defined as follows:

DCiE = 1/PUE = (IT Equipment Power/Total Facility Power) × 100%

For these two equations, the Total Facility Power is defined as the power measured at the utility meter—the power dedicated solely to the data center. (This is important in mixed-use buildings that house data centers among other consumers of power.) The IT Equipment Power is defined as the equipment that manages, processes, stores, or routes data within the data center. It is important to understand the components for the loads in the metrics, which can be described as follows:

1. **IT Equipment Power:** This includes the load associated with all the IT equipment, such as compute, storage, and network equipment, along with supplemental equipment such as KVM switches, monitors, and workstations or laptops used to monitor or otherwise control the data center.

2. **Total Facility Power:** This includes everything that supports the IT equipment load such as the following:

   ♦ Power delivery components such as UPS, switch gear, generators, PDUs, batteries, and distribution losses external to the IT equipment.

   ♦ Cooling system components such as chillers, computer room air-conditioning units (CRACs), direct expansion air handler (DX) units, pumps, and cooling towers.

- ◆ Compute, network, and storage nodes.

- ◆ Other miscellaneous component loads such as data center lighting.

The PUE and DCiE provide a way to determine opportunities to

- ■ Improve a data center's operational efficiency.

- ■ Compare a data center with competitive data centers.

- ■ Assess data center operators' design and process improvements over time.

- ■ Repurpose energy for additional IT equipment.

Although both of these metrics are essentially the same, you can use them to illustrate the energy allocation in the data center differently. For example, if a PUE is determined to be 3.0, this indicates that the data center demand is three times greater than the energy necessary to power the IT equipment. In addition, you can use the ratio as a multiplier for calculating the real impact of the system's power demands. For example, if a server demands 500 watts and the PUE for the data center is 3.0, then the power from the utility grid needed to deliver 500 watts to the server is 1,500 watts. DCiE is quite useful as well. A DCiE value of 33 percent (equivalent to a PUE of 3.0) suggests that the IT equipment consumes 33 percent of the power in the data center.

Total Facility Power is measured at or near the facility utility's meters to accurately reflect the power entering the data center. This reading should represent the total power consumed in the data center. The data center-only portion of a building utility meter should be measured because power not intended for consumption in the data center can result in faulty PUE and DCiE metrics. For example, if a data center is in an office building, total power drawn from the utility is the sum of the Total Facility Power for the data center, plus the total power consumed by the nondata center offices.

In such a case, the data center administrator needs to measure or estimate the amount of power consumed by the nondata center offices. An estimate will obviously introduce some error into the calculations. IT Equipment Power will be measured after all power conversion, switching, and conditioning is completed and before the IT equipment itself. The most likely measurement point would be at the output of the computer room **power distribution units** (PDUs). This measurement should represent the total power delivered to the computer equipment racks in the data center.

The PUE can range from 1.0 to infinity. Ideally, a PUE value approaching 1.0 would indicate 100 percent-efficiency (that is, all power used by IT equipment only). Currently, no comprehensive data sets exist that show the true spread of the PUE for data centers. Some preliminary work indicates that many data centers might have a PUE of 3.0 or greater, but with proper design, a PUE value of 1.6 should be achievable. This theory is supported by measurements completed by Lawrence Berkeley National Labs that shows that the 22 data centers measured had PUE values in the 1.3 to 3.0 range. Other research indicates that PUE values of 2.0 are achievable with proper design. However, currently no comprehensive industry data set exists that shows accurate PUE statistics for data centers.

Furthermore, there is no general agreement on what constitutes an efficient or inefficient data center. In the future, The Green Grid will offer values that profile target PUE and DCiE metrics for a variety of typical data center configurations. In the short term, The Green Grid suggests that data center owners begin using either the PUE or DCiE metrics. Although the measurement points might not yet be clearly defined, The Green Grid recommends measuring data center efficiency, even if the method currently requires data manipulation. In addition, The Green Grid also encourages data center owners to share and compare their respective PUE and/or DCiE results. Such collaboration can help each data center owner to better analyze individual measurement methodology, as well as to understand how the results compare.

Long-Term Green Grid Direction

A mixed-use building can house any number of functions, such as data centers, labs, offices, and such. For these mixed-use environments, separating out the power usage of just the data center environment is difficult. This is particularly true when the utility power grid enters the building through a single entrance point (for example, through a utility room) and is then distributed to various building locations. These building configurations also make it difficult to determine the power losses between the power entry into the building and its delivery to the data center.

To further complicate the calculation of PUE and DCiE, the latest cooling technologies integrate cooling elements such as pumps, refrigeration, blowers, and heat exchangers within the IT equipment. These technologies blur the lines between what has traditionally been a clear delineation between facility equipment and IT equipment. However, equipment used to provide power and cooling to the data center must be accounted for in the metrics described in this chapter.

As part of the effort to promote dramatic efficiency improvements in the data center, The Green Grid can provide clearer distinctions between facility and IT equipment and recommend power consumption measuring techniques throughout the data center, as well as for the equipment.

Data Center Productivity (DCP)

For the long term, The Green Grid is working on metrics to define data center productivity. This is the natural evolution from PUE and DCiE, and such a metric could be in a form that looks as follows:

Data Center Productivity = Useful Work / Total Facility Power

Although data center productivity is much more difficult to determine, members of The Green Grid feel that this is a key strategic focus for the industry. In effect, this calculation defines the data center as a black box: Power goes into the box, heat comes out, data goes into and out of the black box, and a net amount of useful work is done by the black box. This process in some ways parallels the work being done with the EPA and **Standard Performance Evaluation Corporation** (SPEC) at the server level, in which the SPEC working group might produce a standard on the performance of a system, and the EPA provides a process by which to measure power consumed by the server.

The Green Grid hopes to eventually increase the scope of its work to all IT equipment and will require broad participation from the IT community to help guide and define this pursuit of accurate metrics.

Further PUE Developments

The Green Grid will also consider the development of metrics that provide more granularity for the PUE and DCiE metrics by breaking it down into the following components:

PUE = 1/ DCiE = Cooling Load Factor (CLF) + Power Load Factor (PLF) + 1.0

where all factors are ratios that are divided by the IT Load and

- 1.0 represents the normalized IT Load. Effectively, this is the IT Load Factor (ILF) but is always 1.0.

- Cooling Load Factor (CLF) is the total power consumed by chillers, cooling towers, computer room air conditioners (CRACs), pumps, and so on divided by the IT Load.
- Power Load Factor (PLF) is the total power dissipated by switch gear, uninterruptible power supplies (UPSs), power distribution units (PDUs), and so on divided by the IT Load.

These metrics will be designed to address the blurring of the lines between the IT equipment and facility infrastructure as previously discussed.

Component Efficiency Standards

The Green Grid will also work with the industry to define energy-efficiency guidelines for all the components in the data center. Such components include the following:

- Uninterruptible power supplies (UPSs)
- Switch gear
- Chillers
- Computer room air conditioners
- Direct expansion (DX) units
- Pumps
- Cooling tower
- Generators
- Distribution losses external to the racks
- Power distribution units (PDUs)
- Batteries
- Lighting
- Servers
- Storage

The effort to standardize metrics requires close collaboration with other industry bodies such as the American Society for Heating, Refrigeration, and Air Conditioning Engineers (ASHRAE).

In addition to developing best practices, metrics, guidelines, and standards to help improve data center efficiency, The Green Grid also proposes defining metrics at the rack level as rack-level cooling solutions become more prominent. The group will also offer guidance for measuring both power consumption and "useful work" at both the facility and rack levels, and will continue to provide technical updates as these metrics and measurement techniques evolve. In the meantime, The Green Grid recommends the use of either PUE or its reciprocal, DCiE.

So–What's the Future for Green IT Energy-Use Metrics?

As we discussed, there are currently several green IT energy-use metrics, including SPEC, EPA, EPEAT, LEED, and The Green Grid systems. In the United States, green IT and green data center metrics will converge on those developed by the EPA. However, the EPA effort is very much a collaborative effort, and all current measurement systems will play a part. To complicate the problem, some measurement systems and certifications, such as the LEED certificates for green buildings, are outside of the scope of the EPA standards being developed for green IT. In the future, we may have both EPA and SPEC energy-efficiency ratings for servers. That dual-available metric could be beneficial. The EPA ratings will probably be more general (like estimated miles per gallon for an automobile). The SPEC ratings (with controlled tests run by the IT manufacturers) will probably be much more specific, and users will determine more precisely how energy efficient a server will be for their specific server needs (including use of virtual server technology). Ratings for server efficiency—and much more for data center energy efficiency—will always be complicated and dependent on the IT technology needs of each individual customer. Because of this complexity and the continuing evolution of IT technology and user needs, the ratings need to evolve. Having several rating with some overlap can provide the competitive aspect to continually improve green IT metrics and rating systems. We will all benefit.

8

What About Chillers, Cooling Tower Fans, and All That Cooling Equipment Usually Ignored by IT?

"The power and cooling infrastructure that supports IT equipment in data centers uses significant energy, accounting for 50 percent of the total consumption of data centers."

—EPA Report to Congress on Server and Data Center Energy Efficiency, 2007

We know that the cooling of data centers via chillers, cooling tower fans, and such has a significant impact on overall data center energy use and our goal for green IT at data centers. About half of the energy used by data centers goes to cooling and other data center support systems. This chapter looks at methods to improve the energy efficiency of the chillers, cooling tower fans, and other cooling equipment that contribute to 50 percent of the total data center energy consumed.

In general, this chapter focuses on the energy required for data centers other than for IT systems. That remaining energy amounts to about 50 percent and consists of the energy consumed by essential support systems, such as power, cooling, and lighting. Next to technology systems, the cooling system consumes the most energy in the data center, accounting for approximately 37 percent of data center electricity use. Demands on cooling systems have increased substantially in recent years as server densities have risen to unprecedented levels. This change has not only created the need for increased cooling system capacity, but also has exposed inefficiencies in existing approaches to data center cooling. As a result, cooling now represents the second highest opportunity for IT energy cost-savings in many facilities (just after reducing the IT equipment load).

These savings can be significant. For example, a 3 MW IT facility would require 6 MW of power, assuming that support systems consume about the same amount of power as the IT systems. If electricity costs were $.10 per KWH, the total annual energy costs for this facility would be $5.25 million ($600/hour × 8,760 hours). A 10 percent reduction in the IT load would create savings of $260,000, whereas a 30 percent improvement in cooling system efficiency would generate savings of approximately $580,000. This simple example emphasizes the importance of cooling efficiency in our overall goal of reducing energy use at data centers.

One basic concern is that chillers and other data center cooling equipment are not concerns we IT people have had to deal with. My own graduate degrees are in mechanical engineering, so I do have the background. Nevertheless, we IT people usually think of data center cooling as something the Heating, Ventilation, and Air Conditioning (HVAC) engineers will handle. However, for green IT and green data centers in particular, we need to concentrate on all the key areas, and cooling for IT systems is very much a key area. In June 2008, *The New York Times* ran a front-page story in the business section with a headline, "Demand for Data Puts Engineers in the Spotlight." The article went on to state that "In Silicon Valley, the stars have long been charismatic marketing visionaries and cool-nerd software wizards. By contrast, mechanical engineers who design and run computer data centers were traditionally regarded as little more than blue-collar workers in the high-tech world." However, *The New York Times* article went on to state that today data center experts are no longer taken for granted. The torrid growth in data centers to keep pace with the demands of Internet-era computing, their immense need for electricity, and their inefficient use of that energy pose environmental, energy, and economic challenges. So, people with the skills to design, build, and run a data center that does not endanger the power grid are suddenly in demand. Their status is growing, as are their salaries. Expertise in data center cooling is not only critical for energy conservation; it also appears that the status of the engineers working on the data center plumbing will continue to grow.

In considering the topic, the first step is to evaluate and analyze the energy used at your data centers by the cooling equipment. If you have an electric meter that shows your energy use just for the cooling equipment, you're already a step ahead of most data centers. Most data center facilities have meters that give the usage for the whole building.

Starting with the Data Center Cooling Basics

Saving energy for the data center cooling system and building lighting systems should start with the basics. Whenever electrical power is consumed in an Information Technology (IT) room or data center, heat is generated that needs to be removed from the space. Data center and IT room heat removal is one of the most essential, yet least understood, of all critical IT environment processes. Improper or inadequate cooling significantly detracts from the life span and availability of IT equipment. A general understanding of the fundamental principles of air conditioning and the basic arrangement of precision cooling systems facilitates more precise communication among IT and cooling professionals when specifying, operating, or maintaining a cooling solution.

The case studies in Chapter 9, "Green IT Case Studies for Energy Utilities," Chapter 10, "Green IT Case Studies for Universities and a Large Company," and Chapter 11, "Worldwide Green IT Case Studies," indicate some of the basic ways to save energy:

- For one data center, there are 10 chillers, and chillers are powered down when not needed (for example, when outside air in the winter is used for cooling). In the winter, typically at least half the chillers are powered down. This is a basic change in operations that can give an almost immediate payback.

- An energy-savings project to install variable frequency drives for the blowers on the chillers resulted in a 12-month payback.

- Putting the data center lights on motion detectors resulted in a 3-month payback.

New and innovative cooling solutions available would be especially valuable for new data center construction. This chapter discusses methods being developed to store energy including stored cooling.

The use of fuel cells to provide electricity for data centers is receiving a great amount of research attention. Details of this technology, as well as recommendations, will be given in this chapter.

Data Center Stored Energy Including Stored Cooling

One of the new innovative cooling solutions available for the data center is **stored cooling**. Technically, this works something like the old idea of having an icehouse, where during the winter, ice chunks are cut from the frozen lake and stored in an ice warehouse with the ice covered with straw. Then in the summer, the ice is transported to your icebox (replaced by modern day refrigerators). In concept, data center stored cooling is a type of 21st-century technology to replace the 19th-century icehouse. Just like the icehouse, the technology works best when used in a climate where it gets cold in the winter, and you have lots of "cold" to store. Canada, for example, is a good choice for the technology. Because I grew up in North Dakota, I can attest that this state has a lot of winter cold to store for cooling of data centers.

In addition to stored cooling for data centers, innovations are underway for many types of stored energy. One interesting initiative is the partnership between the U.S. DOE Energy Storage Research Program and the New York State Energy Research and Development Authority (NYSERDA) to demonstrate electrical energy storage options. The demonstration projects include electrical energy storage devices at multiple sites in New York State. The projects are described online at http://www.storagemonitoring.com/nyserda-doe/storage-home.shtml.

In the solar power section, Appendix C, "Comparison of Different Power-Generation Methods," describes methods for storing energy. Some of these energy storage methods could be applicable for data centers. The storage methods include the following:

- Thermal storage systems can generate electricity during cloudy weather and at night.

- Thermal mass systems can store solar energy in the form of heat at domestically useful temperatures for daily or seasonal durations. Thermal storage systems generally use readily available materials with high specific heat capacities such as water, earth, and stone. Well-designed systems can lower peak demand, shift time-of-use to off-peak hours, and reduce overall heating and cooling requirements.

- Phase change materials such as paraffin wax and Glauber's salt are another thermal storage media.

- Solar energy can be stored at high temperatures using molten salts. Salts are an effective storage medium because they are low cost, have a high specific heat capacity, and can deliver heat at temperatures compatible with conventional power systems.

- Off-grid photovoltaic systems have traditionally used rechargeable batteries to store excess electricity. With grid-tied systems, excess electricity can be sent to the transmission grid. Net metering programs give these systems a credit for the electricity they deliver to the grid. This credit offsets electricity provided from the grid when the system cannot meet demand, effectively using the grid as a storage mechanism.

- Pumped-storage hydroelectricity stores energy in the form of water pumped when energy is available from a lower elevation reservoir to a higher elevation one. The energy is recovered when demand is high by releasing the water to run through a hydroelectric power generator.

The tried-and-true methods of cooling a data center haven't changed much over the years. You find a large air conditioner or two and bring in a lot of electric power to drive the air conditioners. Across the globe, network and server administrators tend to keep light jackets or sweaters in their cubicles to provide some warmth when they have to spend time in the server room. This is because those massive air conditioners placed in the ceiling, the floor, or along the walls are pumping out 60-degree air and keeping the whole room frigid. It's a solution that certainly works but is obviously wasteful. Why keep the whole room at 68 degrees when the only place you need air that cold is at the front of the racks?

One solution is the use of new in-row cooling solutions. Rather than sitting on the sidelines and blowing cold air everywhere, they're placed between the racks, where they push the cold right where it needs to be: directly into the servers. By going right to the heat source, in-row solutions reduce waste, cut the energy bill, and eliminate the need for the data center parka.

These new cooling solutions can save a significant amount of energy. However, whether it's data center cooling systems or other data center energy-savings solutions, we need enhanced measurement systems for all parts of the data center. Figure 8.1 indicates the scope of power management at a data center. The data center management required would need to include the use of stored cooling or direct use of chillers for cooling. Appendix A, "Green IT Checklist and Recommendations," describes some of the tools available for managing data center energy use.

Data Center IT and Facilities Management

What is the problem we're trying to solve?

- *Constrained resources (space / power)*
- *High cost of infrastructure and operations*
- *No holistic view of IT and facilities infrastructure resources*

Why is it a problem?

- *Inhibits revenue growth and responsiveness*
- *Increased cost of operations reduces competitiveness*
- *Limits ability to drive intelligent business decisions around E2E resource management*

What is the high-level solution?

- *Jointly optimize IT and Facility DESIGN*
- *Jointly optimize IT and Facility OPERATIONS*

> ### *A Green Data Center Energy Management objective is to:*
>
> - *Develop innovative solutions strategy*
> - *Implement deployment plans that integrate IT and facilities infrastructure*
> - *Infuse state-of-the-art hardware and software technologies*
> - *Optimize economically feasible and environmentally responsible data center designs and operations.*

  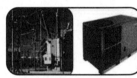

| **IT Assets** | **Data Center Infrastructure** | **Building Systems** |
| *(Servers, storage, network)* | *(UPS, PDUs)* | *(HVAC, power, lighting, security)* |

Source: IBM Big Green Team

Figure 8.1   Managing data center energy use

Back to the Future—Water-Cooled Servers

Not all IT venders are happy about the back-to-the-future trend to use water- (or more generally liquid-) cooled servers. IBM produced its last water-cooled mainframe in 1995. Generally speaking, data center facility engineers are concerned that water leaks in the data center could be devastating. In 2008, Sun Microsystems, Inc., indicated that it would no longer use liquid cooling. That was in significant contrast to 2008 commentary and product rollouts from IBM, HP, and American Power Conversion Corp. (APC), among others. In 2008, Sun rebuffed the view that liquid cooling is necessary now—or even an inevitability in the future. Jeff O'Neal, director of product marketing for Sun Scalable Systems Group, said liquid-as-an-answer is inefficient and described it as Band-Aiding a problem that should be addressed with design at the chip level. "With Niagara, we created a chip with eight-cores...by keeping those threads busy, we could actually run at a relaxed clock speed, which helps keep the heat down.... Retrofitting and greenfielding [a data center for liquid cooling]...add both cost and complexity. The real answer is don't put the heat into the data center and you don't have as much to take out." So, the back-to-the-future direction of using liquid cooling in the data center is not without controversy. In truth, liquid cooling never actually left the data center because computer room air conditioners (CRACs), typically scattered about data centers, use chilled liquid from the chillers (outside the computer room) to generated cold air for cooling the IT equipment. A certain amount of controversy can help assure that standards for the new data center IT liquid cooling technology are well tested.

Strategies for Increasing Data Center Cooling Efficiency

The following data center cooling efficiency strategies were based on a white paper from Emerson/Liebert (see the Bibliography). The white paper indicates that as electricity prices and IT power consumption continue to rise, IT-related energy costs are getting increased scrutiny. Cooling accounts for approximately 37 percent of electricity usage within a well-designed data center and, in many cases, represents a significant opportunity to reduce IT energy costs.

Some proven strategies for increasing data center cooling efficiency are as follows:

- **Proper sealing of the data center environment:** A vapor seal plays a critical role in controlling relative humidity and reducing unnecessary humidification and dehumidification.

- **Optimizing air flow:** Rack arrangement, computer room air conditioner placement, and cable management all impact the amount of energy expended to move air within the critical facility.

- **Using economizers where appropriate:** Economizers allow outside air to support data center cooling during colder months, creating opportunities for energy-free cooling.

- **Increasing cooling system efficiency:** New technologies, such as variable capacity systems and improved controls, are driving increased efficiency of room air-conditioning systems.

- **Bringing cooling closer to the source of heat:** Supplemental cooling systems bring cooling closer to the source of heat, reducing the amount of energy required for air movement.

Together, these methods can reduce cooling system energy costs by 30 percent to 45 percent and generate significant, recurring savings. Coupled with emerging technologies such as higher-efficiency processors and new chip-based cooling technologies, these measures can keep energy costs in line as server densities and the price of energy continue to rise.

Until recently, little attention has been given to the cost of energy used by IT systems. But as power consumption and electricity prices rise, energy costs receive more scrutiny from senior-level executives seeking to manage dollars. In fact, energy costs have now become one of the driving factors in decisions regarding data center location and design.

A recent survey by the Data Center Users Group showed that data center energy efficiency is fast becoming a priority in the industry, with 42 percent of survey respondents saying they have either analyzed efficiency or are currently analyzing it. Respondents perceived significant opportunities for energy efficiency to be in the areas of cooling equipment (49 percent), servers (46 percent), power equipment (39 percent), and storage (21 percent).

EYP Mission Critical analyzed data center energy usage and estimated that 50 percent of data center energy is consumed by information technology systems. It is understood that saving 10 percent of the energy consumed by the IT equipment will create an additional seven percent to 10 percent energy reductions as the cooling and power distribution loads are reduced. Thus, energy reductions in this area have a downstream effect that can almost double savings.

A number of strategies can be evaluated for reducing IT system energy consumption, most notably server consolidation and virtualization. For more information on these strategies, see the Liebert white paper, "Using Virtualization and Digital Control Technologies to Increase Data Center Operating Efficiency," available at www.liebert.com.

1. Proper Sealing of the Data Center Environment

Cooling losses through floors, walls, and ceilings, or the introduction of humidity from outside the critical facility, reduce cooling system efficiency. Therefore, the data center should be isolated from the general building and outside environment as much as possible.

Keep doors closed at all times and use a vapor seal to isolate the data center atmosphere. The vapor seal is one of the least expensive and most important methods of controlling the data center environment and is particularly important in maintaining proper humidity levels. If humidity is too high in the data center, **conductive anodic failures** (CAF), **hygroscopic dust** failures (HDF), tape media errors, and excessive wear and corrosion can occur. These risks increase exponentially as relative humidity increases above 55 percent.

If humidity is too low, the magnitude and propensity for **electrostatic discharge** (ESD) increase, damaging equipment or adversely affecting operation. Also, tape products and media might perform poorly when exposed to low relative humidity.

ASHRAE has defined the optimal relative humidity for a data center environment as 40 percent to 55 percent. CRACs control humidity through humidification or dehumidification as required, both of which consume energy. An effective vapor seal can reduce the amount of energy expended on humidification or dehumidification.

The vapor seal is typically created using a combination of plastic film, vapor-retardant paint, vinyl wall coverings, and vinyl floor systems. All openings in doors, windows, and cable entrances should also be sealed.

This sealing is the first step in any plan to increase efficiency. If the room is not properly sealed, all other measures for improving efficiency will be less effective. A data center assessment, available through various consulting engineering firms or your cooling system supplier, can help identify areas where outside air is entering the controlled environment and recommend strategies for proper sealing.

2. Optimizing Air Flow

After the room is sealed, the next step is to ensure efficient air movement. The goal is to move the maximum amount of heat away from the equipment using a minimum expenditure of energy. Optimizing air flow requires evaluation and optimization of rack configuration, air conditioner placement, and cable management.

- **Rack Arrangement:** Most equipment manufactured today is designed to draw in air through the front and exhaust it out the rear. This allows equipment racks to be arranged to create hot aisles and cold aisles. This approach positions racks so that rows of racks face each other, with the front of each opposing row of racks drawing cold air from the same aisle (the "cold" aisle). Hot air from two rows is exhausted into a "hot" aisle, raising the temperature of the air returning to the CRAC and allowing the CRAC to operate more efficiently.

This approach is most effective when cold and hot air do not mix. Therefore, perforated floor tiles should be removed from hot aisles and used only in cold aisles. Blanking panels should be used to fill open spaces in racks to prevent hot air from being drawn back through the rack.

Some type of cabling grommet should also be used to prevent the cold air from entering the space through cable openings, which are typically at the rear of the rack. Additional steps such as using a return ceiling plenum to draw the air back to the CRAC and physical curtains at the ends of the cold aisles have also proved to be very effective in minimizing mixing of the hot and cold air.

- **CRAC Placement:** When using the hot-aisle/cold-aisle approach, CRAC units should always be placed perpendicular to the hot aisle to reduce air travel and prevent hot air from being pulled down into the cold aisles as it returns to the air conditioner. A return ceiling plenum can be effective in minimizing the mixing of hot and cold air.

- **Cable Management:** The explosion in the number of servers that data centers must support has created cable management challenges in many facilities. If not properly managed, cables can obstruct air flow through perforated floor tiles and prevent air from being exhausted out the rear of the rack. Check the under-floor plenum to determine if cabling or piping is obstructing air flow. Overhead cabling is becoming increasingly popular, which eliminates the potential for obstruction. Deeper racks are now available to allow for increased airflow. Sometimes existing racks can be equipped with expansion channels to add depth for cables and airflow. Be cautious when using cable management "swing arms" because they are not compatible with all IT equipment air-flow patterns.

Finally, but perhaps most significantly, investigate bringing high-voltage three-phase power as close to the IT equipment as possible and increasing the voltage of the IT equipment. These steps will minimize the number and size of the power cable feeds under the floor. This can sometimes be accomplished by using high-voltage three-phase managed power strips within the rack, but it might also require the use of multiple-pole distribution panels or PDUs located within the row of IT equipment racks.

You can add fans to the rear of racks to draw hot air out of the rack, but be aware that these fans consume energy and generate additional heat that must be removed from the room.

3. Using Economizers to Achieve Free Cooling

In many locations, you can use outside cool air to supplement data center cooling and provide "free cooling" during colder months. This is accomplished through the use of economizer systems. A study on building control systems by Battelle Laboratories found that, on average, the normalized heating and cooling **Energy Use Intensity** (EUI) of buildings with economizers was 13 percent lower than those without economizers.

The two basic types of economizer systems are air-side economizers and fluid-side economizers. Choosing the type for a specific project is a function of climate, codes, performance, and preference:

- **Air-side economizer:** The air-side economizer uses a system of sensors, ducts, and dampers to allow entry of the appropriate volume of outside air to satisfy facility cooling requirements. Air-side economizers are available in two types—a "dry air" system and an "evaporatively conditioned" air system. The former is the most common, but its use is restricted to a few geographic locations because of the high cost of energy required to add moisture to the room when the ambient dew-point is below 35° F. The evaporative conditioned solution is an economical method for conditioning the air prior to introduction to the data center, but uncertain reliability and high-maintenance requirements have generally made this approach unattractive to most data center operators.

  The key to either of these solutions is proper control. The control should be based on enthalpy comparisons, not just dry-bulb temperature. Also controls must be implemented to detect incidences of high pollen, dust, or other external contaminants and effectively lock out the economizer during these conditions.

- **Fluid-side economizer:** A fluid-side economizer system is typically incorporated into a chilled water or glycol-based cooling system, and works in conjunction with a heat rejection loop consisting of a cooling tower, evaporative cooler, or drycooler. CRAC units incorporate a conventional glycol-cooled unit, along with a second cooling coil, control valve, and temperature monitor. During colder months, the glycol solution returning from the outdoor drycoolers or cooling tower is routed to the second coil, which becomes the primary source of cooling for the room. As long as the "free cooling" fluid is 8° F below the CRAC return temperature, there is some benefit to having the "free cooling" running because it minimizes the load on the primary cooling method.

Fluid-side economizers are the system of choice for most data center environments because they are not affected by outdoor humidity levels and so are effective in a wider portion of the temperature/humidity band. Also, they do not add any additional air filtration requirements on the data center. For more detailed information on economizers, see the white paper, "Utilizing Economizers Effectively in the Data Center," available at www.liebert.com.

4. Increasing the Efficiency of Room Air Conditioners

Three factors are critical to optimizing the efficiency of CRAC units:

- How efficiently the units operate at partial load
- How efficient the units are at removing sensible heat as compared to latent heat
- How well multiple units work together

Increasing efficiency at part load is a significant issue. Data centers are designed with some level of cooling system redundancy. Plus, the actual capacity of a direct expansion or air-cooled CRAC unit increases as the outdoor ambient temperature decreases below the peak design condition (typically 95° F). This means equipment is operating at less than 100 percent load all the time, creating the opportunity to design systems to operate more efficiently during normal operating conditions. Operating conditions usually aren't stable, so some method of varying capacity based on operating conditions is required.

There are several approaches to providing variable capacity in a direct expansion CRAC unit. The two most common are four-step compressor unloading and Digital Scroll™ compressor technology.

Four-step compressor unloading works by shutting off the flow of refrigerant to some of the cylinders within the system. This minimizes the need to cycle compressors on and off to control capacity. Because unloading essentially changes the compressor operating point, it enables the cooling system to operate more efficiently at lower capacities. For example, a system operating with two compressors "unloaded" will consume approximately 50 percent of the energy of a fully loaded system but will deliver approximately 76 percent capacity because the condenser and evaporator are sized for full load.

Digital Scroll compressor technology offers a newer way to precisely match capacity and power consumption to the desired load and can deliver significantly lower energy consumption compared to standard fixed-capacity compressors.

Traditional modulation technologies (cycling units on and off to match load conditions) often consume close to full-load energy regardless of the required capacity. In a system designed for high reliability, the compressors do not just turn on and off. There is a turn-on delay period and a turn-off pump-down period where the compressor is actually running, ensuring proper oil lubricant to the compressor bearings before power is removed.

Improving Sensible Heat/Latent Heat Removal Capacity: IT equipment generates sensible (dry) heat. Latent heat comes from people and outdoor humidity infiltration (which can be minimized through the vapor seal discussed previously). As server density or capacity increases, it creates a corresponding increase in the sensible heat load. The latent heat load is unaffected. Thus, using cooling solutions that can operate at a 100 percent sensible capacity, except when dehumidification is required, can result in reduced energy consumption. Operating a variable capacity compressor at a lower capacity raises the temperature of the evaporator coil. This means less latent cooling takes place. Under the vast majority of load conditions, the evaporator coil temperature will be high enough to achieve 100 percent sensible cooling. Thus, no energy will be required to add humidity that was inadvertently removed.

Improving Coordination Across Multiple Units: The data center environment has become more diverse as newer high-density servers are deployed alongside older systems. As a result, without proper coordination between room cooling units, air conditioners might be operating in different modes of temperature and humidity control. For example, a unit on the north side of the room might be sensing low relative humidity conditions and adding humidity, while a unit on the south side of the room is sensing high relative humidity and removing moisture from the air. The actual moisture in the air is equal, but because the measurement is a relative measurement, the higher the temperature, the lower the relative humidity. Advanced control systems can be deployed across all the CRAC units in a room to enable the units to communicate and coordinate their operation, preventing the "fighting mode."

5. Deploying Supplemental Cooling

Supplemental cooling is a relatively new approach to data center cooling. Introduced in 2002, this approach gained rapid acceptance as data center managers seek solutions to help:

- Overcome cooling capacity limitations of raised floor systems in high heat density applications.
- Increase cooling system efficiency and flexibility.

Raised-floor cooling proved an effective approach to data center environmental management; however, as rack densities exceed 5 kW, and load diversity across the room increases, supplemental cooling should be evaluated for its impact on cooling system performance and efficiency.

At higher densities, equipment in the bottom of the rack might consume so much cold air that remaining quantities of cold air are insufficient to cool equipment at the top of the rack. The height of the raised floor creates a physical limitation on the volume of air that can be distributed into the room, so adding additional room air conditioners might not solve the problem.

Uptime Institute reports that equipment located in the top-third of a data center rack fails twice as often as equipment in the bottom two-thirds of the same rack. The organization also estimates that, for every increase of 18° F above 70° F, long-term electronics reliability falls by 50 percent. The solution to rising rack densities and high room diversity proved to be a pumped refrigerant cooling infrastructure that supports cooling modules placed directly above or alongside high-density racks to supplement the air coming up through the floor. This solution has a number of advantages, including increased cooling system scalability, greater flexibility, and improved energy efficiency.

Two factors contribute to improved energy efficiency: the location of the cooling modules and the refrigerant used. Higher-density applications require fluid-based cooling to effectively remove the high concentrations of heat generated. From an efficiency perspective, refrigerant performs better than water for high-density cooling. The R134 refrigerant used in the Liebert XD system is pumped as a liquid but converts to gas when it reaches the air. This phase change contributes to greater system efficiency. R134 is approximately 700 percent more effective in moving heat than water, which coincidentally is 700 percent more effective than air. It also ensures that expensive IT equipment is not damaged in the event of a refrigerant leak.

Together, the efficiency of the refrigerant and the location of the cooling modules can reduce cooling system energy costs by 27 percent. Additionally, refrigerant use reduces chiller capacity requirements by 20 percent. This increases energy-savings and also enables additional cooling capacity without adding additional chillers.

Traditional floor-mounted cooling systems with under-floor air delivery will continue to play an essential role in data center environmental management. It is recommended that traditional systems be configured to deliver the required cooling for the first 100 watts per square foot of heat load, as well as solve the room's full humidification and filtration requirements. Supplemental cooling can be deployed for densities beyond 150 watts per square foot.

Fuel Cells for Data Center Electricity

Fuel cells have been proposed to power data centers. For instance, the polluting diesel backup generators that most data centers rely on might be replaced by fuel cells. In 2008, Fujitsu began using a fuel-cell generator to power its data center in Silicon Valley. Fuel cells have also been proposed to be used in an emergency or during peak demand to take some of the load off the grid. Hydrogen-powered fuel cells are environmentally desirable because the only output, in addition to energy, is water. The problem is in obtaining the hydrogen. Currently, hydrogen is usually produced through an energy intensive process using natural gas and immense amounts of electricity. When technological breakthroughs enable us to produce hydrogen efficiently, fuel cells for data center energy will be a significant step forward.

Other Emerging Technologies for Data Centers

Energy costs will likely continue to rise in the future as will the computing requirements of most organizations. Taking steps today to increase the efficiency of the cooling system can offset the impact of rising energy costs when newer, higher-efficiency technologies are deployed. Three technologies, in particular, have potential to significantly enhance data center energy efficiency as follows:

- Multicore processors
- Embedded cooling
- Chip-level cooling

Newer servers are now based on multicore processors that enable a single processor to perform multiple separate tasks simultaneously, run multiple applications on a single processor, or complete more tasks in a shorter amount of time. Chip manufacturers claim that multicore processors can reduce power and heat by up to 40 percent.

Embedded cooling uses the Liebert XD cooling infrastructure to deliver high-efficiency cooling directly inside the rack. This approach brings cooling even closer to the source of heat and allows the cooling system to be optimized for a particular rack environment. An example of how effective this approach can be is the CoolFrame system from Egenera and Emerson Network Power. This system can prevent 20 kW of heat from an Egenera BladeFrame system from entering the room by removing the heat before it leaves the rack.

Chip-level cooling takes this approach to the next level by helping to move heat away from the chip. As embedded and chip-level cooling solutions are deployed, a highly efficient three-tiered approach to data center cooling will emerge. In this approach, heat is effectively moved away from the chip and then cooled in the rack, with stable temperatures and humidity maintained by room air conditioners. These developments are not expected to reduce data center cooling requirements. Instead, they will result in an increase in the amount of computing power that can be supported by a particular facility. As a result, the efficiency improvements made today will continue to pay dividends well into the future as these new developments enable existing facilities to support densities that are not possible today.

The cooling system represents a significant opportunity to improve efficiency. In many cases, relatively simple and inexpensive changes—such as improving room sealing, moving cables or other objects that obstruct airflow, or installing blanking panels—can pay immediate dividends. In addition, new technologies, such as variable capacity room air conditioners and sophisticated control systems, should be considered for their impact on efficiency. Finally, supplemental cooling systems provide a response to increased equipment densities that can increase the scalability and efficiency of existing cooling systems.

Chapter Summary and Conclusions

The following conclusions can be drawn from the previous discussion on green IT:

- Data center cooling technology will continue to grow in importance because about half the energy in a data center goes to cooling.
- Water-cooled systems will continue to make a comeback because the thermodynamics of cooling greatly favors liquid over air from a heat transfer efficiency standpoint.
- New technologies for cooling, including the use of fuel cells, imbedded cooling, and chip-level cooling, will continue to evolve.
- Cooling will continue to play an important role in the new solutions and processes to address the data center energy situation from end to end. The solutions cover the spectrum from the server end through power management features and at the data center ends through integrated IT/facilities modular solutions.

9

Green IT Case Studies for Energy Utilities

"Knowing is not enough; we must apply. Willing is not enough; we must do."

—Goethe

Energy corporations, and especially electric utilities, have an interesting and important role in the establishment of green data centers. As first mentioned in Chapter 5, "The Magic of 'Incentive'—The Role of Electric Utilities," electric utilities have a significant interest in avoiding, when possible, the need to build new electric power plants to meet peak demand. In addition, they can use their experience with their own data centers and green IT initiatives to help their customers evaluate best practices for energy conservation. Then, they can use that experience to establish electric utility rate cases to provide significant incentive for their customers to move to green data centers and green IT in general. The importance of incentives from energy utility rate cases in encouraging green IT was discussed in Chapter 5. This chapter looks at case studies for large energy utilities in their march toward green IT and green data centers.

The energy utility case studies include green IT initiatives within PG&E (Pacific Gas & Electric) in California. Also included are details of the green IT process used for a large energy utility in the Chicago area. The author was involved in the green IT initiatives for the energy utility in the Chicago area.

The Environmentally Friendly Aspect of Green Data Centers

In addition to energy efficiency, case studies for electric utilities bring up the aspect of emissions, global warming, and carbon footprint for data centers. This fits with the overall idea behind green IT—for example, energy efficiency that is also eco-friendly. Typically, corporations don't generate the electricity for their IT systems. Thus, the environmental impact of the generation of electricity for their IT systems is out of their control. Electric utilities are often an exception. However, in the author's experience, many electric utility office buildings and often data centers are not in a region where the utility supplies electricity. In addition to electric utilities, some companies are starting to generate electricity for their data centers using new technology such as fuel cells. Also, the backup systems for data centers (for example, diesel generators) are usually owned and run by each company. An Uninterruptible Power Supply (UPS) based on battery systems provides power backup to outages of up to 15 minutes or 20 minutes. The diesel backup systems are used for longer power outages. Environmentally, the diesel backup systems are a concern, but if they are rarely or never needed, that aspect would and should not be a significant aspect of evaluating green IT for a company.

As discussed previously, electric utilities are also very interesting case studies because the utilities can provide rate cases to give their customers incentives to move to green IT.

Pacific Gas and Electric Company (PG&E)

Pacific Gas and Electric Co. (PG&E) has been active in promoting green IT. PG&E has worked with several IT vendors to consolidate its servers, and the company has developed new ways to measure and reduce heat in data centers. They announced this initiative at a conference in New York City, where companies, such as American Power Conversion Corp., Eaton Corp., General Electric Consumer & Industrial, and others gathered to discuss green computing and power-saving initiatives in 2007.

PG&E also worked with the Lawrence Berkeley Lab to produce a useful white paper giving design guidelines for high-performance (green) data centers. This PG&E document on "High-Performance Data Centers" is listed in the Bibliography, and the URL is also given here for convenience:

http://hightech.lbl.gov/documents/DATA_CENTERS/06_DataCenters-PGE.pdf

The topics covered in the white paper include Air Management, Air-Side Economizer, Centralized Air Handling, Cooling Plant Optimization, Direct Liquid Cooling, Free Cooling via Water Side Economizer, Humidification Controls Alternatives, Power Supplies, Self Generation, and Uninterruptible Power Supply Systems.

According to Brad Whitcomb, vice president, customer products and services at PG&E, "Energy efficiency is the number-one priority for PG&E as we work with our customers to meet our environmental goals. We have a goal of having 20% of our energy come from renewable sources by 2010." PG&E worked with various IT technology consultants on its server consolidation plan to lower energy consumption in its 40,000-square foot data centers in San Francisco, Fairfield, and Diablo Canyon, California, through virtualization.

Before embarking on its server consolidation plan , PG&E teamed with IBM Research to develop a tool to measure the three-dimensional temperature distributions in its data centers. IBM used its new Mobile Measurement Technology (MMT) to survey the relevant physical parameters of PG&E data centers and visualize via 3-D images hot spots, air leakage, and other inefficiencies. The data were then used to build customized thermal and energy models to help mitigate hot spots and rectify imbalances within the data center.

IBM's mobile measurement machine includes a position monitoring system with a network of up to 100 sensors that gather thermal data. A 10,000-square foot data center can be completely surveyed by the machine within a few hours. It would take several weeks for several people to survey the data center manually. Wireless thermal sensor technologies can also be deployed to measure long-term, transient temperature effects in the data center.

PG&E Energy-Efficiency Programs

Several IT vendors have participated in PG&E's Energy-Efficiency Incentive program. Select IT vendor systems from recent product lines are eligible for PG&E's incentive program for server replacement projects. These models exceed efficiency benchmarks established by PG&E for web serving and Java™ workloads. The program is strictly limited to replacement projects, and IT vendors are partnering with PG&E to extend the program for additional IT workload types. See Chapter 5 for details and the Web site for PG&E energy savings and rebates.

Electric Utility in the Chicago Area

This case study is for a large energy utility in the Chicago area. The first step was to evaluate and analyze energy use at the customer's data centers. The energy utility in the Chicago area was already in the process of working with rate case information and was interested in establishing rate case incentives on green data center technology for their customers.

Green data center initiatives for this energy utility cover a broad spectrum, including installation of efficient cooling towers and variable speed blowers, as well as the use of energy efficient IT systems such as virtual servers, blade centers, and virtual data storage.

An important process was to increase energy-efficiency awareness by the customer for all of the customer's IT development and management teams. As part of this energy-efficiency awareness, the IT team is considering modifying some customer architectural document templates to include a section on estimated server energy use. That new section could also contain a subsection on estimated emissions and an estimate of reduced emissions using—for example, virtual servers instead of stand-alone servers.

Data Center Energy Efficiency Process Steps

The first step was to evaluate and analyze energy use at the customer's data centers. The evaluation or diagnose step should be the first step in moving toward green IT. This case study is structured around the five process steps (the "wagon wheel") first described in detail in Chapter 2, "The Basics of Green IT." It should be noted that although the steps are numbered, the steps are often carried out at the same time or in somewhat different order, although the diagnose step should always be the first step.

Step 1. Diagnose

This is the first step. The IBM Project Big Green team was brought in to help kick off the diagnose step with the customer and IBM support team. IT vendors can bring their experience with other customer data centers (and their own data centers) and review best practices and lessons learned. Often this review of experience with other data centers for green IT is presented without financial cost.

There are currently three data centers for this energy utility: the main data center and two smaller data centers. The case study information is based on the main data center. The two smaller data centers will take advantage of the energy-efficiency best practices determined for the main data center.

Along with discussing energy-efficiency best practices with IT vendors and other IT groups, another important early step is to evaluate current server and storage energy efficiency. The energy utility had already been following the standard best practices to provide cost-savings at their data centers, for example, with data center consolidation and server consolidation and virtualization. Those best practices for data center cost reduction are also best practices for energy efficiency.

Server refresh on a typical four-year basis was used to upgrade to virtual servers. The server refresh program had already been underway for two years with new IBM xSeries® (x86) and pSeries® (Unix) servers, all of which were enabled for virtualization. The virtualization technology used for the x86 servers was VMware. The pSeries servers were virtualized using LPARS (logical partitions) with micropartitioning technology that allows the CPU resource to be dynamically allocated among the LPARS based on computation need. The main data center was also refreshing servers using blade servers. In addition to the virtual and blade servers, there were two zSeries® mainframes. The mainframes were moved to the main data center during a data center consolidation project that eliminated the need for a large data center in Ohio. There were also hundreds of legacy stand-alone servers at the main data center that were not yet consolidated.

The storage technology at the data center also followed best practices for energy efficiency. All the newer servers use Storage Area Network (SAN) external disk storage under a SAN Volume Controller (SVC) that allows storage virtualization. Tier 1 SAN storage is provided by an IBM DS8300 (90 terabytes). A new DS4800 is now under the SVC. The DS4800 replaces the older IBM DS4500 and DS4400 devices via the storage refresh program. The strategy calls for a three-tier approach for data storage for optimum performance and cost effectiveness.

At the main data center, the raised floor area is approximately 9,600 SF. The tape area is approximately 4,000 SF, and the mechanical area (UPS, air handlers, and such) is approximately 9,000 SF. The data center is considered the raised floor—approximately 10,000 SF. There are also conference rooms and office area at the main data center. The customer facilities manager estimates that 80 percent of the annual energy consumption is for the data center.

Step 2. Build
The 20-year-old Uninterruptible Power Supply (UPS) has been replaced by building an addition to the current data center building (using the current tornado proof construction with very thick walls and protected roof).

This was done to ensure availability of the data center; however, an added benefit is a high-efficiency UPS that should boost efficiency to 95 percent from the 80 percent efficiency that is typical of 20-year-old UPS systems. This should result in a significant gain in energy efficiency because power for almost all IT devices flows through the UPS. For additional information on the impact of the UPS on data center energy utilization, see the upcoming section "The Energy Impact of the UPS."

Another energy-saving project was to place all data center lights on motion detectors. This was a simple low-cost project with a significant return on investment because previously the data center lights were always on.

Step 3. Virtualize

As discussed in Step 1 (and extensively in Chapter 6, "A Most-Significant Step—'Virtualizing' Your IT Systems"), server and storage virtualization is the strategy for all new servers and new storage. The virtualize step is recognized as the most significant way to improve the efficiency of the IT portion of the data center. Server virtualization provides the flexibility to allocate only the server resource required for an application. The data center virtual servers are based on LPARS on the pSeries boxes and VMware for the xSeries servers. AIX® 5.3 and Micro-Partitioning™ allow re-allocation that can be dynamic and can be in fractions of a CPU.

The typical virtual server configurations at the main data center are as follows:

- VMWARE or Windows virtual servers (typical configuration):
  - Four-way dual core xSeries (IBM 3850) (newer boxes are eight-way).
  - 16GB memory (newer boxes have 32GB).
  - Four to 10 virtual servers.
  - Energy savings: The VMware Web site gives case studies of 25 percent to 75 percent energy-savings consolidating stand-alone Intel servers onto VMware virtual servers. Case studies also indicate significant increase in CPU utilization (at least double).
- P570 pSeries for AIX virtual servers:
  - Eight-way dual core p570.
  - 64GB memory.
  - Micro-partitioning.

- Six to 10 LPARS (including two VIO LPARS).
- Energy savings: The IBM pSeries Web sites give case studies of more than 50 percent energy reduction consolidating stand-alone pSeries servers onto pSeries virtual servers (LPARS).

Step 4. Evaluate Cooling

In July 2007, Variable Frequency Drives were installed for all the cooling system blowers. There are 10 chillers, and they are powered down when not needed (for example, when outside air in the winter is used for cooling).

Step 5. Manage and Measure

There is only one meter for the data center building. In addition to the data center, the building includes some conference rooms and a few offices. It is estimated that more than 80 percent of the electrical energy consumption is due to the data center. The IT team plans to use Active Energy Manager (AEM) to measure, monitor, and manage the energy components built into the servers and other IT systems (see information in the "Next Steps for This Energy Utility's Green Data Centers" section).

The main data center energy use versus the IT server and storage capacity has been reduced due to server and storage virtualization and other technology (including cooling and lighting, and so on) to increase efficiency. As analysis of the energy use indicates, the KWH usage increased over three years by two times due to data center consolidation, and such. However, the IT team estimated that server capacity over the same period increased 4 to 5 times. Server capacity increase is not easy to determine, especially with virtual servers and when there is a mix of x86, UNIX®, and mainframe machines. SPEC Marks discussed in Chapter 7, "The Need for Standard IT Energy-Use Metrics," do provide some comparison metrics, and this is an area to be further explored. Chapter 7 also discusses the new SPEC information being gathered on server power and performance, which will prove to be useful for building green data centers.

KWH per month energy consumption at the main data center increased from an average of 217K KWH in 2005 to an average of 555K KWH in 2008 (through 11/08). Thus, the average KWH per month at the main data center increased approximately 2.5 times from 2005 through 2008. Server capacity during that period increased by 4 to 5 times. There was a noticeable peak in the KWH graph during September 2006, when the two large mainframes were moved from the Ohio, data center to the main data center as the final part of a data center consolidation project.

A month-by-month KWH comparison from 2007 to 2008 indicated that monthly electric use was reduced for most months despite an increase in the number of virtual servers. The virtual server growth from 2007 to 2008 is indicated in Table 9.1.

Table 9.1 Main Data Center Virtual Server and Blade-Server Counts

Virtual Server Type	Dec. 2008 count	Dec. 2007 count	Comments
VMware	180	140	First VMware server installed at main data center in Dec. 2005.
AIX LPAR	195	185	Reduction in AIX LPARS due to Oracle/DB2/SQL Server Farm concept. First p570 installed at main data center in Nov. 2005.
Blade Server	060	060	
Total	435	385	

Additional Energy Efficiency for the Energy Utility's Data Center

There are several projects for the main data center that will continue to improve energy efficiency, as follows:

- **New UPS:** As discussed under the "Build" step, the facility manager for the main data center drove the process to replace the 20-year-old UPS. This was completed at the end of 2008. Because power for almost all IT devices flows through the UPS, the efficiency improvement of the UPS (up to 15 percent) will significantly help reduce electrical use at the data center during 2009 and beyond.

- **Continued IT virtualization:** There are still several hundred legacy stand-alone servers at the main data center. The plan is to continue to consolidate and virtualize these servers based on the ongoing server refresh and server consolidation programs.

Next Steps for This Energy Utility's Green Data Centers

The next steps for this utility's green data centers include monthly reports on server energy use correlated with server CPU utilization and thermal information. These reports will give us the trends to help answer the question on how data center virtualization has increased server CPU utilization and reduced server energy use.

AEM would allow energy utilization reporting for each server. This will work well at the data center because Active Energy Manager is an IBM Director extension that supports the following endpoints: IBM BladeCenter®, POWER™, System x®, and System z® servers. IBM storage systems and non-IBM platforms can be monitored through PDU+ support. In addition, Active Energy Manager can collect information from select facility providers, including Liebert SiteScan from Emerson Network Power and SynapSense (the preceding linked content resides outside of ibm.com®). The Active Energy Manager server can run on the following platforms: Windows on System x, Linux® on System x, Linux on System p®, and Linux on System z. Active Energy Manager uses agent-less technology and, therefore, no agents are required on the endpoints. The IT team plans to implement AEM along with the current Netcool® system during 2009.

The IT team will continue to measure energy use and enhance reporting. The IT team will also continue to emphasize that data center energy savings (green data centers) are ongoing initiatives where the measurement process will be continually improved to better quantify the savings due to energy initiatives.

The IT team needs to continue to look at emerging technology for server and storage enhancement. These technology areas include Information Lifecycle Management (ILM), overall storage management, tiered storage, Power6 technology, VMware enhancements, and enhanced cooling technology. The IT team will also continue to work with IT vendors and other groups/utilities on green data center technology.

The Energy Impact of the UPS

The replacement of a 20-year-old UPS was one of the initiatives in the preceding case study. Updating old, inefficient UPS systems to high-efficiency models can have a significant impact on your data center efficiency. It is estimated that efficiency losses in a data center's UPS represent about

5 percent to 12 percent of all the energy consumed in data centers. This estimate is from the Lawrence Berkeley National Lab Web site on data centers: http://hightech.lbl.gov/DCTraining/emerging.html. Manufacturer specifications can differ widely from measured results because of differences in loading conditions and test procedures. There can also be differences between efficiencies measured under reference conditions and under in-use conditions in data centers. Work is underway to estimate how much energy could be saved by improving UPS efficiency, developing standardized efficiency testing protocols, measuring the efficiencies of UPSs across a range of load conditions, and proposing efficiency metrics for use by the marketplace in comparing units for purchase.

Chapter Summary and Conclusions

The following conclusions can be drawn from this chapter's discussion on green IT for energy utilities:

- Energy utilities have an important role in encouraging data center energy efficiency.
- Energy utilities have a significant incentive to encourage energy efficiency for both their own IT and customer IT to avoid building additional power-generation plants to meet an increasing power demand. This is due to both the significant expense and the social aspects of building new power plants.
- Rate cases from electric utilities provide an important way for the utility to encourage data center energy efficiencies.
- Case studies as described in this chapter confirm the importance of green IT strategies for electric utilities.

10

Green IT Case Studies for Universities and a Large Company

"Ah, to build, to build! That is the noblest of all the arts."

—Henry Wadsworth Longfellow, from the poem, "Michael Angelo" (pt. I, II, 1.54)

The case studies described in this chapter include "lessons learned" and information on the evolution of best practices for building green data centers and leveraging green IT. The case studies include universities (Bryant and Columbia) and a large (61,000 SF) corporate data center.

The first case study is the well-publicized green data center project for Bryant University (http://biz.yahoo.com/iw/070713/0277526.html). The Bryant University project was with a scalable modular data center design. In addition to the modular data center design used by Bryant, other innovative data center designs are discussed (including Google's "Data Center in a Box" concept).

The Columbia University case study includes information on plans for a green data center that can be applicable to almost any organization. In analyzing the opportunity at Columbia University for green IT, the IT team discussed many proposed solutions that range—in their words—from "bleeding edge" to "common sense." Many of the solutions involve the university's expanding requirement to support **High-Performance Computing** (HPC) based on a centrally administered and shared server cluster of high-density blade systems for space and power efficiency. Universities offer a rich environment for such innovations and best practices. Not only do they have the administrative systems common to any large organization, but also with computation increasingly being a key element of all research projects, the need for centralized and energy-efficient computing has never been greater. Historically at large universities, many of the computers used for research are dispersed throughout the campus, often in spaces not designed for the multinode clusters required for HPC. In most cases, these dispersed computers are administered by graduate students rather than IT professionals. Also, each group of dispersed computers usually operate at much less than full capacity because the computer resource for one research project cannot be shared with other research projects because each have their own computer systems.

In my experience, universities are similar to any organization in that different groups with their own computer resource are often skeptical about the benefits versus the loss of flexibility and control in moving to a centralized, shared computer resource. Different groups in a corporation or university often question the benefits of shared computing from performance, accessibility, and security aspects. However, the global economic meltdown in the second half of 2008 has provided a substantial additional motivation to move to green data centers because of the promise of substantial economic savings in addition to the societal necessity of reducing energy consumption to benefit the environment. The Columbia University case study discusses the university's proposed solution for addressing these concerns.

The Lexington, Kentucky, corporate data center case study should give valuable lessons learned for improving the energy efficiency of any large legacy data center. This data center, originally at 61,000 square feet and bursting at the seams, is far larger than any of the data centers I've worked on and should give encouragement to any IT group looking at creating a green data center out of a very large data center that at first might appear to be "beyond repair."

Bryant University Scalable Modular Approach to a Green Data Center

The Bryant University (Smithfield, Rhode Island) green data center is a state-of-the-art project based on the concept of a "Scalable Modular Data Center." The IBM modular data center used at Bryant is similar in concept to Google's "Data Center in a Box" design. The modular design concept is to build small and easily expand as needed. Google's design is a container solution that also can be readily expanded. Sun Microsystems also has a Data Center in a Box concept, called Project Blackbox. During its debut in 2007, Sun installed a Blackbox—essentially a cargo container for 18-wheelers— outside of Grand Central Station in New York City, to show how easily one of its data centers could be installed. In addition, Rackable Systems has a similar data center design it calls ICE Cube. These modular and container designs will be a significant help for the predicted worsening space crunch for data centers due to high-performance demands and expensive real estate prices. In this section, we first look at the details of the Bryant University modular data center design and then further discuss the future of that type of data center design approach.

The modular data center technology allowed Bryant University to meet the school's technology requirements for its growing enrollment while simultaneously becoming more energy conscious by implementing a green data center. The Scalable Modular Data Center proved to be a cost-saving, energy-efficient solution that was rapidly deployed as a pre-engineered data center.

Founded in 1863, Bryant University has a history of excellence and innovation, both academically and technologically. The university prides itself on being wired with "one port per pillow" in each of its dorm rooms; however, as the university grew, its three data centers couldn't handle enterprise information technology (IT) for either communication or computing. The IT vendor services included a data center strategy, data center design, server and storage integration, relocation planning, project management, infrastructure equipment sourcing, installation services and management, data center testing, and start-up management. A modular data center solution can usually be implemented in 8 to 12 weeks and is usually about 15 percent less expensive than traditional data center builds.

The modular design solution integrates power, cooling, rack, management, services, and security, allowing for selection of standardized components to create a solution through modular configurations. By using standardized components, the architecture easily scales to meet the evolving needs of the university.

Summary, Bryant University Scalable Modular Data Center

Rapid deployment of a traditional data center at 20 percent less cost than a traditional data center raised floor design.

Client Requirements

- Centralized IT infrastructure to replace costly and inefficient decentralized infrastructure that proved to be increasingly unable to scale to growing demands for IT services.
- Consolidation of systems in an enterprise-class data center.

Solution

- Implementation of a Scalable Modular Data Center solution with advanced InfraStruXure architecture from APC.
- Standardized blade servers for virtualized Microsoft Windows and Linux systems.
- Savings on power and cooling costs; ability to provision new virtual servers in less than one day.

Benefits

- Reduced physical servers from 75 to 40.
- 40 percent to 50 percent reduction in floor space requirements.
- Reduced carbon footprint and reduced power consumption/cooling.

Bryant University Modular Data Center Design Details

Rhode Island's Bryant University sees its fair share of snow and cold weather. All that cold outside air is perfect to chill the liquid that cools the university's new server room in the basement of the John H. Chafee Center for International Business. It's just one way that Bryant's IT department is saving 20 percent to 30 percent on power consumption compared with a year ago.

Art Gloster, Bryant's VP of IT for the last five years, stated that before a massive overhaul completed in 2007, the university had four data centers scattered across campus, including server racks stuffed into closets with little concern for backup and no thought for efficiency. Now Bryant's consolidated, virtualized, reconfigured, blade-based, and heavily automated data center is an early example of green data center initiatives.

For Bryant, it's more than cheap or even clean power. Previously, most power outages would shut down the network. The last power outage before Bryant opened its new data center took out the air conditioning, but not the servers themselves. Bryant was forced to use portable air conditioners just to get basic apps up and running. Alarms that register poor power or problematic temperatures went off all the time, but the university could do nothing about them because there was no managed air conditioning distribution system. Now the data center has a closed-loop cooling system using ethylene glycol, chilled by outside air when it's cold enough. On a cold December day, the giant APC chiller sits encased in snow, cooling the ethylene glycol. Mitch Bertone, a Bryant technical analyst, estimates a 30-percent to 40-percent savings on cooling costs compared with more common refrigerant-based air conditioning.

Consolidation was one of the main goals of Bryant's data center upgrade. The initial strategy was to get everything in one place, so the university could deliver on a backup strategy during outages. Initially little thought was given to going green. However, as Bryant worked with the data center consultants, going through four designs before settling on one, saving energy emerged as a value proposition.

The final location was the right size, near an electrical substation at the back of the campus, in a lightly traveled area, which was good for the data center's physical security. Proximity to an electrical substation was key because the farther away the power supply, the less efficient the data center.

Bryant has also deployed software that automatically manages server clock speed to lower power consumption. Now, APC technologies monitor and control fan speed, power level used at each outlet, cooling capacity, temperature, and humidity. Power is distributed to server blades as they need it.

When power goes out, Bryant no longer has to take the data center offline or bring out the portable air conditioning. A room near the data center hosts an APC Intelligent Transfer Switch that knows when to switch power resources to batteries, which can run the whole system for 20 minutes. If power quality falls out of line, the data center automatically switches to generator power and pages Bertone. The generator can run for two days on a full tank of diesel.

Because Bryant doesn't now have to worry constantly about data center reliability, it can focus on new strategic initiatives. It's working with Cisco, Nokia, and T-Mobile to set up dual-band Wi-Fi and cellular service that will let students make free phone calls on campus. The university is also home to the Cisco IPICS communication center that links emergency responders in

Rhode Island and Connecticut. In addition, the university is moving toward providing students with unified communications and IPTV and is in talks with an accounting software company to host apps in the Bryant data center to bring in extra cash.

Rich Siedzik, director of computer and telecommunications services at Bryant, indicated that before the new data center was created, just reacting to problems was the major focus. Now, with the new data center, his team has more time to be innovative. The university IT services group has moved from an operational focus to a strategic one. With all the IT projects, Bryant is now considered one of the most wired campuses in the country. Bryant is also considering ways to further save energy.

Other Modular and Container Data Center Designs: Google, Sun, Rackable

As mentioned at the beginning of the section describing the modular data center for Bryant University, other IT vendors offer similar designs: designs similar in concept to the IBM design used for Bryant, including Google's Data Center in a Box design, Sun Microsystems' Project Blackbox, and Rackable Systems' ICE Cube. Google has a patent for its Data Center in a Box concept. One of the convenient ways to search for patents is with Google's patent search engine located at: http://www.google.com/patents. The following URL was obtained from the Google patent search engine based on a search on Google's Data Center in a Box patent: http://www. google.com/patents?id= 7TypAAAAEBAJ&dq=patent+number+7,278,273.

Google's patent covers "modular data centers with modular components that can [be] implemented in numerous ways, including as a process, an apparatus, a system, a device, or a method." The patent also covers a method for deployment that includes building one module within a ready-to-ship container, shipment via a transport infrastructure, several computing systems mounting within the container, and transporting the container to a new site via the infrastructure. Finally, it states that deployment will involve connecting at least one resource connection—like electricity, natural gas, water, and Internet access—to at least one module.

In 2008, Microsoft announced that it had completed the first phase of its new, container-based data center in the Chicago area. The new facility is being built on modular, shipping-container-based data centers. The testing phase indicated the data center to have a **Power Usage Effectiveness** (PUE) rating of 1.22. In 2008, Google also released PUEs for some of its data centers, finding an average of 1.21, with one test facility going as low as 1.13. A perfect PUE would be 1—all the energy going into a data center is used for IT functions instead of support infrastructure. Some of the details released on the Microsoft container-based data centers include information that Microsoft is using standard-sized shipping containers that can each house as many as 2,500 servers. Containers have the potential to drive significant cost benefits and green benefits. The use of containers is one method of expanding data center infrastructure to help prevent overbuilding. The competition among IT vendors on PUE results for their data center designs will continue to help drive innovation in the designs.

Columbia University Green IT and New York City Green Plan

This case study is based on information provided by Alan Crosswell, Associate Vice President and Chief Technologist for Columbia University's Information Technology. In addition to Alan, the other members of the Columbia team who contributed to the information were Victoria Hamilton, Lynn Rohrs, and David Millman.

The Columbia University green data center analysis involved many of the unique green IT issues within a large research university. (For example, each research project often has its own servers in its own labs because the funding model works best that way.) In addition, the green IT analysis included New York City Mayor Michael Bloomberg's ten-year plan for New York City on reducing carbon emissions by 30 percent based on 2007 levels. Columbia University has committed to that 30 percent reduction even in the face of greatly increased growth in High Performance Computing (HPC) requirements fueled by the worldwide research community.

The implementation of much of the Columbia University green data center strategy is just getting underway as of early 2009. Because the main idea behind this book is to first look at the business and environmental aspects of green IT with the technical (engineering) aspects secondary, the Columbia University green IT case study fits this goal and should be of value not only to other universities in their pursuit of green IT, but also to all groups looking at the road to green data centers.

As discussed at the beginning of this chapter, Columbia University's challenge of getting the many different administrative and research groups to agree to share computer resources is similar to the challenge faced at most large companies in getting all their separate business groups to give up their "fiefdoms" and agree to share computer resources. In many cases, the different groups also need to give up their long-established business process applications to consolidate not only on shared hardware but, where possible, also on common application software. By standardizing as much as possible, these organizations achieve cost reduction that includes energy reduction. Consolidation and resource sharing not only give significant cost reduction but also provide benefits in greater system availability (larger systems usually include failover), performance (through larger servers), and disaster recovery (since all business groups on a consolidated system share the same robust disaster recovery plan). The following sections give details on Columbia's green data center plan.

Columbia University's Analysis and Plan for Creating a Green Data Center

Columbia University's IT team analyzed the financial and political costs of energy in addition to environmental concerns. Opportunities for energy conservation included equipment, infrastructure, and managerial practices. These opportunities are indicated in the well-known Lawrence Berkeley National Lab pie-chart, as shown in Figure 10.1.

Columbia University's green IT plan includes a pilot of an Advanced Data Center. That data center will be used for rigorous before-and-after measurements of recommended best practices and innovative equipment and infrastructure improvements. The Advanced Data Center will be a production environment. All university groups will participate.

Columbia's plan seeks to improve the energy efficiency and environmental impact of the administrative systems currently in a centralized data center and, at the same time, significantly expand the available capacity in the centralized data center. Included in the plan are provisions to make sure that lessons learned on green IT are widely applicable and broadcast first to the community and later to peer universities and organizations. Students from Columbia's School of Engineering and the School of Business will help with the communication. This will help lay the foundation for plans to submit the results to a number of educational and government groups. The opportunity to rigorously measure recommended best practices and technological innovations in a real-world environment, validated by the scrutiny incorporated from the beginning, will be a significant benefit to both Columbia and, potentially, many other universities and organizations in their quest for green IT.

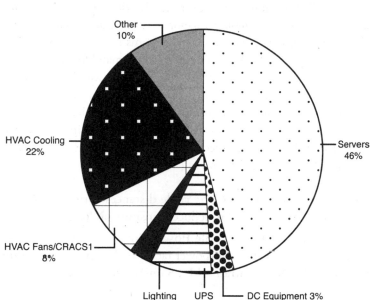

Source: Lawrence Berkeley National Lab (LBNL)

Figure 10.1 Average power allocation for 12 benchmarked data centers (LBNL 2007)

High Performance Computing (HPC) at a Large Research University

This area of the Columbia University green IT plan is especially interesting to me. For my Ph.D. thesis at U.C. Berkeley, the HPC facilities at U.C. Berkeley and LBNL were available for the Monte Carlo simulations I used to determine mechanical failure probabilities under random vibration. (My studies were based on airplane sonic boom signatures.) At that time, I never considered the electric power required to perform those intense computations! As pointed out by the Columbia University IT team, in the past several years, HPC has been growing at every research university, government research laboratory, and high-tech industry, nationally and internationally. HPC is a cornerstone of almost all scientific research disciplines, many of which had previously used little or no computing resources. Researchers are now performing simulations, analyzing experimental data from sources such as the Large Hadron Collider at CERN, genetic sequencers, scanning-tunneling electron microscopes, econometric and population data, and so on.

These applications have led to an explosion of computing clusters being deployed throughout Columbia, its peer research institutions, and organizations in industries such as biotechnology, nanotechnology, and finance. Frequently this has required construction of new server rooms or put pressure on space in existing data centers. All this has led to increased demand for energy.

Columbia operates a 5,200 square-foot data center in support of the University's administrative and instructional computing needs. It is one of several large and many small data centers at the University. The data center, originally built in 1963, has been identified as having significant deficiencies, especially with respect to electrical distribution and air conditioning. These deficiencies include the following:

- Low voltage distribution over long cable distances with no **Power Distribution Units** (PDUs) to reduce transmission losses.
- Lack of a central **Uninterruptible Power Supply** (UPS) with instead multiple individual inefficient (power factor of 70 percent) UPS units in each server rack. (New centralized UPS units can be up to 95 percent efficient.)
- Lack of hot and cold aisles, obstructed under-floor airflow, many unsealed openings in floor tiles, and other methods of preventing mixing of hot and cold air (multiple thermal inefficiencies).
- Many old energy inefficient servers.

The computing resource required for research at Columbia will continue to grow, especially as it is fueled by the explosive growth in HPC needs. In spite of these growing needs for computing power, Columbia has committed to reduce its greenhouse gas footprint by 30 percent by 2017 (relative to a 2007 baseline). As mentioned earlier, this planned reduction is part of Columbia's commitment to New York City Mayor Bloomberg's PlaNYC challenge. New York City has some of the highest energy costs and most limited energy production and transmission capacity in the nation, so this challenge is extremely important to the city's environmental sustainability. It also emphasizes the need for green data centers for all organizations in the city.

During its analysis, the Columbia IT staff identified the following potential solutions to help reduce data center energy consumption:

- Improve the efficiency and server density of the current data center to make space for the new programs in as efficient a means as possible.

- Reduce or eliminate servers being hosted in what is better used as wet lab or faculty office space, an especially important issue in a space-constrained New York City location.

- Encourage sharing of research clusters to more efficiently utilize available computing cycles.

- Replace older, less-efficient servers with newer models that take advantage of recent vendor improvements in power efficiency.

- Use cogeneration. This is planned for a new campus in New York City and is being researched and prioritized for the main campus.

- Participate in regional and national consortia, including the New York State Grid Consortium to further attain the benefits of sharing resources.

- Investigate cloud computing and outsourcing computational needs to areas that have abundant renewable power sources, such as hydroelectric generating facilities.

Green IT Techniques to Be Analyzed and Verified

Columbia University's IT staff plans to test several techniques for data center energy efficiency, applying rigorous testing and measurement discipline—as best as can be accomplished in a live data center, rather than a controlled, artificial laboratory environment. These techniques include the following:

- Higher input voltage results in more-efficient operation. Most of Columbia's servers are connected to 120V power sources but are capable of 208V operation.

- New servers are more efficient than three-year-old and older servers. Many of the servers are much older.

- Active server power management (for example, reducing CPU speed) can result in significant reductions. As is typical of most serve administrators, BIOS and more advanced software power management techniques have not been applied to those servers.

- Cold-aisle containment and ducting improvements for conventional forced-air cooling systems increase efficiency.

- In-row cooling technology can be 30 percent more efficient than conventional forced-air cooling. This is a common industry claim.

- Increasing the chilled-water set-point 5 degrees results in 5 percent efficiency improvement.
- Other advanced cooling technology, such as variable speed CRAC unit fans and zoned cooling control systems, yields efficiency improvements.
- Sharing of research clusters (server consolidation) results in greater efficiency without having a negative impact on research productivity. Consolidation and virtualization of conventional commercial IT workloads has like benefits.

Columbia's Green IT Test Plan

The test plan includes measurements to establish initial state benchmarks. These benchmarks will be updated as incremental improvements are made. After instrumentation and baseline data collection are completed, the test plan includes the following:

- Replacing old servers using best practices to include 208V e-phase power distribution (current servers are 120V); efficient UPS; efficient server power supplies; low power CPUs and memory; and consolidation and virtualization.
- Adjusting IT server power-saving settings on all clusters and measure expected reduction in power consumption.
- Implementing in-row, high-power density rack cooling and measure actual reduction in cooling load.
- Adjusting chilled-water set point for in-row racks' Cabinet Power Distribution Unit (CDU) and measure actual reduction in cooling loads.

The test objectives include a validation of industry claims of energy savings (with respect to Columbia's IT environment) for a number of best practices and advanced techniques. As part of its analysis, the Columbia IT team will utilize standard tools and practices for implementing energy-efficient data centers. The tools will include the DOE DC Pro tool. Measurement techniques will include those identified in the ASHRAE Workshops on Improving Data Center Energy Efficiency and Best Practices. Other standardized techniques, such as potential new ENERGY STAR server and LEED data center metrics, will also be utilized.

Columbia University Green IT Plan Summary

The Columbia University plan for green IT will provide valuable input for IT energy-efficiency projects for all organizations:

- The project goal of leveraging current best practices and latest lessons learned from all the organizations involved in green IT fits with the key need to have wide collaboration across many organizations so that everyone can benefit. In addition, the plan to communicate lessons learned to peer higher education institutions and other groups will help us all.

  The challenge of the green computing and the increasing demands of HPC might be unique to research universities and research companies. However, concepts used to meet the requirements of these computationally intensive systems in an environmentally friendly way will prove to be valuable to all IT teams.

- The plan includes testing of power and cooling efficiency techniques via a pilot data center before deciding which techniques would be best for Columbia's central data center. This will provide valuable lessons learned for all data center teams. Establishing a baseline and continuous measurement of variables is fundamental to success and should be a best practice for all groups.

Lexington, Kentucky, Large (61KSF) Data Center

As data centers are becoming more constrained, it is essential that capacity managers step to the forefront and help out. This case study analyzes one such very constrained, very large data center. It describes a five-step approach to mitigating data center constraints, delaying a costly data center upgrade and data center relocation. Best practices will be described, including data center level metrics in the industry and recent governmental work in the data center metrics. The case study is based on information provided by Chris Molloy, an IBM Distinguished Engineer from Raleigh, North Carolina, who led the IT team on this green data center project.

In an IT environment of on-demand computing with virtualization getting a significant amount of attention, it is easy to forget that IT equipment requires physical resources. That is, until they run out. In the early days of distributed computing, many IT organizations took the throw-another-server-at-it approach because servers were inexpensive compared to the proper capacity planning needed to optimize hardware equipment utilization.

Back in the 1980s, the author of this case study, Chris Molloy, was personally involved in this approach. It wasn't until the financial approval for the 2,501st server was requested that the finance team asked if there were room for the workload on the first 2,500 servers. The answer was not available as capacity management tools were not installed at that time. In agreement to provide funding for future server requests, we agreed to install capacity management tools and to demonstrate that utilization of existing servers justified the investment in new servers for new workload. Even so, the multitier distributed applications ran at low utilization because capacity planners were required to size servers for peak utilization versus average utilization. In those days, space, power, and cooling were not an issue because improvements in miniaturization of IT resources exceeded the physical growth requirements.

Much has changed since those days. Virtualization techniques have allowed companies to share reserve capacity between multiple workloads, increasing server utilization. There has been a rapid increase in the demand for IT resources, with current studies showing a 6X growth in servers and 69X growth in storage resources in this decade. The cost dynamics have changed, with electricity costs in the data center increasing in double-digit percentages for the past two years. Equipment manufacturers have responded to these challenges by making larger, more-efficient hardware. Unfortunately, the physical characteristics of power, space, and cooling have become an issue because previous data centers cannot contain the new physical requirements of these larger servers or cannot contain the volume of servers needing to be installed for new IT requirements.

Such was the case with the data center that is the subject of this study. To install a new piece of IT equipment, you need to have the space to put it in, the power to run it, and the cooling to dissipate the heat generated from the power consumed. The installation of a piece of equipment requires power, space, and cooling. Additionally, the applications had a high-availability requirement. Each watt of utility power was backed up by UPS, batteries that provide power for about 15 minutes. This time allows for longer-term generators to start and stabilize until utility power resumes. Any of these physical components can become constrained, preventing additional equipment from being installed.

As of 2006, the subject data center contained 61,000 square feet of wall-to-wall data center space. With the space required for aisles and equipment maintenance clearance, usable space was reduced to 44,000 square feet. As of April 2008, 43,000 square feet of the data center was in use, with demand requests for more than the remaining 1,000 square feet. The UPS unit was running at 92 percent (2,227 kilowatts of 2,430 kilowatts installed). The generators were running at 85 percent (4,229 kilowatts of 4,988 kilowatts installed, noting that additional devices are supported on the generators that are not supported on the batteries). The chillers were running at 94 percent (1,175 tons of 1,250 installed).

Something had to be done to address the growth requirements. For this situation, we return to the IBM five-step process described previously in this book.

A Five-Step Approach for an Energy-Efficient Data Center

The continuous five-step process, first described in detail in Chapter 2, "The Basics of Green IT," is summarized in Figure 10.2. Four out of five of these steps involve improving the facilities portion of the data center. The virtualize step involves improving the IT portion of the data center. It's ironic that virtualization is the most promising IT technology to affect the physical data center in such a positive manner. The reason for this is that virtualization allows an IT environment to significantly reduce the amount of resources being reserved to handle the times when workload peaks. It does so by allowing multiple workloads to share resources, including the resources reserved for growth. Typical distributed server virtualization projects plan to quadruple the equipment utilization, resulting in a 75 percent reduction in equipment requirements. This translates to freeing up 75 percent of the power, space, and cooling resources used by distributed servers. IT business models such as Information Technology Infrastructure Library (ITIL) include capacity planning for both facilities and IT as updated in ITIL version 3.

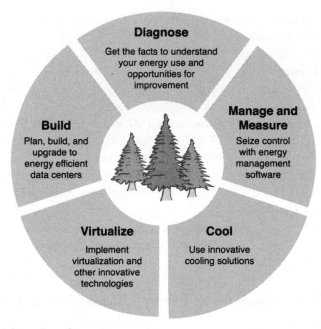

Source: IBM Green Data Center

Figure 10.2   Five-step process for data center energy efficiency

The following sections describe what was done for each of these steps.

Step 1. Diagnose

The first step was to baseline the environment to understand the current situation and to have a baseline to measure future improvements against. The IBM IT Delivery organization that runs the data center brought in the IBM GTS Site and Facilities organization to perform an energy assessment. PUE, as described in The Green Grid, was one of the major metrics used to measure the efficiency of a facility. This metric computed the ratio of the power used by the data center divided by the power used by the IT equipment in the data center. It was typical in the industry to have a metric of 3, indicative of one-third of the power going to IT equipment, one-third of the power going to cooling, and one-third of the power going to other uses (for example, lighting, power losses converting from AC to DC, and charging batteries).

This particular data center had a PUE rating of 1.8. Normally, this would have been considered excellent, but what drove the ratio was the denominator (IT power used), which was abnormally high because the data center was full.

In 2008, The Green Grid modified the PUE metric to make it simpler to understand. The new metric is called **Data Center Infrastructure Effectiveness** (DCiE). The following graphic (see Figure 10.3) describes both metrics.

DCiE— Data Center (Infrastructure) Efficiency

PUE— Power Usage Effectiveness

$$\text{DCiE} = \frac{\text{IT Equipment Power}}{\text{Total Raised Floor Power}} = \frac{1}{\text{PUE}}$$

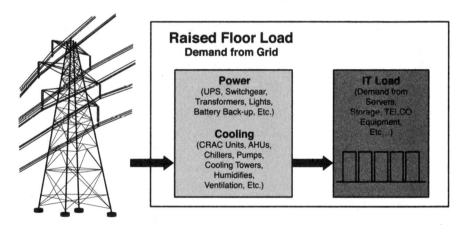

Raised Floor Load
Demand from Grid

Power
(UPS, Switchgear, Transformers, Lights, Battery Back-up, Etc.)

Cooling
(CRAC Units, AHUs, Chillers, Pumps, Cooling Towers, Humidifies, Ventilation, Etc.)

IT Load
(Demand from Servers, Storage, TELCO Equipment, Etc.)

Source: IBM Green Data Center

Figure 10.3 Data center metrics DCiE and PUE

The PUE of 1.8 translated to a DCiE of 0.56, meaning 56 percent of the power coming into the data center was going to IT equipment.

Step 2. Build

The subject data center resided in a leased facility. As the landlord did not want to make significant improvements, the options were limited. The decision was made to limit the amount of build activity of new data center space because the parking lot was not considered a viable option.

Fortunately, the "Build" step includes upgrading some of the constrained components other than space. In this case, additional power could be added. The additional power enabled the replacement of servers with servers of the same size but more compute capacity; therefore, the amount of space required for a particular compute capacity was reduced, effectively doubling the space in the data center.

To justify the upgrade, the business case normalized the 170 kilowatt power addition to 4,250 square feet, using a conversion factor of 40 watts per square feet, the average density of the existing data center.

Because we did not create physical space with this additional power, we had to replace servers with higher-density servers. We continued our direction to replace single CPU servers with multiple CPU servers. The dominant new server was a 16-processor server that took about 8U of rack space. Physical space was not created with the additional power. Existing servers were replaced with higher-density servers. The direction was to replace single CPU servers with multiple CPU servers. This improvement led to requiring half of the space that the 1U servers required. The combination of additional power and denser servers reclaimed space for additional equipment.

Step 3. Virtualize

The subject data center consisted of many different accounts. Each of these accounts had architectural control over the type of hardware they used in their part of the data center. Over the years, we started working with the accounts to right-size their servers during server-refresh periods, and to move to a scale-up model (larger servers) so that we could leverage virtualization techniques to increase server utilization.

In the beginning of 2006, a study was conducted on the 1,500 UNIX variant servers that were in the data center. The survey indicated that 59 percent of the single CPU servers had a monthly utilization of less than 5 percent! The majority of the servers were single-processor servers that had been sized for the peak workload of the application. The following chart (see Figure 10.4) provides further insight into the distribution of utilization for the one-way, two-way, and four-way physical servers that were installed at that time.

In essence, what that meant was that on average, we had 20 times the amount of distributed equipment on the floor than was needed. Imagine finding a way to leverage those untapped resources and eliminate 80 percent of your equipment!

Significant increases in the penetration of virtual technology began at this site. This included installing 8-way and 16-way servers. By March 2007, the percentage of servers with less than 5 percent monthly utilization had dropped to less than 25 percent. By March 2008, this number had dropped to less than 14 percent.

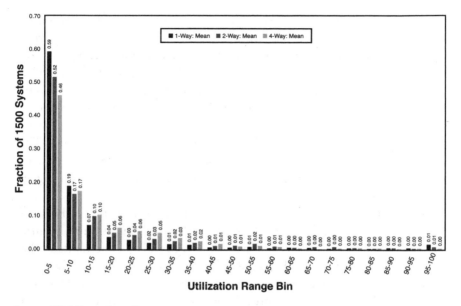

Source: IBM Green Data Center

Figure 10.4 Original distribution of CPU utilization for one-way, two-way, and four-way UNIX physical servers

Even if only 10 percent of your servers average less than 5 percent monthly utilization, there is still room for improvement. One technique used to minimize cost on the larger multiprocessor servers was to use capacity-on-demand technology. Capacity-on-demand technology allows for servers with extra capacity that can be turned on if the application requires additional resources. This keeps down the cost without increasing the risk of running out of resources to run an application.

One of the accounts in the data center has been aggressively pursuing virtualization over the last two years. This included senior management support of the default direction to virtualize all workloads unless architecturally constrained from doing so. This account had more than a thousand servers. Approximately two-thirds of the virtual images were located in the subject data center for their test and development workload. Their production servers were in another data center. The account leveraged virtualization technology to use the test and development site to be the backup for the production site.

In the UNIX environment, a large number of 16-processor servers were installed on this account, leveraging capacity on-demand technology to keep four processors turned off for future growth. The account was originally risk averse to the risk associated with shared resources in a virtual environment. To reduce the original risk, the processor and storage resources of the virtual images were oversized. After the virtual images were put into production, several months of data were collected to establish a usage baseline and understand the effects the load on the images peaking at different times. Tools were written to analyze the data and determine which virtual images needed more physical resources and which virtual images needed less physical resources. The account approved the right sizing of the virtual images. This was accomplished in a controlled fashion using contemporary change management processes, including back-out capability should something go wrong.

Several 16-processor servers were freed up as a result of this rightsizing. Some of these servers are being redeployed in that account for future requirements, and some of the servers are being given to the other accounts in that data center. The redeployment to the other accounts in that data center dramatically improves server installation time, as the servers are already on site, already installed, already accounted for in space, power, and cooling allocations, and already cabled into the network and disk storage.

In the x86 environments, we performed a similar exercise. We leveraged a virtualization technique that allowed us to nondisruptively move an image from one physical server to another. We were previously using this function to move the virtual images around to enable us to take physical servers down for microcode updates. We can now use this function to move the virtual images around to enable us to increase the physical server utilization. Through this movement, we could also reduce the server utilization to zero on several of the servers and position them for reuse.

Based on the success of the early adopter account, we started approaching each of the other accounts to virtualize their environment. Although each of the lines of business was receptive to virtualization, none were prepared to take as aggressive an approach. Several of the lines of business had already piloted virtualization on some of their workloads. We are currently working with two of the lines of business to create a business case for virtualization in their environment. We refined the business case template used for the accounts from the experience we gained from the virtualization of more than 50,000 images that we had previously installed. As we have cost-justified several virtualization projects already for those installations, we expect a positive return on investment with the business case. We will work with the accounts to make sure that the investment funding and people are available to execute the proposals.

As the IT organization should also set a good example for its own customers by demonstrating implementation of its strategy within its own resources, the IT organization should virtualize the systems management servers in the subject data center. We created a project to virtualize those servers and submitted the project in the Fall plan for 2008 implementation. We received funding for this project, and have begun implementing the project creating standard deliverables for how to build and maintain the internal infrastructure virtual images.

Step 4. Manage and Measure

The next step was to implement power management software. Previously, a data center space request tool was implemented that allowed the accounts to indicate when they had new data center requirements. This tool was enhanced to not only handle space requests but also to determine the power and cooling requirements. The management system was enhanced to report on power (utility, UPS, and generator), space, and cooling.

Prior to the physical resources being constrained, the name-plate power for the equipment was used for planning. The name-plate power was a conservative estimate of the amount of power needed to run a fully configured system. Unfortunately, many of the servers we ordered were not fully configured, causing us to oversize the power and cooling requirements. Equipment manufacturers recognized this problem and have provided power calculators that allowed us to more accurately size the power requirements because the calculators enabled us to specify equipment that was not fully configured.

This improvement still represented an overstatement of our power usage, as many servers do not use maximum power at all times. For example, power supplies do not use all their power when the servers are not running at maximum utilization. To improve the accuracy of the power consumption, we worked with our real estate organization to provide us with monthly measurements of the actual amount of electricity consumed in the data center.

The IT team started basing demand on actual data versus estimated data. There was still the concern on what percentage of name-plate power we should use to size new requests. Analysis was performed on the power usage of the existing equipment. The analysis team determined that using an overall 60 percent of name-plate power would provide more accurate sizing than the 80 percent they had previously used for new demand requests.

As equipment manufacturers implement the energy savings features we are familiar with in notebook computers (along with new server-based energy management features), server energy use will vary widely during the day. Just using the server name-plate power will become more and more inaccurate. Manufacturers have provided additional software to record equipment power and temperature. We have installed data center energy management software for a set of the servers as part of determining the best practices from the project for all data centers we manage, including the one in this analysis.

As legacy equipment that will not be refreshed for several years does not have this capability, we will have to use a combination of planned and actual measurements for the next several years. To increase the accuracy of understanding energy usage of legacy servers, we are installing metering at different levels of the power distribution. This will enable us to reconcile the difference between the newer equipment we have data on and the older equipment that we don't have data on.

Step 5. Cool

Cooling improvements to the data center were provided by implementing the recommendations of the energy assessment. Many of these suggestions were tactical in nature and did not have a significant amount of investment required for the return. Other suggestions were more long term in nature. The team provided information on the estimated amount of savings, the implementation cost, and the return on investment period. In total, the team identified improvement opportunities that would result in saving 10 percent of the power in the data center.

Most people in IT are familiar with the cooling implementations where data centers are air-cooled using **Computer Room Air Conditioners (CRACs)**. What they might not be familiar with is that simple air leaks resulting in inappropriate air flow can dramatically reduce the efficiency of this type of cooling solution. The two most common air leaks are in the floor-based cable cutouts and in the spacing between servers that are installed in racks. To mitigate the cutout leaks, brushes were installed in the cutouts. Rack-spacing leaks were mitigated by installing panel blanks in the racks. Most IT equipment is designed to be cooled by having cold air come in the front of the equipment and leave heated through the back. Without panel blanks installed, hot air recirculation was misdirected.

The next area of tactical cooling improvement was the actual placement of perforated tiles. These tiles are designed to go into the cold aisles so that cold air can enter the front of the IT equipment. Over time, aisles were moved and equipment reinstalled so that the perforated tiles were not in the optimal location. The team took a look at this problem and recommended what tiles needed to be moved and which perforated tiles needed to be replaced with solid tiles. Medium flow tiles were installed in areas where additional air flow was needed.

As we moved to longer-range improvements, the team recommended turning off some of the redundant CRAC units. Extra CRAC units had been installed initially to ensure sufficient cooling and compensate for maintenance and unplanned failures. It is not uncommon to have 20 percent more units installed than are needed to handle the cooling capacity. Turning off extra CRAC units would save electricity and extend the life of those units not in use. To ensure that no problems were introduced by turning off particular CRAC units, a three-step process was used. A total of 11 units were turned off, five in the first step and three in each of the subsequent steps. At $0.04 per kilowatt hour, this results in an estimated annual savings of $19,250. More important, the 481,250 kilowatts saved can be applied to run other equipment as a result of this best practice.

Other changes such as increasing the chilled water temperature and increasing the supply air temperatures from the CRAC units were implemented, providing additional savings.

Recent analysis of DCiE metrics has shown that data centers that leverage free cooling technologies have a variability of up to 20 percent improvement for the same IT load depending on the time of day and time of year. Free cooling leverages the outside temperature when it is colder than the inside temperature (for example, nights and winter). Unfortunately, this data center did not leverage free cooling.

Other options such as free cooling continue to be investigated. It is estimated that the outside temperature at this specific location is colder than the inside data center temperature approximately 40 percent of the year.

Future Plans and Government Involvement

Because water conducts heat 3,700 times better than air, several equipment manufacturers are making liquid cooling devices that move the liquid cooling closer to the IT equipment than the CRAC units, which are liquid-cooled. Options now exist for in-row cooling, overhead cooling, rear-door cooling, and aisle-based heat containment systems. These techniques have the added benefit of having the cooling closer to the equipment being cooled, further increasing cooling efficiency. The trade-off is that chilled water pipes now need to be installed closer to the IT equipment aisles, decreasing the amount of flexibility in IT aisle changes.

Highly virtualized resources are one of the key elements of the energy-efficient data center model. The next evolutionary step for many data centers is to understand the utilization of the servers and create projects to address the utilization of their equipment. Idle servers with no productive work on them should be turned off, redeployed, or disposed. Low-utilization servers should have their workload virtualized onto other servers, freeing those low-utilization servers to be redeployed or disposed. Medium-utilized virtual servers with high-variance workload should be periodically energy-capped so that their physical resources can be redeployed for the majority of time the resources are not needed. High-utilization servers can be created by moving multiple virtual images to a single physical server. Accounts can then evolve more toward cloud computing by moving from static virtual images they have placed on physical servers to dynamic virtual image placement using policy-based systems management image workload balancing for even higher levels of utilization.

Governments are increasing their activity in this space. In the United States, the EPA and DOE are currently working with the IT industry to develop ENERGY STAR ratings for components such as power supplies, ratings for equipment such as servers, and ratings for the enterprises such as data centers. For example, the draft for the ENERGY STAR rating for servers has been published, and it is anticipated that the final version will be published in 2009. Similar work has been done by the European Union, creating the European Union Code of Conduct for IT.

Lexington Green Data Center Conclusions

The following conclusions can be made from the preceding discussion on data centers:

- IT capacity planners are becoming increasing involved in mitigating facilities capacity planning requirements.
- Data centers can be monitored to create a baseline to determine their current efficiency and affect of future changes to them.
- Data center upgrades of constrained components such as power can be used to effectively gain more space in the data center when combined with installing physically smaller higher-capacity equipment.
- Virtualization continues to be one of the key technologies for companies to reduce their power, space, and cooling requirements and significantly lower their TCO.

- Improvements can be made in to the supply-demand model by using a combination of actual data from newer equipment with the planned data from older equipment.

- Legacy equipment that will not be refreshed for several years often does not have this measurement data capability, so we might have to use a combination of planned and actual measurements for several years.

- As cooling consumes a significant amount of power in the data center, tactical and longer-term cooling improvements can be made to conserve energy and reallocate that energy to additional IT equipment.

- Significant mitigation of IT growth was achieved by conserving electricity due to improvements in cooling, adding space by using denser equipment enabled via the addition of power, reducing the number of servers through virtualization, and more accurately measuring the resources available.

- No one technology will mitigate the explosive growth of IT in the industry; gaining space through the use of denser equipment and additional power will address a portion of the problem. It is the sum of the application of these individual technologies that will significantly address the mitigation of growth.

In summary, the IT team managed the requirements for significant IT growth in the data center by conserving electricity, adding power and denser equipment to effectively gain space, virtualizing the environment to require fewer servers by increasing server utilization, more accurately measuring the facility's resources, and improving cooling by redirection of air flow.

Chapter Summary and Conclusions

From the discussion on green IT for several types of data centers, you can reach the following conclusions:

- There are many types of green IT initiatives, ranging from installing smaller modular data centers to retrofitting large data centers. The case studies in this chapter demonstrate a significant range in green data center types and size.

- University green IT case studies can provide important lessons learned. Not only do they have the administrative systems common to any large organization, but with computation increasingly important for all research, they can also provide a rich proving ground for green IT innovations and best practices. Energy efficiency for High Performance Computing (HPC) is an especially important area where research universities will provide valuable lessons learned.

- IT companies such as Sun, Google, and IBM can provide valuable case studies because they use their own data centers to serve as models for their customers. All the large IT vendors and IT providers, such as Google, are providing data center innovations such as modular (data center in a box) designs.

- An iterative approach to data center energy efficiency, including pilots of energy-saving techniques, is usually the best approach. The common sense approach of first going after the energy-efficiency areas with quick payback should be one of your best practices. The Columbia University plan should provide valuable input for IT energy-efficiency projects for all organizations.

11

Worldwide Green IT Case Studies

"What we have to learn to do we learn by doing."

—Aristotle, *Ethics*

The challenges in implementing green IT and green data centers can vary considerably based on the part of the world where the data center is located. Challenges include government regulations, the cost of electricity, and the social/political environment relating to the environment and energy efficiency. The first few chapters discussed these aspects of green IT. The case studies in this chapter include green IT for countries around the world, including countries in Europe and Asia. The case studies include the use of a worldwide computing grid to make green use of unused computer power in thousands of laptops and other computers around the world. Also included in this chapter are case studies for data centers in Montpellier, France; Istanbul, Turkey; and a company with over 30 data centers in India. Although the social and political environments of the particular country do have an impact on implementing green data centers, the technical challenges remain the same. The basic five steps (diagnose, build, virtualize, cool, manage, and measure) discussed for data centers in the case studies in Chapter 9, "Green IT Case Studies for Energy Utilities," and Chapter 10, "Green IT Case Studies for Universities and a Large Company," still apply no matter where the data center is located or how big it is. The great value in looking at green IT case studies should be to take advantage of lessons learned.

World Community Grid™—A Green IT Grid for Good

Grid computing was first mentioned in Chapter 6, "A Most-Significant Step—'Virtualizing' Your IT Systems," as the ultimate in the use of server virtualization for green IT. Grid computing and its offshoot, cloud computing, are discussed in detail in Appendix B, "Green IT and Cloud Computing." In this case study, we examine the use of a global grid computing system used for addressing environmental concerns. Thus, this case study is the use of green IT to help solve environmental problems, or, in other words, to hit two green birds with one stone!

IBM's World Community Grid uses idle computer power to address world hunger, disease, environmental problems, and more. Rising costs of food and oil put heavy pressure on consumers around the world and severely strain governments' capability to provide relief. The author's laptop is one of the more than one million PCs in this grid, so I can tell you from first-hand experience that this is an interesting way for anyone to be involved in green IT with the added benefit of addressing global environmental and health concerns. When this paragraph was written in September 2008, the World Community Grid project running in the background on the author's laptop was an application on research to fight AIDS, sponsored by The Scripps Research Institute. To learn more and join, visit the Web site: http://www.worldcommunitygrid.org/index.jsp.

The global food crisis is particularly acute in Asia, where the World Bank estimates demand for food will double by 2030, forcing as many as 100 million people deeper into poverty. The crisis is real, as is the need to develop workable, real-world solutions. The World Community Grid uses the power of idle computers around the world to perform humanitarian research that wouldn't otherwise be possible because of the high cost of the required computing power. More than one million participants worldwide—including more than 95,000 IBMers—are plugged into the World Community Grid. Their idle PCs are helping researchers battle cancer, analyze human proteome folding, compare genomes, fight AIDS and muscular dystrophy, and much more.

Researchers from the University of Washington and IBM are working together to harness the 167-teraflops of grid computing power in a new initiative, Nutritious Rice for the World. The project will study rice at the atomic level and assess traditional cross-breeding techniques to help farmers around the world breed better rice strains with higher crop yields and research greater disease and pest resistance. According to Dr. Ram

Samudrala, associate professor in the Department of Microbiology at the University of Washington, and principal investigator on the Nutritious Rice for the World project, there are between 30,000 and 60,000 different protein structures to study. "Using traditional experimental approaches in the laboratory to identify detailed structure and function of critical proteins would take decades. Running our software program on the World Community Grid will shorten the time from 200 years to less than two years." Figure 11.1 shows the World Community Grid status icon.

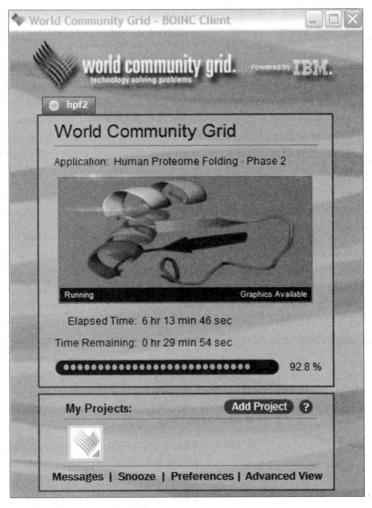

Source: IBM World Community Grid

Figure 11.1   World Community Grid status icon on user laptop

Understanding the Structure of Rice

The Nutritious Rice for the World project will run a three-dimensional modeling program created by computational biologists at the University of Washington to study the structures of the proteins that make up the building blocks of rice. Understanding the structure is necessary to identify the function of those proteins and to enable researchers to identify which ones will help produce more rice grains, ward off pests, resist disease, or hold more nutrients. The project will create the largest and most comprehensive map of rice proteins and their related functions, helping agriculturalists and farmers pinpoint which plants should be selected for cross-breeding to cultivate better crops.

"This project could ultimately help farmers around the world plant better crops and stave off hunger for some," said Stanley Litow, vice president of Corporate Citizenship and Corporate Affairs, and president of the IBM International Foundation. "People who want to be a part of something big can take a small step today by donating their unused computer time. Volunteers can personally effect how quickly this research is completed and can make a significant difference for farmers and people in great need."

The Clean Energy Project

This is a new World Community Grid project from researchers at Harvard University. The mission of The Clean Energy Project is to find new materials for the next generation of solar cells and energy storage devices. By harnessing the power of World Community Grid, researchers can calculate the electronic properties of tens of thousands of organic materials—more than could ever be tested in a lab—and determine which promising candidates can develop more affordable solar energy technology. With this information, scientists expect to create successful materials to produce efficient and inexpensive solar cells that will serve as viable solutions for our future energy needs.

This short discussion on the World Community Grid is certainly not a typical green IT case study. However, the idea of implementing a worldwide computing grid to make use of unused computer power in thousands of laptops and other computers around the world fits well with the most important method to implement green IT at data centers—that is, use virtualization to make more efficient use of computer resources and reduce the periods of very low CPU utilization that is typical of traditional stand-alone servers. World Community Grid is designed to not require the donor machines to remain powered on any more of the time than they normally would and limits CPU utilization by the grid computations so energy consumption is not significantly increased. In this way, World Community Grid is environmentally friendly, making better use of otherwise wasted energy as well as CPU time.

A Green Data Center in Montpelier, France

This case study was based on information from Dr. Jean-Michel Rodriguez of IBM France. Jean-Michel is the World Wide Lead Architect for the Systems Technology Group Green Data Center and one of the ITO Lead Architects based at the IBM customer center in Montpelier, France.

This is another nontraditional green IT case study because it is based on a data center specifically built to demonstrate innovative approaches to improve utilization and energy-efficiency costs in other data centers. The demo data center in Montpelier is called the PSSC (Products and Solutions Support Center) Green Data Center of the Future. The main idea was to create a customer friendly real time green showcase production data center that will demonstrate a large percentage of the currently available best practices in IT and facilities energy conservation, integrating at least one bleeding-edge major conservation technology. The live camera, thermal camera, and green IT energy use real-time dashboards available to IT personnel through a portal are interesting innovations that can help communicate the energy efficiency of the data center to all interested employees.

Customer Pain Points

As mentioned previously in this book, the availability and price of electricity have become the number-one concern for data center operators, according to surveys at the Gartner Data Center Conference in Las Vegas in 2007. Power moved ahead of its close cousin, data center cooling, as the number-one pain point for customers. Forty-seven percent of respondents cited power availability as their top concern. Insufficient cooling slipped to second at 27 percent. The cost of power will become a huge issue, and even if you don't have to pay for the power, the power costs being visible will have significant impact. In the meantime, data center operators will cope by continuing to expand their infrastructure. To address the issue, many different approaches coexist, from relocating current data centers to another facility, expanding an existing site, renovating a current facility, to eventually outsourcing data center operations. As a consequence, we see different ways to address customer requests and pain points.

Strategy, Best Practices, and Solutions

The basic green IT strategy for any organization is based on the goal of reducing IT energy consumption throughout the business. Emerging infrastructure technologies, such as service-oriented architecture, virtualization, and distributed computing, continue to offer businesses greater levels of flexibility and efficiency of resource allocation and should provide the scalable platform that every business requires. IT teams need to point to consolidation strategies as popular techniques for fighting the flab in the data center. Virtualization is also key because it allows for innovative and responsive approaches for the allocation of computing resources. We also need to understand that most of the time, corporations have mixed hardware environments—unlike the environments in **High Performance Computing** (HPC). This heterogeneous environment includes: various storage units (NAS, SAN) and servers (high- and low-density, various IT vendors), networking components, tape units, and robots. They have also mixed or incomplete software environments, and IT infrastructure and IT resources supervision are often disconnected. They are facing common limitations: limited space, limited ceiling height in older building, limited height for raised floor, new and old equipment mix, old cabling, and water pipes. Back-end cooling changes might not be an option.

PSSC Green Data Center of the Future Implementation

The main objective of the Products and Solutions Support Center (PSSC) Green Data Center of the Future is to create a customer friendly real-time green showcase production data center that can demonstrate a large percentage of the currently available best practices in IT and facilities energy conservation, integrating at least one bleeding-edge major conservation technology.

The objective of the PSSC Green Data Center of the Future is a data center dedicated to clients that will be an innovative leader in green data center strategy. The showcase is based on a worldwide set of business scenarios and demonstrations, and a dedicated room for new technologies introduction has been implemented. An important point is that the Green Data Center of the Future is being used in PSSC production mode, expecting energy consumption economy.

The main specifications of the PSSC Green Data Center are the following:

- Target a PUE of 1.5.

- Implement low- and high-density zones and a dedicated and isolated technical area, and implement Schneider APC solution for high-density zones.

- Use latest technology for CRAC (variable speed), implement water cooling, and use a rear-door heat exchanger.

- Use one supervision solution for facility, infrastructure, and IT resources.

Figure 11.2 shows the implementation of the data center with the resources hosted.

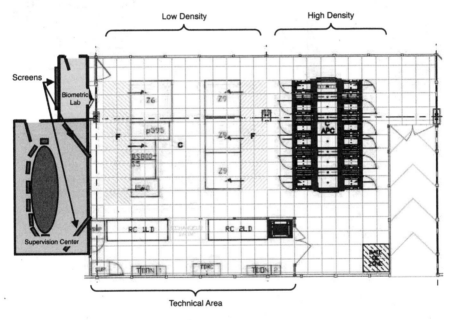

Source: IBM Montpelier PSSC Green Data Center Team

Figure 11.2 Montpelier PSSC Green Data Center area implementation

Innovation for Green IT—Local or Remote Access to the Supervision Room

The PSSC green data center has several very innovative features. Included is a web camera showing the implemented technologies. In addition, there is a "live camera" to track people and assets. The live camera is described in the following section with a graphic showing the camera setup.

Live Camera

The PUE is affected by any physical access to the room. Having a live, sophisticated camera can reduce the need for frequent physical access. For demo purposes, it helps to remotely present the technologies to customers. Figure 11.3 shows the capabilities of the live camera.

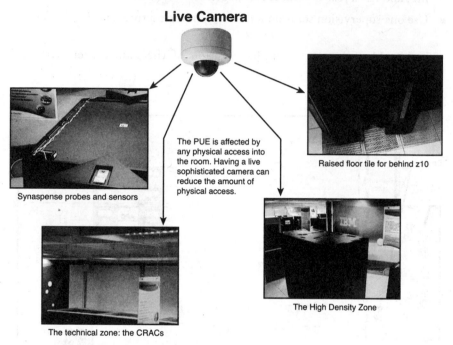

Source: IBM Montpelier PSSC Green Data Center Team

Figure 11.3   Montpelier PSSC Green Data Center live camera

In addition to the live camera, a thermal camera visualizes hot spots at the server, rack-room levels. The following section describes the thermal camera.

Thermal Camera

This technological advanced camera can show hot spots in a data center. For demo purposes, you point the camera to any data center components and graphically visualize the temperature of it. Figure 11.4 shows pictures from the thermal camera.

PSSC Montpelier Thermal Camera

This very technological advanced camera can show hot spots in a data center.
For demo purposes, you point the camera to any DC components and graphically visualize the temperature of it.

Source: IBM Montpelier PSSC Green Data Center Team

Figure 11.4   Montpelier PSSC Green Data Center thermal camera

Energy-Use Dashboards at Montpelier

The **Power Usage Effectiveness** (PUE) is the metric used to measure the energy efficiency of a data center. Both IT and non-IT resources' energy consumption are gathered. Two PUEs are measured: overall and high-density zone.

For demo purposes, you can show in real time the PUE of the PSSC Green Data Center. Although the PSSC Green Data Center is for demo purposes, these energy-use dashboards would be useful for any data center to raise company awareness on IT energy efficiency. These dashboards remind me of the real-time gas mileage graphics on the Toyota Prius automobile I recently rented. The graphics on the Prius' dashboard constantly reminded me that I was getting around 42 miles per gallon and informed me when the car was using the electric motor and when it was using the gas engine (and charging the battery). The data center energy-use dashboard for the Montpelier demo center is shown in Figure 11.5.

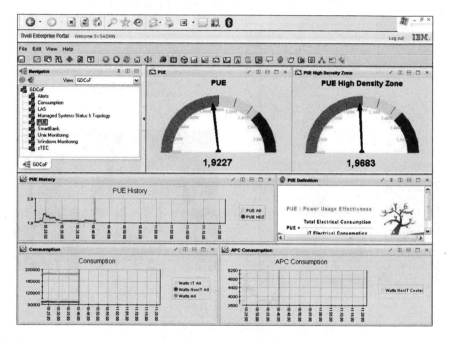

Source: IBM Montpelier PSSC Green Data Center Team

Figure 11.5   Montpelier PSSC Green Data Center energy-use dashboard

Smartbank–Monitoring at the Solution Level

Monitoring can be done at the solution level. Smartbank is a live showcase involving many platforms.

For demo purpose, the monitoring of an entire solution can be demonstrated.

Active Energy Manager is implemented for the energy management of z10® and Blades. The Smartbank solution-level monitoring is shown in Figure 11.6. As stated for the previous dashboard, these data center energy dashboards can communicate current energy efficiency to interested IT team members just as the hybrid automobiles constantly remind the driver with dashboard gas mileage graphics. The real-time dashboard can give the IT team immediate feedback on how data center energy management techniques impact data center energy use, just as the hybrid automobile gas mileage dashboard gave me immediate feedback on how my driving technique impacted automobile energy use.

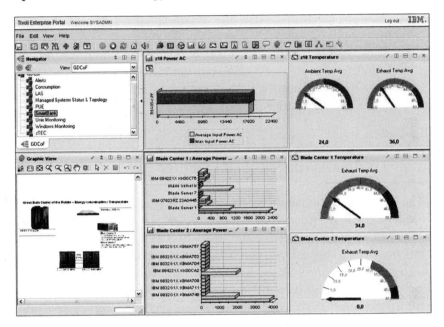

Source: IBM Montpelier PSSC Green Data Center Team

Figure 11.6 Montpelier Green Data Center Smartbank—solution-level monitoring

Innovation at the PSSC data center is summarized in the following list:

- Web camera showing the implemented technologies.
- A solution to track people and assets.
- Dynamic and graphic visualization of the temperature, pressure, and humidity in the green data center.
- A thermal camera to visualize hot spots at the server and rack-room levels.
- A modelization and visit of the data center in Second Life.

- TEPS (Tivoli® Enterprise Portal Server) workplaces have been defined. They will be used to show the monitoring and management of IT and non-IT resources:

  1. PUE (Global, HDZ, IT resources): Show in real time the PUE of the data center.
  2. Alerts: All the alerts coming from IT and non-IT resources are monitored.
  3. Managed resources Status and Topology: What are the resources managed by Tivoli?
  4. Windows GreenDemo monitoring. ITM UNIX monitoring.
  5. LAS: Integration of the LAS solution in TIVOLI.
  6. Smartbank: Monitor real PSSC solutions.
  7. zTEC: Monitor real PSSC solutions.

Istanbul, Turkey–Data Center Case Study

The case study information in this section is from Serkan Sahin of IBM Turkey. As you'll see from this brief green data center case study, the data center in Istanbul offers some unique challenges. The Turkish IT market is very competitive. This competition brings challenges in designing IT solutions, especially for designs for outsourcing. In Turkey, the most popular server strategies to meet customer requests are to set up dedicated servers for each customer application. However, many data centers in Turkey have problems with electricity capacity and resilience, and those problems are exacerbated with the dedicated server strategies that lead to very low-server utilization. In addition, the Turkish IT infrastructure is continuing to grow rapidly, and electricity is expensive (2008 costs of 15 cents / KWH) when compared to similar growth-market countries.

The data center in Istanbul run by IBM Turkey has furnished data center services since 1992. The data center started with mainframe hosting, but in recent years, the IT services for the small and medium outsourcing markets have taken center stage for outsourcing projects. In 2006, the data center started to provide Shared Virtual Infrastructure hosting services for outsourcing customers. This solution brought with it cost benefits to customers but, in addition, the virtual IT systems also provided aspects of green IT for all those shared resource solutions. Many IT service companies in Turkey continue to sell dedicated solutions but will undoubtedly converge on shared resource virtual systems based on competition. Since 2006, IBM Turkey has made IT virtualization (the green IT approach) its standard for outsourcing of managed services.

The Istanbul Green IT Data Center Solution for Cost-Saving

The Istanbul green IT data center solution is based on IT virtualization techniques for server, disk, and network. At the same time, the solution provided the opportunity to extend the shared solutions to system monitoring, system management, and backup and recovery, all of which are now part of the standard data center service. The standard High Available (HA) UNIX systems at the data center require virtual servers on two separate physical servers, two different SAN switches, and at least one SAN disk and one tape library system. This typical UNIX solution requires a minimum of 3.1 kW electric power, not including other necessary systems like monitoring, system management, and backup and recovery. If we looked at CO_2 emissions using the UK-based recommended conversion procedure, this solution would release 1 kg of CO_2 every hour to the atmosphere. In 2008, the cost per KWH in Turkey is approximately 15 cents. Using that 2008 electricity cost, the HA UNIX system would require a daily electricity cost of about $12 (U.S.), without considering the other services such as monitoring and backup.

The IBM Istanbul IT team used the information on CO_2 emissions to compare a dedicated UNIX system with a UNIX system based on IT virtualization. Figure 11.7 shows a comparison of kW and CO_2 emissions for a one, two, and three HA UNIX server solution using the dedicated physical server approach versus the virtual server approach. The results in Figure 11.7 include estimates for system monitoring, management and backup, and recovery. The IT team calculated that the virtual IT system would emit 0.25 kg CO_2 per day for the monitoring, and so on, compared to 1.0 kg CO_2 a day with the dedicated HA UNIX system used at the Istanbul data center in 2006 prior to the migration to virtual IT systems. Note that the calculation shown in Figure 11.7 was done only for the HA UNIX solution.

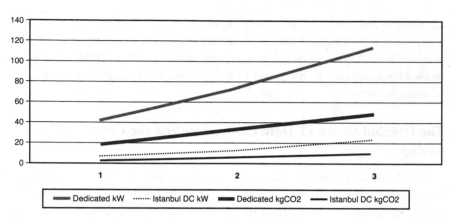

Source: IBM Turkey Green Data Center Team

Figure 11.7 Electric power (kW) and CO2 emission comparison chart for a 1- 2- and 3-server dedicated UNIX solution versus the Istanbul Data Center shared virtual server solution

Large Project in India (Over 30 Data Centers)

This green data center case study is for a large project involving 35 data
centers of about 200,000 sq. feet of data center space. Most of the case study
information was provided by Ramesh Goel and Chris Molloy of IBM.

Primarily driven by the need for improved efficiency and cost reductions,
the case study includes the results of consolidating the 35 data centers to
seven data centers. In addition to data center consolidation, server consolidation and virtualization were among the many efficiency and cost-saving
improvements. However, this was a green data center project, and the electric
power savings due to these data center efficiencies were part of the project
and goals from the beginning.

The Solution: Work with the Experts

As the company's business grew, there was increasing pressure on the management to focus on IT in terms of planning, budgeting, and implementation to scale it to support business growth. As IT became more complicated,
it seemed more prudent to hand it over to a trusted partner that could manage all the requirements including applications, networking, hardware, IT
staff, and the data centers.

IBM realized the following challenges, as soon as it took over the client's IT:

- **The physical space in 35 data centers was not enough.** Newer applications needed to be introduced, and automation had to be continued. This required more hardware to be introduced and at an unimaginable pace. About 200,000 sq. feet of data center space might not have been sufficient for this growth.

- **Multiple vendors simply don't integrate.** There were multiple hardware vendors at the data centers. Although at the application integration level, there were definite challenges, there were bigger problems at the hardware compatibility level.

- **No optimized hardware environment.** IBM realized that hardware compatibility was a big challenge and so was getting the non-IBM vendors to agree on costing. IBM was also ahead on newer and better technology and computing power architectures.

- **Even bigger hardware problems.** IBM also realized that most of the existing hardware (almost 80 percent to 90 percent) in client environment was with non-IBM vendors. The core and mission-critical applications were running and were locked on a non-IBM environment. The challenge for us was to integrate the systems and find a way to introduce better products in the environment.

- **More challenges.** There were multiple issues in most areas and specifically related to the existing 35 data centers; each had a different challenge that needed to be addressed individually, including the following:

    - Building Management System (BMS).
    - Supporting secondary power sources—UPS systems, generators, and such.
    - Supplies—transformer, fuel (diesel), cabling, telecommunication, and so on.
    - Individual inventory management.
    - Supporting staff and supporting environment.

In addition to the preceding challenges, there were a lot of environmental concerns that the team needed to address while working out a solution, as follows:

- Performance enhancement
- Lesser DC floor area

- Lesser energy usage
- Lesser cooling requirement
- Lesser cost to IBM

The IBM team was confident of its capabilities to address these challenges. The support and cumulative expertise available within IBM would surely make it a profitable and global reference resource for IBM. It would also contribute meaningfully to the environment and IBM's green initiative.

The Organization's Initiatives and Innovation

The IT vendor-client team proceeded enthusiastically with continuous innovation in the solutions provided. Following is an outline of the key initiatives implemented:

- **Buildings, data centers, and production processes**
  - Data center build
  - Data center consolidation
  - Server consolidation
- **Products**
  - Use of energy-efficient and EPA-approved products
- **Services and solutions**
  - Automation
  - Virtualization
  - Optimized disaster recovery solution
  - Energy-saving solutions for users

The following sections give the details on the preceding outline.

Buildings, Data Centers, and Production Processes

Data Center Build   The client entrusted the data center build to IBM, given its expertise in building and deploying world-class data centers. The following initiatives were taken up for the data center build, with a view to a green environment and energy conservation:

- Use of R407C EPA certified refrigerants in the XD units on the basis that their release does not pose a threat to the environment.

- Precision air conditioners are installed with high-efficiency scroll compressor from Copeland Scroll (part of Emerson Climate Technologies), instead of conventional reciprocating compressor.

- Condensers used in precision air conditioners are provided with fan speed control for energy saving due to ambient temperature variation.

- Dehumidification is built in within the precision air conditioners and do not require reheat and thus save energy.

- Precision air conditioners supplied from ISO-14000 manufacturing units.

- XD units installed are with highest efficiency digital scroll.

- XD units installed are designed for SHF of 1 and thus do not waste energy in unnecessary removal of moisture.

- Localized cooling for high-density servers requiring fan energy of 25 watts/ Kw of heat removal against conventional 80 watts/ Kw of heat removal.

- UPS installed at data center has efficiency of 92.3 percent at 100 percent load.

- Twelve pulse rectifiers used in UPS against conventional 6 pulse, which ensures THD less than 10 percent at rated load–enabling lower thermal loss.

- Output isolation transformers in UPS are designed for minimum losses, even at part load.

Data Center Consolidation   The consolidation plan was to reduce the total numbers of data centers from 35 to 7 (two large- and five-medium sized data centers). IBM worked out the plan to migrate the applications in these seven new data centers. All the data centers are ready, and migration was completed successfully. IBM won the contract for the data center, which was a major achievement because it demonstrated the client's confidence in our capabilities and expertise in building and deploying world-class data centers. IBM's green initiatives planned were realized during this construct and migration.

Server Consolidation   "Server Consolidation" is another initiative that IBM undertook to minimize the DC floor, electricity, and cooling requirements. Some of the major areas in which work has happened or is being addressed include the following:

1. Consolidation of 10+ servers installed at distributed locations to eight System P servers at central locations for one application.

2. Consolidation of 73 Intel servers at 20+ locations to just three System P servers at one central location for another of the company's tools.

3. 200+ distributed Intel servers to just four blade centers for Citrix farm.

Products

Use of Energy-Efficient and EPA-Approved Products   World-class energy-efficient and EPA-approved products were used in building the data center. Some of the key products are as follows:

1. Cooling systems: Highly energy-efficient precision air conditioners from Emerson and the environmentally friendly EPA-compliant refrigerant R407C.

2. DG set: MTU (Germany) engines for DG set used as secondary source of power. These engines are EPA, tier -3/ EU stage 3A certified.

3. UPS: Highly efficient UPS systems from Emerson, Italy. The efficiency ratio is more than 92.3 percent at 100 percent load.

4. Use of ENERGY STAR-compliant CFLs.

Services and Solutions

Automation   The IBM team planned and implemented Tivoli tools for automation in remote support, patch management, asset inventory, performance monitoring, network monitoring, and so on. This led to reduced manpower and optimization of the computing requirements.

In phase-II, IBM has planned to centralize, consolidate, and integrate all the tools under the overall umbrella of an enterprisewide command center. The Tivoli suite of products along with various other tools are planned to be integrated to provide a centralized management. This will result in further reduction in manpower and optimization of the computing requirements.

Virtualization   Virtualization results in effective utilization of residual computing powers and storage disks. This directly results in DC space-savings, energy-savings, and usage of less hardware.

IBM has planned to use IT virtualization technology for dynamic allocations of computing resources such as LPARs in the servers and virtualizing storage and using it as a pool. P series will be using the virtualization feature that has been planned for implementation.

Optimized Disaster Recovery Solution   Rather than using the exact replica of production systems at the Disaster Recovery (DR) site, IBM has successfully convinced the client to optimize the DR solution. This has resulted in reducing the computing power to about 50 percent for batch applications.

Energy-Saving Solutions for Users   The client has a large base of employees and expanding. IBM did an analysis of working atmosphere and patterns and suggested that the client should convert most of the PCs into laptops. The benefits of using laptops are multifold with increased mobility of workforce, greater work efficiency, and business continuity.

Using laptops also helped the client in larger aspects of green environment contribution with reduced energy, reduced work area, reduced residuals, and health benefits for employees, and so forth.

The customer is making these changes with the refresh of PCs that are taking place. (For example, laptops are used for new purchases when refreshing PCs.)

Compilation of the Organization's Results

Table 11.1 below gives the compilation results of positive impacts on IBM. Table 11.2 gives the positive impacts on the client. This is an indicative table, and there are many other areas where such an impact can be demonstrated.

Table 11.1 Positive Impacts on IBM

System	Impact on IBM
Blue project (overall)	Increased the processing power by 80%, creating global reference bases for various Telco applications. Cost reduction.
Billing	Global reference for the application.
Server consolidation	Reduced support staff.
Data center consolidation	Huge operating expense savings Heavy reductions in support staff.

continues

Table 11.1 Positive Impacts on IBM   continued

System	Impact on IBM
On-demand capacity enhancement	Cost reductions.
Automation	Reduction in manpower. Optimization of computing requirements.
Virtualization	Reduced hardware requirements, resulting in cost savings.
Optimized disaster recovery solution	Huge cost savings.
Lesser manpower deployment	Energy-saving solution for users. Additional business realization for IBM.

Table 11.2 Positive Impacts on Client

System	Impact on Client
Blue project (overall)	Decreased the power requirement by 40%. Decreased the floor space by 30%.
Server consolidation	Reduced DC floor space. Reduced cooling requirements. Reduced electricity requirements.
Data center consolidation	Considerable savings in energy. Considerable savings in space.
On-demand capacity enhancement	Optimization of energy consumption.
Virtualization	Energy-savings. DC space savings.
Optimized disaster recovery solution	Huge DC space savings.
Energy savings	Energy-saving solution for users. Increased mobility of workforce. Greater work efficiency. Implementation of business continuity. Reduced energy requirements. Reduced work area. Reduced residuals. Health benefits for employees.

Future Plans During 2009

As highlighted in the preceding segment, various projects are being planned to be undertaken in 2009. Some of these include the following:

- Ongoing data center consolidation
- Virtualization of computing power and storage
- Centralization of an enterprisewide command center
- Enhanced server consolidation
- Implementation of Business Continuity Program

These projects contribute highly to the green environment efforts of IBM, and lead to significant cost and performance benefits.

Chapter Summary and Conclusions

The following conclusions are from the discussion on green IT for data centers around the world:

- Although the challenges in implementing green data centers around the world can vary considerably based on factors such as the cost of electricity and social/political environment, the basic best practices remain the same—for example, data center consolidation, server consolidation, IT virtualization, and so on.
- Green data center show cases such as the PSSC Data Center at Montpelier can provide some valuable innovation ideas. Real-time dashboards showing data center energy use (PUE) can help IT teams evaluate the impact of different energy management policies (like the hybrid car's miles per gallon dashboard). Also, live cameras and thermal cameras can reduce physical access and identify current data center hot spots, as indicated in the Montpelier study.
- The brief green data center discussion for Istanbul helps indicate the growing worldwide interest in green IT and the cost and environmental benefits of energy efficiency in all parts of the world.

- The large green data center case study for a company in India provides an example of the lessons that can be learned for data center projects that dwarf any of our data center efficiency concerns. That case study can help us all understand that no green data center project is too big!

- The basic green data center steps of diagnose, build, virtualize, cool, manage, and measure apply for data centers anywhere in the world and of all sizes, and case studies can help us evaluate best practices for our green data centers.

12

The Future of Green IT for Corporations

"What's past is prologue."

—William Shakespeare, *The Tempest*

The future of green IT is being shaped now—based on university, corporate, and government research, regulations, incentives, and so forth. Because of the dynamic aspect of IT, we have already made significant progress with green computing and can build on that past. This chapter gives a summary of what we have discussed in the preceding twelve chapters and takes a look at the future of green IT.

For success with green IT, it needs to continue to be a collaborative endeavor. The IT hardware and software manufacturers (Dell, Sun, HP, IBM, Fujitsu-Siemens, Intel, EMC, Microsoft, and so on) have a great deal of competitive incentive to market and improve the energy-efficiency aspects of their products. Energy utilities, government regulators, environmental advocates, and the groups involved in helping build data centers—including the infrastructure technology providers—all need to collaborate with IT providers and IT customers.

One of the most important arenas for development of green IT is that we must have better measurements to better manage energy use at data centers and throughout the corporation. We will see great strides here: for example, like gas mileage monitoring on the Toyota Prius hybrid. Currently, we can use the data network "sniffer" concept to determine network bandwidth and response time for each user of a server. That same sniffer concept will be developed for power and energy used. There will be an inexpensive power/energy monitoring appliance that will act like the network sniffer and give us information on the power and energy use for each IT device. That appliance will send the information to an energy monitoring system (a server). Then we can see actual energy reduction results of using virtualization and other energy-saving initiatives. The electric power/energy monitoring device will also be in our homes and will have the capability of sending information to our laptops. We can see the actual power and energy-use history of our refrigerators or window air conditioners. We then can better manage our energy use by measurements and trending.

Review of IT Steps to Help Save the World!

According to the research company Gartner, the green wave has only begun to rise. The company predicts that by 2009, more than one-third of all IT organizations will place environmental concerns within their top six buying criteria. By 2010, Gartner says, three-quarters of companies will use carbon-footprint considerations with their hardware-buying strategy, and by 2011, large enterprises will develop policies requiring their suppliers to prove their green credentials through an auditing process.

Remember, many companies are talking a good game but are not being as aggressive in going green as will be necessary to make the difference needed to solve our energy and climate crisis. According to a survey of 124 IT operations by Forrester Research in May 2007, some 85 percent of respondents said environmental factors are important in planning IT operations. But only one-fourth of survey respondents have actually written green criteria into their company's purchasing processes. Enterprises that have started the green journey, however, have found that reducing total energy requirements can be accomplished through some fairly straightforward improvements that don't take years to implement or bring return.

Chapter 1, "The Importance of Green IT," lists six steps that apply to all companies and organizations in going to green IT. These steps from Chapter 1 that have been discussed throughout the book are reiterated here.

1. Communicate Green IT Plans and Appoint an Energy Czar

A first step is to measure current energy use and establish a baseline. Chapter 2, "The Basics of Green IT," and Appendix A, "Green IT Checklist and Recommendations," give details on measurement options and a checklist to get started. Chapter 7, "The Need for Standard IT Energy-Use Metrics," describes the different energy-efficiency metrics. Communicating to all employees your organization's plans and goals to save energy via green IT is an important step. That communication, in addition to plans and goals, needs to include the organization that will be driving the effort. It is a good idea to designate a focal point, with a title. The title doesn't need to be officially "energy czar," but, in essence, that should be the role of the focal point.

2. Consolidate and Virtualize

The significance of consolidating and virtualizing IT is the topic of Chapter 6, "A Most-Significant Step—'Virtualizing' Your IT Systems." Consolidation of IT operations and using virtualization to reduce server footprint and energy use are the most well-recognized and most-often-implemented efficiency strategies of the past few years. The checklist in Appendix A provides a good way to start with an inventory of where you are with green IT, and this checklist emphasizes consolidation and virtualization as key steps.

3. Install Energy-Efficient Cooling Units

Chapter 8, "What About Chillers, Cooling Tower Fans, and All That Cooling Equipment Usually Ignored by IT?," describes the significance of energy-efficient cooling (cooling accounts for half of data center energy use). Although energy-efficient data center cooling is not something we IT people usually are involved with, the significance of an energy-efficient data center needs to be appreciated as part of your green IT plan.

4. Measure and Optimize

Chapter 7 describes IT energy-use metrics. Over the past two years, The Green Grid has grown from 11 founding members to a consortium of more than 150 companies working to improve data center energy efficiency.

In 2009, the group is expected to release some of its most important deliverables in the form of metrics that businesses can use to measure the power usage effectiveness of facilities infrastructure equipment. Most businesses can already readily identify areas where infrastructure optimization can achieve increased efficiency by simply monitoring and measuring their existing infrastructure equipment. Additionally, the Environmental Protection Agency (EPA) is stepping in to help create metrics as well. About 100 companies have indicated they will provide raw power data and other information to the EPA for use in developing its new benchmark. The EPA indicated that the results of the benchmark should be available by 2010.

Until widely accepted metrics become available, businesses should make sure the utility costs associated with their data center operations are broken out separately from those for other corporate facilities. In addition, metering specific equipment racks or types of equipment such as servers can provide valuable insight into which specific consolidation, virtualization, and optimization projects would yield the best ROI going forward.

Energy optimization software is discussed in Chapter 2 in the section, "You Can't Manage What You Can't Measure." This discusses energy management software such as IBM's Active Energy Manager (AEM) and HP's Insight Control. Appendix A further discusses available energy monitoring and management software tools.

5. Implement Efficient Applications and Deduplicate Data

Chapter 2 discusses the significance of software and application efficiency for green IT. Data storage efficiency such as the use of tiered storage is also significant, as described in Chapter 9, "Green IT Case Studies for Energy Utilities." Data deduplication (often called intelligent compression or single-instance storage) is a method of reducing storage needs by eliminating redundant data. Only one unique instance of the data is actually retained on storage media, such as disk or tape. Redundant data are replaced with a pointer to the unique data copy. For example, a typical e-mail system might contain 100 instances of the same one megabyte (MB) file attachment. If the e-mail platform is backed up or archived, all 100 instances are saved, requiring 100MB storage space. With data deduplication, only one instance of the attachment is actually stored; each subsequent instance is just referenced back to the one saved copy. In this example, a 100MB storage demand could be reduced to only 1MB.

6. Make Use of Rebates and Incentives

Chapter 4, "The Government's Role—Regulation and EPA Activity," and Chapter 5, "The Magic of 'Incentive'—The Role of Electric Utilities," describe the rebates or other incentives that encourage businesses to update equipment and adopt efficient operational practices. These practices can help reduce peak and total power demands, and that's what makes the electric power utilities happy.

Chapter 3, "Collaboration Is Key for Green IT," describes how going to green IT on a worldwide basis requires the collaboration of many different groups, including electric utilities, government agencies, IT technology vendors, data center design and build businesses, and all companies and organizations worldwide, including your company. That's one of the best things about green IT as a step toward solving the energy crisis—we can all participate. The case studies in Chapter 9, Chapter 10, "Green IT Case Studies for Universities and a Large Company," and Chapter 11, "Worldwide Green IT Case Studies," and Appendixes A through D give details on how other companies have implemented green IT.

Green IT for the Future

According to a 2008 article in *ComputerWorld*, "Green computing promises an enormous win for IT: a chance to save money—and the environment. Many companies are trying to go greener, but a few truly stand out." Many companies have begun to address some of these challenges head on. In fact, between 30 percent to 50 percent of large enterprises have consolidated or started to consolidate during 2008, and most are doing some level of virtualization. Those that have really advanced these efforts are seeing significant returns or savings. Some customers have shown the ability to do the following:

- Triple asset utilization
- Provision new resources in minutes
- Reduce heat by up to 60 percent
- Reduce floor space by as much as 80 percent
- Reduce disaster recovery time by 85 percent

The following section describes one vision for a green IT future.

A Roadmap for Green IT

This section is based on the article "IBM's Vision for the New Enterprise Data Center," March 2008 (see Bibliography). You can't make the world move more slowly. Or change where markets are headed. Or hold back new technologies while focusing on day-to-day IT operational issues. But there is something you can do, right now.

The fact is that not all of today's IT infrastructures were built to support the explosive growth in computer capacity and information. Many data centers have become highly distributed and somewhat fragmented. As a result, they are limited in their capability to change quickly and support the integration of new types of technologies or to easily scale to power the business as needed. So how do you find the time and resources to drive the innovation required to keep your company competitive in a rapidly changing marketplace? How can you react to business needs faster?

Because today's distributed approach to the enterprise data center is challenged to keep up in a fast-paced business environment, a new centralized IT approach is needed. We must rethink IT service delivery to help move beyond today's operational challenges to a new data center model that is more efficient, service-oriented, and responsive to business needs.

This vision for the new enterprise data center is an evolutionary model that helps reset the economics of IT and can dramatically improve operational efficiency. It also can help reduce and control rising costs and improve provisioning speed and data center security and resiliency—at any scale. It will enable you to be highly responsive to any user need. And it aligns technology and business, giving you the freedom and the tools you need to innovate and stay ahead of the competition.

Through our experience with thousands of client engagements, we have developed an architected approach based on best practices and proven implementation patterns and blueprints. And our own data center transformation provides first-hand proof that embracing this new approach simply makes good business sense.

Right now, technology leaders are challenged to manage sprawling, complex distributed infrastructures, and an ever-growing tidal wave of data, while remaining highly responsive to business demands. And, they must evaluate and decide when and how to adopt a multitude of innovations that will keep their companies competitive. IT professionals spend much of the day fixing problems—keeping them from applying time and resources to development activities that could truly drive business innovation. In fact, many say they spend too much time mired down in operations and precious little time helping the business grow. These operational issues include the following:

- **Costs and service delivery:** Time is money—and most IT departments are forced to stretch both. There is no question that the daily expense of managing operations is increasing, as is the cost and availability of skilled labor. In fact, IT system administration costs have grown four-fold, and power and cooling costs have risen eight-fold since 1996. And in today's data center, data volumes and network bandwidth consumed are doubling every 18 months, with devices accessing data over networks doubling every 2.5 years.

- **Business resiliency and security:** As enterprises expand globally, organizations are requiring that IT groups strengthen the security measures they put in place to protect critical information. For good reason, enterprise risk management is now being integrated into corporate ratings delivered by organizations such as Fitch, Moody's, and Standard & Poor's. At the same time, companies are demanding that users have real-time access to this information, putting extra—and often conflicting—pressure on the enterprise to be both secure and resilient in the expanding IT environment.

- **Energy requirements:** As IT grows, enterprises require greater power and cooling capacities. In fact, energy costs related to server sprawl might rise from less than 10 percent to 30 percent of IT budgets in the coming years. These trends are forcing technology organizations to become more energy efficient—to control costs while developing a flexible foundation from which to scale.

The bottom line is that enterprises report that IT operational overhead is reaching up to 70 percent of the overall IT budget. And that number is growing, leaving precious few resources for new initiatives.

If you're spending most of your time mired in day-to-day operations, it's difficult to evaluate and leverage new technologies available that could streamline your IT operations and help keep your company competitive and profitable. Yet the rate of technology adoption around us is moving at breakneck speed, and much of it is disrupting the infrastructure status quo. Consider some examples: In 2007, there were 3 billion mobile subscribers worldwide, and that number is estimated to grow by 2010. Between 2003 and 2006, stock market data volumes rose by 1,750 percent in financial services markets. And by 2010, it is estimated that medical imaging will consume 30 percent of the world's data storage. Increasing speed and availability of network bandwidth is creating new opportunities to integrate services across the Web and recentralize distributed IT resources. Access to trusted information and real-time data and analytics will soon become basic expectations. Driven by the expanding processing power of multicore and specialty processor-based systems, supercomputing power will be available to the masses. And it will require systems, data, applications, and networks that are always available, secure, and resilient.

Further, the proliferation of data sources, RFID and mobile devices, unified communications, SOA, Web 2.0, and technologies like mashups and XML create opportunities for new types of business solutions. In fact, the advancements in technology that are driving change can be seen in the new emerging types of data centers, such as the Internet and Web 2.0, which are broadening the available options for connecting, securing, and managing business processes. Ultimately, all these new innovations need to play an important role in the new enterprise data center.

The vision for the new enterprise data center provides for a new approach to IT service delivery. Through it, you can leverage today's best practices and technology to better manage costs, improve operational performance and resiliency, and quickly respond to business needs. Its goal is to deliver the following:

- **New economics:** The new enterprise data center helps you transcend traditional operational issues to achieve new levels of efficiency, flexibility, and responsiveness. Through virtualization, you can break the lock between your IT resources and business services—freeing you to exploit highly optimized systems and networks to improve efficiency and reduce overall costs.

- **Rapid service deployment:** The ability to deliver quality service is critical to businesses of all sizes. Maintaining a positive customer experience—and ensuring cost efficiency and a fast ROI—relies on your ability to see and manage the business, while leveraging automation to drive efficiency and operational agility. Therefore, service management is a key element in the new enterprise data center approach.

- **Business alignment:** A highly efficient and shared infrastructure can enable you to respond instantaneously to new business needs. It creates opportunities to make sound decisions based on information obtained in real time, and it provides the tools you need to free up resources from more traditional operational demands. With a new enterprise data center, you can focus on delivering IT as a set of services aligned to the business, freeing up time to spend on IT-driven business innovation.

What makes this approach for efficient IT service delivery unique? As businesses move toward a recentralization of the data center environment, a holistic integrated approach needs to be considered. We need to capture an end-to-end view of the IT data center and its key components. Although we understand that incremental improvements to each element of the new enterprise data center can improve overall operations, we take into account that modifications to one component might strain the performance of another.

For example, upgrading the enterprise information architecture to provide integrated and trusted information to users will likely require changes to security and business resiliency approaches. And creating highly virtualized resources are most effective along with a stronger, more integrated service management approach. As such, the strategy for the new enterprise data center needs to be holistic and integrate the following key elements:

- **Highly virtualized resources** that are flexible to adjust to changing business needs to allow for more responsive provisioning and help deliver efficient resource utilization. Virtualization removes the bind between applications and data and underlying physical resources-granting IT organizations more flexibility and freedom in deployment options and the ability to exploit highly optimized systems.
- **Business-driven service management,** in which a complex and difficult-to-manage environment is transformed for improved transparency and cost-efficient, easier management. This transformation involves raising management tasks from the simple monitoring of individual resources to the orchestration of the entire environment to be more responsive and efficient. When transformed, the environment can be fully aligned with business needs and controls to ensure that customer priorities are met, business controls are maintained, and availability and performance is maximized across the entire enterprise.

- **Security and business resilience approaches** and best practices that become increasingly important with the consolidation of data centers and recentralization of systems and data while providing secure, open access across and beyond organizational boundaries.

- **Efficient, green, and optimized infrastructures and facilities** that balance and adjust the workloads across a virtualized infrastructure and align the power and cooling consumption with business processing requirements across all IT and data center facilities. The result is balanced energy demands to help avoid high-peak energy use and the associated higher energy billing rates and meet SLAs based on business priorities. Through the introduction of an optimized infrastructure, the number of systems and networks in the data center can be reduced, cost efficiency improved, and energy efficiency enhanced.

- **Enterprise Information Architecture.** Data that was typically contained in disconnected, heterogeneous sources, and content silos are virtualized through flexible enterprise information architecture. Therefore, IT can deliver trusted information to people, processes, and applications to truly optimize the business decision making and performance.

Conclusions

As you've seen throughout this book, green IT promises a significant win for IT: a chance to save money—and the environment. Collaboration with governments on all levels, energy research organizations, universities, energy utilities, IT vendors, and all the nonprofit green organizations that keep springing up is key. And it's not just for organizations dealing with IT. Almost everyone worldwide can collaborate on green IT, since almost everyone is now, or soon will be, a user of IT through PCs, the Internet, and cell phones. We all need to contribute to energy efficiency to help solve the climate crisis. Energy conservation will remain the best and easiest way to save energy—and, of course, that applies to energy conservation for our IT systems and for every other energy-consuming device we use.

Green IT Checklist and Recommendations

"...you can't make a product greener, whether it's a car, a refrigerator, or a traffic system, without making it smarter—smarter materials, smarter software, or smarter design."

—Thomas L. Friedman, author of *Hot, Flat, and Crowded*

This appendix includes a green IT checklist and information on various green IT areas.

A Green IT Checklist

The green IT checklist in this section was developed by Dave Anderson, who is a green architect for IBM's Energy-Efficiency Initiative. One of Dave's passions has been to travel around to different companies, schools, and other organizations, giving talks on green IT. Dave's background as an engineer, which includes Professional Engineer (PE) certification, gives him the background to address all aspects of green IT. This checklist was developed as a result of Dave's speaking engagements.

Tips on Creating Sustainable Data Centers (Dave Anderson)

Everywhere I go, from the grocery store to the carpool parking place outside IBM's mega data centers, I am now reminded to be green.

Whether purchasing alternative green products for everyday use or taking care of business in a sustainable way, we now have the opportunity to change for the better. I simply define better as doing operations with less energy and creating longer lasting value. Green is all about doing the right thing *and* saving costs. How can you spruce up your data center? Here are some tips and examples of green IT users:

1. **Begin with an enterprise goal in mind.** Create lasting greenness. Small scale will yield small results. Large scale will yield bigger results. Often every project looks good and green by itself, but when added up, a suboptimal data center and complex infrastructure has been created. IBM has a vision that can become a green blueprint for a data center that has state-of-the-art capabilities while using less energy and space. The New Enterprise Data Center exploits virtualization and service management with automation and aligns with business goals. The journey of transformation includes being simplified, shared, and dynamic. Start a green program with goals in mind.

2. **Exploit virtualization to reduce the number of servers and improve flexibility.** Virtualization or using software or hypervisor technology to represent virtual servers rather than physical servers is a very green technology. Reducing the number of power drawing components in the data center to a minimum directly slashes the amount of energy consumed as well as reduces the cooling requirements. **Logical Partitioning** (LPAR) and virtualization technologies such as VMware, PowerVM, and z/VM®, to name a few, break the physical boundaries of servers and drive up utilization reducing the need for many servers. Starting with pilot or proof of concept projects is easier than ever before because IT vendor services and virtualization technologies on all platforms have matured. From open source virtualization to mainframe z/VM virtualization, both implementation services and technologies abound to start eliminating the wasteful approaches of one server per application and a variety of servers for every production server. Many applications can be hosted on a physical server and still have the autonomy because of virtualization. How many servers can be eliminated? Compression ratios of 1 to 8 are common, and 1 to 50 compression ratios are often achieved with the best virtualization technologies.

3. **Exploit virtualization to reduce the amount of storage networking equipment.** This includes SANs and using virtual I/O connections within servers such as IBM's HiperSockets™, Virtual Ethernet for Systems p and i, and OSA integrated layer 2 and 3 switching.

4. **Use integrated approach to server consolidation to optimize savings.** More than a single methodology needs to be applied to get the fewest number of servers. IBM's Enterprise Computing Model for reducing thousands to about 30 large centralized servers used the following approach to consolidation:

   ♦ Migrate servers delivering largest savings first (for example, stranded infrastructure). This primes the pump and generates enthusiasm and savings for other green projects.

   ♦ Eliminate assets with lowest utilization first. These assets are not pulling their weight when measured by watts/logical image or other common metrics to compare servers.

   ♦ Identify assets with an upcoming compelling event to mitigate expense (upgrade, move, asset refresh). It is always easier to have a positive ROI and be green within the normal refresh of assets.

   ♦ Aggregate by customer work portfolio to leverage strong customer buy-in. Ease of migration assists speed and successful workload migrations.

   ♦ Start with oldest technology first because it uses the most power and provides the least performance.

   ♦ Focus on freeing up contiguous raised floor space. This enables growth and the addition of energy-efficient new IT and facilities equipment.

   ♦ Provision new applications to the mainframe or another large centralized server.

5. **Drive to high-utilization rates.** Virtualization and management of workloads are key. The operating system must manage W/L to business priorities and dispatch in an automated manner. The average Wintel server is used only 5 percent to 15 percent of the time. No manager would allow his people to work 5 percent to 15 percent of the time. With new technologies and automation, utilization rates can go beyond 50 percent and at the same time improve flexibility and responsiveness as more resources can be tapped for peaks.

6. **Consolidate on large servers.** Fewer larger servers will convert AC to DC more efficiently than many smaller servers with smaller and less-efficient power systems. Power supplies of large servers are capable of operating at very high efficiencies (+90 percent). Large servers can also take advantage of high voltages and eliminate a conversion loss that robs efficiencies when stepping down to smaller voltages. The ability to more efficiently share resources makes running on a few larger systems more efficient than many small ones. Workload can be balanced, driving up utilization and reducing the number of watts needed to run applications, day or night.

7. **Eliminate redundancy but keep high availability and disaster recovery capabilities.** High availability and disaster recovery can be efficient and in a green way be designed into server configurations. Engines can now add nondisruptively to almost all platforms, reducing the need for extra servers. No longer is an idle server needed for what-if scenarios. Production servers can back up other production servers. Configuring the ability to nondisruptively add (and reduce) capacity for production or disaster recovery without having idle or underutilized servers significantly reduces the number of footprints and slashes the energy consumed in the data center. Commonly used technologies include IBM's On/Off Capacity on Demand (add engines by the day) and Capacity Backup Upgrade (CBU) for Disaster Recovery. A data center can be greened and the bottom line affected by using fewer servers while having the ability to increase capacity without adding server and the associated facility infrastructure.

8. **Measure and put the costs of energy where they are incurred.** Automated measuring and billing of energy consumption makes usage part of cost and green decisions. Without energy and cooling knowledge, requirements are unknown, inaccurate, and often overplanned leading to inefficiencies. An example of new technology to optimize energy use is IBM's **Active Energy Manager** (AEM). Monitoring energy usage and developing trends is key to understanding how energy is being used. This first step to optimizing energy use opens up the potential to become more efficient and optimizing for performance / watt. Managing energy use is an evolving concept in the data center. Capping power at the server level and optimizing to deliver the right performance per watts can be achieved using AEM. In the future, the most efficient data centers

will treat servers like you treat lights in your house, turning them off when not in use or at least turning on only what you need. Linkage to **Total Cost of Ownership** (TCO) ensures that green is part of every decision. Benchmark the entire data center as well as local areas for continuous improvement. Use commonly accepted methodologies such as the Power Usage Efficiency ratio (Total power / IT equipment power = PUE) from Green Grid Consortium or the Energy-Efficiency ratio.

9. **Use the concept of hierarchical storage.** Picking the right media and format for storing data is like picking the right vehicle for a trip. Not every trip needs an 18-wheeler or a motorcycle. A combination of disk, tape, and hybrid technologies optimizes the use of energy while giving your data a secure and extendable home. Tape, a green storage equipment star, uses the least amount of energy and should be part of the storage constellation. Disk storage should be for demanding applications that require frequent updates. The virtual tape server can mask latency with many applications and is another green star in the storage constellation. Larger and slower disks use less energy, and if their latency can be masked, the energy efficiencies gained by their use is worth it. For less-demanding apps, MAID might be appropriate, and the elimination of spinning disks when not needed can substantially reduce wasted watts.

10. **Use the latest equipment.** Newer generations of IT equipment are more energy efficient and give better performance than older IT equipment. Begin greening your data center with replacing *the oldest and most inefficient equipment first*. Newer generations of servers and storage are built with more efficient power supplies, processors, memory, and I/O. Just about everything in newer servers and storage provides more performance or stores more data with fewer watts. We all have experienced how digital cameras have provided more memory, functions, and better performance in the last five years. Servers and storage are on similar technology-improvement trajectories. Servers scale higher in performance while using fewer watts per logical image. Decommissioning older servers that never were designed for virtualization or energy efficiency can be one of the most cost-effective ways to green your data center. Like the gas-guzzling clunker that needs to be replaced with a hybrid, there are better ways now to run applications. There is a *big* difference between IT and your automobile. The new servers enable you to

replace 8 to 80 servers. The simplicity in running fewer physical servers is a no-brainer. The System z10™, IBM's new generation of energy-efficient, large centralized servers can replace approximately 1,800 distributed servers. The energy efficiency and space-savings enable the data center to add capacity within the four walls.

II. **Do not wait for the 11th hour. Start a sustainable data center now.** The biggest savings of all for going green is to create a culture and infrastructure that exploits technology for creating a sustainable data center. With green concepts and projects, a data center can grow in capability / capacity while continuing to use the same or less space and energy. Conducting or having a third party conduct an energy audit can benchmark where you are and identify projects with ROIs that can be prioritized to give cascading green returns. For every watt you save in IT equipment, you reduce the infrastructure (UPS, cooling, and so on) load and generate savings for future projects. Conserving energy in the data center allows the dollars to be used for adding more value to the business. Use energy like a precious commodity. Turn it up (and on) when needed and throttle back (turn off) when not needed. Create a culture and data center that is intrinsically green.

Following are some additional green ideas for sprucing up your data center. Some you may have already done. Others can yield small to massive energy savings. All of them I have observed in various data centers in the past 18 months:

✓ Know the new (revised as of 2008) ranges of the temperature and humidity specs of ASHRAE. Stop running too hot or cold. Yes, you can run your data center between 60°F and 80°F. Let the hot aisles be hot.

✓ Place equipment so that it is in hot and cold aisles with two floor-tiles width. Stop mixing hot and cold air whereever possible.

✓ This includes keeping openings in the server ranks and the servers to a minimum. Inspect each cabinet to make sure that for all empty slot positions where no equipment is installed, filler strips or blanking plates are installed to eliminate turbulence inside the cabinet (allowing proper cooling of the installed hardware). In some cases, where a cabinet is by itself, devices such as "snorkels" might be used to direct either cold air into or hot air out of the cabinet as a tactic to provide the most-efficient cooling for that cabinet. This is especially useful where a hot side of a cabinet faces a cold side of an adjacent cabinet.

✓ If you need enclosures for additional cooling, you still should have two floortiles-width for servicing. One is tight and three is wasteful.

✓ Do an assessment that looks at both temperature and air flow. IBM has advanced tools and models to assist this baselining of what the cooling profile is.

✓ Use free cooling. Outside air can substantially reduce energy required by computer room air conditioners. Data center site selection will enable more days of free cooling when the climate has big difference between day and night temperatures. Colorado is an example of an excellent climate to exploit free cooling.

✓ Enable Active Energy Management (IBM Power Director Active Energy Management with Tivoli). If you do not measure, you miss understanding easy opportunities to improve. Measuring enables new charging methodologies that include energy consumption.

✓ Charge for usage and have a surcharge for equipment at peak demand (or a reduced rate at off hours).

✓ Larger than code copper distribution (wiring for data center).

✓ Whereever possible, *eliminate* conversion losses. This includes using high-voltage power, as well as rotary UPS.

✓ Plan for use of 480V (or 600V) to equipment. The mainframe uses these today.

✓ Enable dynamic provisioning of server and storage resources. This can reduce, as well as turn off, the number of servers drawing power.

✓ Modeling suggests at least 24 inches of unobstructed raised floor. Optimize air flow, putting less stress on CRACs. Fewer than 24 inches will need higher velocities of air.

✓ Plan for water. It will be used on high-end equipment to reduce energy requirements and hot spots on the raised floor.

✓ Capture rain water for onsite storage of water.

✓ Putting water closer to heat loads can minimize the need for more air conditioning.

✓ Control hot air rising. How? Ceiling return of hot air, row air curtains, or use card board or plastic if you want to really go cheap. Block for recirculation, but make sure you can use sprinklers. Dividers to the ceiling can prevent hot air from escaping into cold aisles.

✓ Plugged openings (cables, power) not in cold aisle. Block at the server or other IT equipment cable tailgates and cable openings in the raised floor to prevent cold air losses and improve efficiencies.

✓ Two tiles on both hot and cold aisles. Enables both tiles to be pulled up to ease access to underneath floor. Having tiles with many perforations (holes) in the cold aisle is a must.

✓ Tile and CRAC placement can be optimized (temperature and air flow) with fluid dynamic analysis. Moving air with fewer direction changes is best. Watch out for too many perforations, and do not place any perforated tiles within four tiles from CRAC.

✓ Cables overhead—even power. Leave under floor for pumping and air flow. When laying out cables, make sure they do not impede airflow if under raised floor (or above). A tray or trough can be made.

✓ If cables are already under the floor, manage them. Remove cables when no longer needed. Keep "rats nesting" of cables to a minimum.

✓ Auto lights out. Lights need to be on only when someone is inside the data center.

✓ Shock and vibration support for racks. This is a must-do for earthquake regions and can be planned when refreshing equipment or greening the data center.

✓ Lighting on back of racks for ease of servicing.

✓ New generation battery, flywheel, and diesel generator backup. Flywheel can provide a very green way to keep up the power system until generators start. Equipment has substantially improved in energy efficiency in the last year. Use the latest generation of UPS, flywheel, and generators. Newer generations of UPS are much more efficient than older generations.

✓ Negotiate with the electric utility for going off grid (use generators) in rare peak-demand situations. Utilities will pay for the capability to shed load that might potentially cause a brownout or a blackout. The data center can contribute to the electric grids resilience by working with the utility.

✓ Redundancy design for power and cooling. Eliminate common cause failures whereever possible, including UPS, by having flywheel and batteries rather than redundant battery UPS.

✓ Liquid cooling for hot equipment with rear door heat exchanger or side car technologies.

✓ Enough water cooling taps built into water system for new growth.

✓ Minimize impedance of piping (water or air) to reduce pumping power required.

✓ Leak detection under raised floor for water distribution system.

✓ Variable frequency drives on all pumps and air-conditioning equipment.

✓ Do not build out all facilities at once. Be modular and strive for high utilization of IT and facilities equipment.

✓ Easily displayed power and thermal monitoring for data center. Large displays to highlight success / energy saved. Take pride in using less.

✓ Where possible, measure overall data center Power Unit Efficiency and plan on ways to keep reducing as new state-of-the-art equipment and processes become available.

✓ Physical: Fire protection system FM—200 or wet sprinkler + security system with "man trap" to keep potential intruders from entering the raised floor.

✓ Liquid side economizer. Efficiently control humidity.

✓ Thermal storage to optimize use of chillers and reduce energy cost at peak hours.

✓ High-efficiency pumps, chillers, and fans for cooling towers.

✓ If possible, use cooling towers in summer and reuse waste heat to reduce energy in winter.

✓ When designing a new facility, place the infrastructure in the basement. Position the water piping and electric cables in the ceiling of the basement below the raised floor, leaving the first floor raised flow clear of obstructions.

✓ Use virtualization for testing and potentially actual disaster recovery. Where possible, architect and build active solutions (production in two places that can nondisruptively add capacity to back up and scale when needed).

✓ Virtualize servers, storage, and network.

✓ Link facilities and IT. Offer new types of service level agreements based on performance / watt and not just performance.

✓ Be open to cogeneration of electricity. Fuel cells, gas turbines, wind turbines, solar arrays, and even small nuclear reactors (such as the Toshiba 4S) can generate electricity to augment or supply all the needs of a data center.

✓ Use IT as a green catalyst for organizational efficiencies. Examples are telecommuting, virtualizing desktops, travel optimization, and supply-chain management.

✓ Set both tactical and strategic green goals. Educate your team and have the entire team devoted to achieving green goals.

✓ Celebrate your green successes. Whether it is posting of reductions in the electric bill as you walk into the data center or Energy-Efficiency Certificates in the annual report, taking pride in accomplishments generates enthusiasm for the next project and fosters an energy-saving culture.

✓ Learn from others. IBM was rated top green IT vendor. Client examples include the following:

    A. Highmark, Inc.: LEEDs-certified. Underground storage, virtualization exploitation of mainframe virtualization.

    B. Discovery Com: Energy efficiency is part of every purchase decision.

    C. First National of Nebraska, Inc.: Fuel cell technology, consolidation onto System z IFLs, virtual PCs.

    D. Perkins + Will: Every office has a green team and a green operations plan for six areas (transportation, office water use, office energy use, office consumables, indoor air quality, and office renovations and new construction).

    E. Snohomish Public Utility District: EZ GPO control power management settings using resident APIs. Turnoff puts equipment to sleep.

    F. World Wildlife Federation: Energy-saving designs for servers, notebooks, and desktops.

    G. Wellpoint: Utilize IBM for best practices and green tape.

    H. Ryder: Know who is using, for example, every KW/sq ft.

    I. Austin Energy: Dynamic management with customer partnership.

    J. Marriott International, Inc.: Virtualization of IT equipment and underground facilities.

    K. Monsanto: Consolidate to fewer data centers and virtualize.

    L. Wachovia: SOA and using managed services reduced power consumption by a factor of 5.

Tools and Information to Help with Green IT

This section lists tools and information available online to help with your analysis of green IT.

DOE DC Pro Tool

The Department of Energy (DOE) Data Center (DC) Pro (Profile) tool is an online software tool designed to help organizations worldwide quickly diagnose how energy is used by their data centers and how they might save energy and money. The tool is available at no cost from http://www1.eere.energy.gov/industry/saveenergynow/printable_versions/partnering_data_centers.html.

Carbon Footprint Tool

This site provides a calculator tool for both your personal and business carbon footprint: http://www.carbonfootprint.com.

ASHRAE Information

The American Society of Heating, Refrigerating, and Air Conditioning Engineers (ASHRAE) has a variety of energy-efficiency information available on its Web site: http://www.ashrae.com.

Server Power Calculator Tools

The various IT vendors provide power calculation tools on their Web sites. The IBM xSeries power configuration tool—used for basic xSeries stand-alone and blade server power estimates—can be accessed at http://www-03.ibm.com/systems/bladecenter/powerconfig/.

NYSERDA Clean Power Estimator

NYSERDA (New York State Energy Research and Development Authority) has made available a Clean Power Estimator, developed by Clean Power Research. This is an economic evaluation tool that provides an estimate of the benefits and costs associated with a solar-electric or photovoltaic (PV) system. A wind power estimator is also being developed. The estimator can be accessed at http://www.clean-power.com/nyserda/.

Worldwide Electricity Used in Data Centers

Jonathan Koomey of the Lawrence Berkeley National Lab (LBNL) and Stanford University has been active in helping to estimate worldwide electricity use in data centers. His papers on the subject are listed in the Bibliography. In this section, a summary from his September 2008 paper, "Worldwide Electricity Used in Data Centers," available at http://stacks.iop.org/1748-9326/3/034008, is discussed.

Table A.1 shows installed base and power use per server by major world region and server type. Typical power use per server was derived from a detailed analysis of the most popular server models reported by IDC. Koomey's analysis estimated the actual electricity used by the six most popular models in the installed base for each major class of server (volume, mid-range, and high end) for the U.S. and the world. Power use was based on manufacturer data, measurements, or engineering estimates of servers typically configured and operated. Power use per server for non-U.S. regions was inferred from the world and U.S. installed base and power use per server numbers.

Table A.1 Installed Base and Server Power per Unit in 2000 and 2005 by Major World Regions

Installed Base	Units	Volume	Mid-Range	High-End	Total/ Avg.
2000					
U.S.	Thousands	4,927	663	23	5,613
Western Europe	Thousands	3,332	447	15	3,794
Japan	Thousands	1,140	250	15	1,405
Asia Pacific (ex. Japan)	Thousands	1,416	132	4	1,552
Rest of World	Thousands	1,425	317	8	1,750
Total	Thousands	12,240	1808	66	14,114

Installed Base 2005	Units	Volume	Mid-Range	High-End	Total/ Avg.
U.S.	Thousands	9,897	387	22	10,306
Western Europe	Thousands	6,985	356	15	7,355
Japan	Thousands	2,361	185	12	2,558
Asia Pacific (ex. Japan)	Thousands	3,553	137	4	3,694
Rest of World	Thousands	3,162	199	7	3,368
Total	Thousands	25,959	1264	59	27,282

Average Power Used per Server 2000	Units	Volume	Mid-Range	High-End	Total/Avg.
U.S.	Watts/server	186	424	5534	236
Western Europe	Watts/server	181	422	4517	227
Japan	Watts/server	181	422	4517	271
Asia Pacific (ex. Japan)	Watts/server	181	422	4517	212
Rest of World	Watts/server	181	422	4517	246
Total	Watts/server	183	423	4874	236
2005					
U.S.	Watts/server	219	625	7651	250
Western Europe	Watts/server	224	598	8378	258
Japan	Watts/server	224	598	8378	289
Asia Pacific (ex. Japan)	Watts/server	224	598	8378	247
Rest of World	Watts/server	224	598	8378	263
Total	Watts/server	222	607	8106	257

As indicated in Figure A.1, worldwide electricity used by data centers doubled from 2000 to 2005. This represented an aggregate annual growth rate of 16.7% per year for the world. About 80% of this growth is attributable to growth in electricity used by servers (almost entirely volume servers), with ten percent of growth in electricity use associated with data center communications and about the same percentage for storage equipment. The overall increase in server electricity use is driven almost entirely by the increase in the number of volume servers, with a small component associated with increases in the server power used per unit.

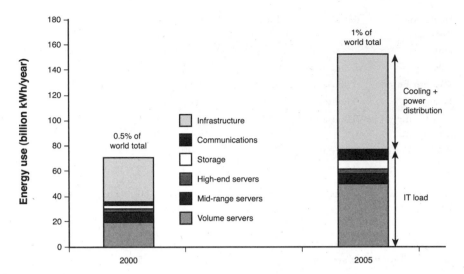

Source: Koomey report from Lawrence Berkeley National Lab (LBNL)

Figure A.1 Summary results for worldwide IT electricity use—total electricity use (billion KWH/year)

Data center communications use electricity as indicated in Figure A.1, including only those for internal networking equipment to data centers. It does not include the electricity use of the networks connecting data centers to the Internet as a whole or to the other parts of that broader network.

Infrastructure energy use includes cooling and air handling, as well as loss in power distribution. This component is characterized by what the Uptime Institute calls the Site Infrastructure Energy Overhead Multiplier (SI-EOM), also known by the somewhat less-intuitive term Power Utilization Effectiveness (PUE). This concept characterizes the ratio of total data center loads to information technology (IT) loads.

Figure A.1 shows that on a worldwide basis, cooling and power distribution accounts for approximately half of data center energy use, with various IT used accounting for the remaining 50 percent of energy use. This corresponds to the estimates given throughout this book on the significant amount of energy required for data center cooling.

IT Power Management with the
Active Energy Manager (AEM) Tool

Overview

The IBM Active Energy Manager (AEM) is an update to the IBM PowerExecutive™ that was previously available from IBM for x86 systems only. IBM Systems Director Active Energy Manager supports multiple IBM platforms and provides new capabilities that build upon the functions previously available with the IBM PowerExecutive tool.

AEM measures, monitors, and manages the energy components built into IBM systems enabling a cross-platform management solution. AEM is an IBM Director extension that supports the following endpoints: IBM BladeCenter, POWER, System x, and System z servers. In addition, both IBM storage systems and non-IBM platforms can be monitored through PDU+ support.

The AEM server can run on the following platforms: Windows on System x, Linux on System x, Linux on System p, and Linux on System z. AEM uses agentless technology and, therefore, no agents are required on the endpoints.

Monitoring and management functions apply to all IBM systems that are enabled for IBM Systems Director Active Energy Manager V3.1. Monitoring functions include power trending, thermal trending, and PDU+ support. Management functions include power-capping and power-savings mode.

AEM also provides a source of energy management data that can be exploited by Tivoli enterprise solutions, such as IBM Tivoli Monitoring and IBM Tivoli Usage and Accounting Manager. It is a key component of IBM's Cool Blue™ portfolio within Project Big Green.

How Active Energy Manager Works and the Benefits

This solution helps customers monitor energy consumption to allow better utilization of available energy resources. The application software enables customers to trend actual energy consumption and corresponding thermal loading of IBM systems running in their environment with their applications. This helps customers do the following:

- Allocate less power and cooling infrastructure to IBM servers.

- Lower power usage on select IBM servers.

- Plan for the future by viewing trends of power usage over time.

- Determine power usage for all components of a rack.

Having a better understanding of energy usage across your data center can

- Identify energy usage.

- Measure cooling costs accurately.

- Monitor IT costs across components.

- Manage by department and user.

Figure A.2 indicates some of the server energy monitoring and management options available from the AEM tool, for example, monitoring, collecting, measuring, and trending server power and energy use, managing server power use, and developing better strategies to have continuous improvement of your data center operations.

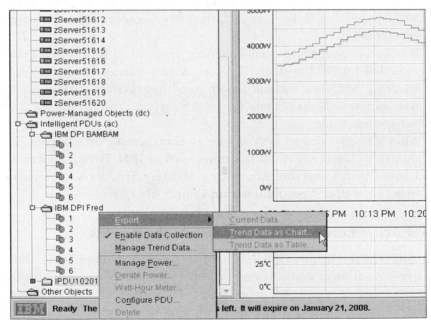

Source: IBM Active Energy Manager Product

Figure A.2   Trend server energy use chart from AEM Tool

Integration of Energy and Systems Management

In an overall systems management environment, power management is only one aspect of many. This section discusses how to integrate AEM into the IBM Tivoli systems management platform.

The IBM Tivoli Monitoring tool can monitor the status of your IT environment. It enables you to monitor your operating systems, databases, and servers throughout distributed environments through a flexible, customizable portal. A monitoring agent sits in place to tap the desired data from the monitored system. With this agent in place, IBM Tivoli Monitoring can monitor the power, temperature, and CPU usage of the respective systems. Figure A.3 shows how the components interact.

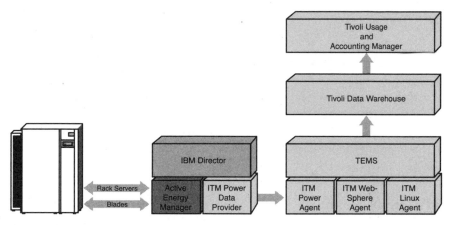

Source: IBM Active Energy Manager Product

Figure A.3   Integration of AEM with Tivoli systems management tools

Having this entry point into the Tivoli environment enables you to employ all the well-known features of IBM Tivoli Monitoring and other tools with which it interacts. You can also add the performance aspect of energy efficiency.

Optimizing for power and performance might include the following scenarios:

■ Reprovisioning a server based on the machine's environmental temperature or overall rack power consumption to another rack in a cooler area of your data center. On a temperature alert in ITM, you would trigger the reprovisioning in IBM Tivoli Provisioning Manager.

- Power-capping a single server having a temperature problem, perhaps because of an obstructed airflow, until the problem is solved
  onsite.

- Feeding power, temperature, and CPU usage data into the IBM
  Tivoli Monitoring Warehouse. Using IBM Tivoli Usage and
  Accounting Manager, this data can be correlated with accounting
  data. Charge the IT users according to their CPU and correlated
  power usage.

The opportunities are many, after the AEM data is available to the
Tivoli environment. As energy management begins to play an important
role, additional integration products from Tivoli are evolving. Due to
the flexible nature of the Tivoli toolset, user setup might be complex.
IBM services can help you find the best-fit solution.

Computer Manufacturers and Green Computing

All computer manufacturers are busy not only reducing energy use in
the servers they produce, but are also working on making their own data
centers green computing examples. Here are case studies for some of the
major manufacturers based on news articles. Although there's a marketing aspect to these articles, the emphasis on green IT is significant.

HP Green Computing

In 2008, HP announced initiatives to promote green computing and
reduce the company's environmental footprint. HP's goal is to reduce
power consumption 20 percent below 2005 levels by 2010 through
energy-efficient products and operating practices. The company, which
operates in more than 170 countries around the world, plans to meet its
energy reduction goal through more efficient products, internal operations, and supply-chain management. Recent innovations that should
help HP customers reduce power consumption include PCs with power
supplies that are 33 percent more efficient than their predecessors.
Furthermore, redesigned print cartridge packaging for North America
will reduce greenhouse gas emissions by about 37 million pounds in
2007, the company reported.

HP has also introduced an energy management system for data centers, called Dynamic Smart Cooling, which delivers 20 percent to 45 percent savings in cooling energy costs, the company reported. "Cooling is about 60 percent of the power costs in a data center because of inefficiency," Perez said. "The way data centers are cooled today is like cutting butter with a chain saw. The air-conditioning system in my home is more efficient than cooling systems in data centers today. HP plans to practice what it preaches in its operations by consolidating 85 of its data centers worldwide into just six larger data centers using virtualization and blade servers, combining applications, and smart planning," Perez said.

The company is also looking at less-conventional ways to obtain power. Wind power, water, and methane gas are on the HP radar, as they are for other data centers. HP is looking at supply management of power and other ways to generate it, such as cogeneration of power or whether to generate power using a grid or through local sources.

In 2007, HP purchased 11 million kWh of renewable energy for use in its operations and also joined the U.S. Environmental Protection Agency's (EPA) Green Power Partnership program—a challenge to Fortune 500 companies to double their renewable energy purchases by the end of 2007. HP plans to increase renewable energy purchases by more than 350 percent by procuring 50 million kWh of renewable electricity during 2007, the company reported. HP also established an initiative with the World Wildlife Fund-U.S to reduce greenhouse gas emissions from its operating facilities worldwide.

Sun Green Computing

In 2007, Sun Microsystems unveiled a green data center that has resulted in a dramatic decline in electricity use. Deploying new server technology and state-of-the-art cooling systems, Sun consolidated its Silicon Valley data centers, halving the square footage while cutting power consumption nearly 61 percent. Although Sun reduced the number of servers from 2,177 to 1,240, computing power increased 456 percent, according to the company.

Here are some highlights of Sun's Santa Clara campus's next-generation data center. Through virtualization—enabling one server to do the work of multiple machines—Sun slashed the number of computers in the data center and the heat they generate. Sun has invested in smart-cooling technology to reduce the considerable energy that typically goes to cool hot-running servers. For instance, in one data center room on the Santa Clara campus, servers are arrayed in long black pods called hot aisles. Hot air from the machines blows into the interior of the closed pod where it is captured by heat exchangers.

Sun is continuing to explore other ways to further green its data centers. For instance, the polluting diesel backup generators that most data centers rely on might be replaced by fuel cells—or converted to run on biodiesel.

Chip Technology and Green IT

More-efficient processors can be a significant energy-saving element, as IBM, Intel, Advanced Micro Devices, and Sun Microsystems all have green chips. Where chip makers used to compete entirely on speed, now they also compete on performance per watt. Microprocessors often have built-in energy-efficiency features, such as the ability to reduce power to idle cores, sleep mode to power off inactive cores and restore power when needed, and thermal tuning. Almost all modern microprocessors are being designed with "hooks" for virtualization built in.

Energy Efficiency for Computer Networks

Servers and cooling equipment consume the largest fraction of data center power by far. Little attention is given to network components, but they also consume power and produce heat. Here's information on saving energy on your networks from a 2008 article by David B. Jacobs of The Jacobs Group (http://users.rcn.com/djacobs/). Network integrators can provide a valuable service by analyzing and offering ways to lower network energy consumption, whereas resellers can replace old network hardware with new, more energy-efficient components. Use these energy-saving tips as a starting point. Each network is different, so not all will apply.

- **Shut off unneeded equipment.** If server virtualization has resulted in fewer physical servers, the switch ports that supported the now-removed servers are no longer needed. Staff reductions might have resulted in fewer workstations and, therefore, fewer switch ports are required. If some switches have a few active ports and others have unused ports, consolidate connections and unplug one of the switches.

■ **Replace old, inefficient network hardware.** Concerns about network energy consumption have led manufacturers to design higher-efficiency power supplies. Newer equipment consumes less power while delivering the same or improved function. Use the local cost of power to evaluate each potential replacement to calculate the payoff period.

■ **Consolidate multiple small switches, which might have been purchased as the network grew, into a single larger switch.** A single high-port-count switch is more energy efficient than many smaller switches.

■ **Calculate actual power requirements in switches with modular power supplies.** Switches might have been over-provisioned when first installed, because power consumption was not a major consideration in the past. Power supplies operate more efficiently at a higher percentage utilization of available capacity. An unneeded supply increases available capacity, so at a given level of utilization, percentage utilization is lower, resulting in reduced efficiency. Put another way, using 40 watts of a 50-watt supply is much more efficient than using 40 watts of a 100-watt supply. If possible, remove one or more of the supplies. If the additional supply was put in place to provide redundancy, however, removing it might not be an option.

■ **Review use of stand-alone virtual private networks (VPNs), firewalls, and DHCP servers.** These stand-alone appliances have proliferated, and each contains a power supply, takes up rack space, and produces heat. Moving these functions into a modular switch can reduce power and heat.

■ **Determine whether 100Mbps is sufficient for workstation users.** Most new workstations come with 1Gbps Ethernet ports, which consume roughly 2 watts more than 100Mbps. Configuring 1Gbps on the workstation and on the corresponding switch port adds 4 watts to each workstation. Although not significant for a small- or medium-sized site, the unnecessary power use and heat can add up for a large site.

■ **Evaluate use of Power over Ethernet (PoE).** It is an efficient way to power IP phones, wireless access points, and security cameras. It is not necessary on all switch ports, however, because it cannot be used to power workstations or servers. If PoE is available on all switch ports, make sure that it is configured off for ports that do not use it. When provisioning the power supply of a new modular switch, keep in mind that not all ports will require PoE.

- **Properly place all components to efficiently draw in cool air and exhaust hot air.** Although components might have been placed correctly when first installed, the addition or removal of adjacent equipment might have resulted in less-efficient airflow. Use blank panels or move components to fill in gaps in racks that allow cool and hot air to mix.

- **Remove unnecessary terminals from switch console ports.** Most switch management is done via the network, but a console port terminal might still be in place and powered up even though no longer needed. If for some reason it must be left in place, shut it off.

- **Conduct a component-by-component review of your customer's network to identify additional ways to lower energy costs.** Many methods of achieving lower energy costs are common sense and will appear obvious when identified. While reviewing the customer's network, you can also suggest equipment upgrades and operational changes that will result in improved network operation.

B

Green IT and Cloud Computing

"Cloud computing is reshaping the IT marketplace, creating new opportunities for suppliers, and catalyzing changes in traditional IT offerings."

—IDC, October 20, 2008

Cloud computing has been receiving a great deal of attention in IT during the past year. It is, in actuality, a new label (as of late 2007) for the subset of grid computing that includes utility computing and other approaches to the use of shared computing resources. Cloud computing is an alternative to having local servers or personal devices handling users' applications. Essentially, it is an idea that the technological capabilities should hover over everything and be available whenever a user wants. Cloud and grid computing were introduced in Chapter 6, "A Most-Significant Step—'Virtualizing' Your IT Systems." This appendix expands on the subject and was mostly written by Ravi Subramaniam, IBM Software IT Architect.

The concept of grid computing has been around for a decade. It's defined by the Global Grid Forum (www.gridforum.org) as "distributed computing over a network of heterogeneous resources across domain boundaries and enabled by open standards." The IT industry has used server cluster technology and distributed computing over networks for many years; however, grid and cloud computing are major steps forward because of their use of open source middleware to virtualize resources across domains.

Cloud Computing, Both Public and Private Possibilities

Cloud computing is a style of computing where IT applications and business functionalities are provided as services and accessed through the Internet. Consumers pay for the services as a subscription on a periodic basis or through a pay-for-usage model. The term cloud originated from the popular depiction of the Internet in architecture diagrams as a cloud. **Internet service providers** (ISPs) and application service providers (ASPs) can be thought of as the earliest users of this style of computing. An Internet service provider (ISP, also called Internet access provider or IAP) is a company that offers its customers access to the Internet:http://en.wikipedia.org/wiki/Internet. An example of a service provided by an ISP is to provide Internet e-mail (http://en.wikipedia.org/wiki/E-mail) accounts to users that enables them to communicate with one another by sending and receiving electronic messages through the ISP's servers (http://en.wikipedia.org/wiki/Servers). An **application service provider** (ASP) is a business that provides computer-based services to customers over a network. Typical examples are web hosting, credit card payment processing, medical practice application services, advertising services, and so on. The concepts have now evolved to be called "cloud computing." Terms such as **cloud storage**, **cloud services**, and **cloud collaboration** denote specialized forms of cloud computing.

Cloud computing is grounded in the concept of sharing the costs of procuring, setting up, and maintaining an IT computing infrastructure over a large number of consuming participants. In a way, this is similar to the concept of microselling perfected by the **Fast Moving Consumer Goods** (FCMG) industry. The FCMG industry realized that there is a significant portion of the population in developing economies, such as China, India, The Philippines, Mexico, and Brazil, that had aspirations to use their products such as soap, shampoo, and laundry detergent but could not afford the cost of buying a large package of the product. For such markets, the industry perfected the concept of selling products in affordable portions, sachets, or sizes. For example, in Brazil, FCMG giant Unilever (http://www.unilever.com) sells Ala, a brand detergent created specifically to meet the needs of low-income consumers who want an affordable, yet effective, product for laundry that is often washed by hand in river water. In India, Unilever successfully markets Sunsil and Lux shampoo sachets sold in units of 2–4 dollar cents, Clinic All Clear antidandruff shampoo sachets at 2.5 rupees each, and 16-cent

Rexona deodorant sticks. In Tanzania, Key soap is sold in small units for a few dollar cents.

Cloud computing has reduced the barrier to entry for providers of innovative applications. Let's consider the case of a small business that developed an innovative Internet application. To bring this application to market for its consumers on its own, it needs to procure hardware related to providing Internet connectivity, such as application servers and routers, purchase servers for support functions and e-mail, hire staff to maintain the infrastructure, and create and manage plans to upgrade infrastructure software and other related aspects, such as disaster recovery, high availability, and security. Moreover, if the application becomes successful and there is exponential growth of customers, the business needs to address and manage the scalability requirements of the infrastructure. All this translates to large initial fixed cost and recurring operational costs and puts pressure on the business model. However, using web hosting services provided by an ASP, the business can convert this to a variable, periodic subscription cost at a fraction of the cost of setting up and running the infrastructure on its own. The provider typically has a huge amount of available bandwidth, a trained staff to monitor and fix problems with the infrastructure 24 hours a day, will back up the data on a regular basis, and is responsible for disaster recovery. Moreover, more capacity is available on demand with an adjustment to the subscription fee.

Another aspect of cloud computing is the manner in which it represents a shift in the way information is stored, interrogated upon, and delivered. This is akin to a computing equivalent of the evolution in electricity a century ago when large utilities started producing and distributing power in an efficient manner. Farms and businesses shut down their own generators and instead bought cheaper power from these utilities. The founders of Google, Inc., Sergey Brin and Larry Page, had the vision a decade ago "to organize the world's information and make it universally accessible," which translated into the popular Google search engine and then to providing services related to Internet advertising using that information. To grow and update its information bank, Google spiders crawl the Internet looking for new Web sites and pages. A spider is a program that visits Web sites and reads their pages and other information to create entries for a search engine (http://searchsoa. techtarget.com/sDefinition/0,,sid26_gci212955,00.html) index.

Another large, successful Internet retail company, Amazon, Inc., uses the cloud computing approach to provide a variety of infrastructure-related services (cloud services) to consumers. Amazon Simple Storage Services, also known as Amazon S3, is storage for the Internet (cloud storage). Amazon S3 provides a simple web services interface that stores and retrieves any amount of data, at any time, from anywhere on the Web. It gives any developer access to the same highly scalable, reliable, fast, inexpensive data storage infrastructure that Amazon uses to run its own global network of Web sites. The service aims to maximize benefits of scale and to pass those benefits on to developers. In a similar manner, Amazon Elastic Compute Cloud (Amazon EC2) provides a virtual computing environment and enables a consumer to ramp up capacity with new server instances easily.

During October 2008, IBM announced the availability of a free beta version of a web-based software suite called Blue House for collaboration (cloud collaboration). The software suite is accessible from the Internet and can be used for scheduling meetings and projects, storing and sharing documents, instant messaging, and making PowerPoint-like web presentations. The applications providing the software suite are hosted on IBM's servers and made available on-demand. The approach addresses the issue of using the Web for driving greater business collaboration. Blue House services will eventually be based on paid subscriptions and will help companies that cannot afford to set up and run a detailed infrastructure for providing collaboration services for its employees and business partners.

The cost benefit nature of services provided by independent organizations such as Amazon through cloud computing enables the model to be readily accepted by small and medium businesses and individual consumers. However, security concerns relating to Internet threats and application vulnerabilities and loss of control over data and infrastructure can prevent the approach from being used by large companies. Such companies can afford the cost of setting up and running the infrastructure in exchange for some of the advantages such an approach brings. However, the "sharing-of-resources" aspect of cloud computing and the advantages thereof is giving shape to **private cloud computing**, which is a different take on the mainstream Internet-based version. A **private cloud** is a smaller cloudlike IT system within a corporate firewall that offers shared services to a closed internal network. Consumers of such a cloud would include the employees across various divisions and departments, business partners, raw-material suppliers, resellers, and other organizations that participate in one or more business processes of the corporation. Shared services on the infrastructure side such as computing power or data storage services or on the application side such as a single customer information application shared across the organization are suitable candidates for such an approach.

Because a private cloud is exclusive in nature and limited in access to a set of participants, it has inherent strengths with respect to security aspects and the control over data. Also, the approach can provide advantages with respect to adherence to corporate and regulatory compliance guidelines; therefore, the concept of a private cloud is expected to gain further interest for adoption among large organizations.

Business and Technology Drivers for Cloud Computing

Business and technology drivers are influences or solution view points that can spur the adoption of cloud computing approaches by organizations. Some of the key drivers are summarized in the following:

- Provides a flexible business and pricing model for small and medium customers.
- Helps outsource non-core competency functions such as IT provisioning and infrastructure management.
- Promotes business agility by providing massive scaling capabilities (infrastructure can grow or shrink elastically to manage business requirements).
- Helps a customer accomplish more business functionality with less onsite IT resources.
- From a provider's perspective, virtualized, efficient infrastructure promotes energy efficiency and cost benefits, which can be passed on to consumers.
- Usage of open standards and common components drives standardization and lowers costs over the long run.

Types of Cloud Computing Offerings

Figure B.1 depicts the various kinds of offerings based on cloud computing prevalent today. The offerings are based on three broad layers or categories, namely i) Platform or Infrastructure Basis, ii) Business Applications, and iii) Business Services.

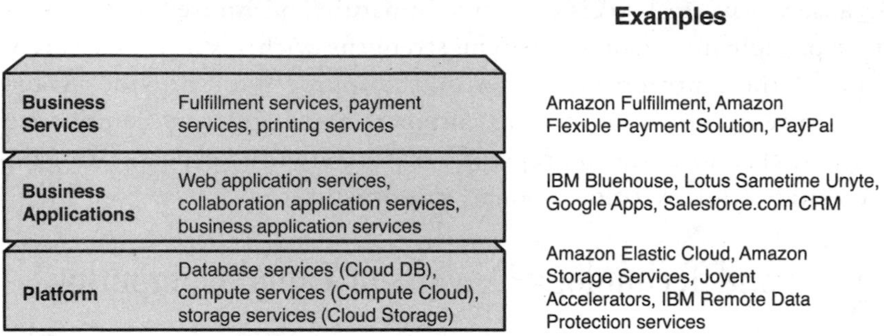

Examples

Business Services	Fulfillment services, payment services, printing services	Amazon Fulfillment, Amazon Flexible Payment Solution, PayPal
Business Applications	Web application services, collaboration application services, business application services	IBM Bluehouse, Lotus Sametime Unyte, Google Apps, Salesforce.com CRM
Platform	Database services (Cloud DB), compute services (Compute Cloud), storage services (Cloud Storage)	Amazon Elastic Cloud, Amazon Storage Services, Joyent Accelerators, IBM Remote Data Protection services

Source: IBM Software Group

Figure B.1 Types of cloud computing

Platform-based offerings focus on providing storage services (Cloud Storage), computing capacity (Compute Cloud), and database services (Cloud DB). Cloud storage is a model of networked data storage where data is stored on multiple virtual servers, generally hosted by third parties, rather than being hosted on dedicated servers. Hosting companies operate large data centers; and people who require their data to be hosted buy or lease storage capacity from them and use it for their storage needs. The data center operators, in the background, virtualize the resources according to the requirements of the customer and expose them as virtual servers, which the customers can themselves manage. Physically, the resource may span across multiple servers. Nirvanix, offers a storage delivery service used by developers for storing content and data and making them available worldwide at low latency. In the case of Nirvanix, the system may span multiple data centers or even continents.

Amazon.com is probably the first company to sell cloud-based computing in the form of its Amazon Elastic Compute Cloud, a part of Amazon's web services platform. It provides computing capacity in the cloud to run applications. Another company, 3tera, has created a network of partners with its AppLogic system in the U.S., Asia, and Europe who provide resources for developers to run their applications in the cloud. Joyent provides a highly scalable on-demand infrastructure for running Web sites, including rich Web applications written in Ruby on Rails, PHP, Python, and Java. Joyent Accelerators are next-generation virtual computers that can grow and multiply (or shrink and consolidate) depending on the real-world demands faced by your Web application. Currently, 25% of Facebook's page view runs on Joyent, and they just launched a program to provide infrastructure for OpenSocial developers. IBM Remote Data Protection services provide a highly reliable, distributed data protection strategy that helps ensure business continuity and effective disaster recovery on a pay-as-you-use cost structure.

There are a variety of cloud offerings in the Business Applications arena. A few examples are discussed here. IBM's "Bluehouse" was the first web-delivered collaboration cloud service for social networking. It provides online collaboration tools to help business users to share documents, contacts, engage in joint project activities, host online meetings, and build social network communities. Lotus® Sametime® Unyte® helps businesses communicate in real-time with a worldwide network of employees, customers, and partners by helping arrange quick and easy web conferences, including the sharing of document, presentations, or applications in real time. It also provides multi-language support, specialized alerts and prompts for meeting hosts. Through Google Apps, Google provides web-based communication, collaboration, and security applications such as Gmail for email, Google talk for instant messaging, Google calendar for organizing schedules, and Google Docs for online documents, presentations, and spreadsheets. Salesforce.com provides Customer Relationship Management software as a service.

Amazon Fulfillment, Amazon Flexible Payment Solution, and PayPal are examples of business services cloud offerings. Consumers of Amazon Fulfillment can send their products for storage at an Amazon Fulfillment center. Orders received for the products from either amazon.com or through consumer-provided order information are then fulfilled by Amazon through Amazon's process. Amazon Flexible Payment Solution and PayPal provide third-party payment solutions, which consumers can incorporate into their business processes for order completion or for making payments.

Conceptual Architecture and Infrastructure for Cloud Computing

The conceptual architecture behind a cloud computing platform layer represents a massive network of "cloud servers" interconnected as if in a grid running in parallel, sometimes using the technique of virtualization to maximize computing power per server. A front-end interface enables a user to select a service from a catalog. This request gets passed to the system management, which finds the correct resources, and then calls the provisioning services, which carves out resources in the cloud. The provisioning service may deploy the requested stack or web application as well:

- **User interaction interface:** This is how users of the cloud interface with the cloud to request services.
- **Services catalog:** This is the list of services that a user can request.
- **System management:** This is the piece that manages the computer resources available.
- **Provisioning tool:** This tool carves out the systems from the cloud to deliver on the requested service. It may also deploy the required images.
- **Monitoring and metering:** This optional piece tracks the usage of the cloud so the resources used can be attributed to a certain user.
- **Servers:** The servers are managed by the system management tool. They can be either virtual or real.

The underlying infrastructure for cloud computing can be based on either virtualization or grid computing or a combination of both. Grid computing (or the use of a computational grid) is the application of several computers to a single problem at the same time—usually to a scientific or technical problem that requires a great number of computer processing cycles or access to large amounts of data. It is a form of distributed computing whereby a "super and virtual computer" is composed of a cluster of networked, loosely-coupled computers, acting in concert to perform very large tasks. This technology has been applied to computationally-intensive scientific, mathematical, and academic problems through volunteer computing, and it is used in commercial enterprises for such diverse applications as drug discovery, economic forecasting, seismic analysis, and back-office data processing in support of e-commerce and web services. However, this arrangement is thought to be well-suited to applications in which multiple parallel computations can take place independently, without the need to communicate intermediate results between processors because various processors and local storage areas may not have high-speed connections. In grid computing, the computers and resources involved can be heterogeneous. They can run different operating systems and use different server and storage platforms that may even be owned by different individuals, companies, labs, or universities. Grids may include clusters, individual servers, or entire data centers as part of the resources that are virtualized for sharing with other members on the grid. Grids are capable of massive scaling to share and manage applications, data, and storage resources among local, campus, regional, and international locations. Google search engine technology is supposed to use thousands of servers in the form of grid computing for processing search requests, crawling the web for new sites, storing documents, and managing advertisements.

On the other hand, virtualization is about abstracting computing resources in such a manner that a larger computing resource can be apportioned and provided as smaller resources. The concept was pioneered by the time-sharing concepts of the mainframes of the sixties, and there are various forms of virtualization today. For example, IBM System z mainframes are capable of multiple levels of virtualization. A single machine can be divided into several logical partitions (LPARs), and each logical partition is a separate virtual machine running a separate operating system instance. The same capability is available in midrange computers, such as IBM's System p and others. VMWare is a frequently quoted name in the arena of server virtualization. VMWare provides software solutions that partition a physical server into multiple virtual machines. VMware plans to expand the reach of its virtualization platform offering to integrate with other aspects of the data center, such as network and storage. System management, provisioning, workload management, monitoring, metering, and security are other technologies that are needed for both grid computing and virtualization.

The Ultimate in Server and Data Storage Virtualization

Let's step back a bit and look at the history of grid and cloud computing. Grid computing was a major evolutionary step that virtualized an IT infrastructure. It's defined by the Global Grid Forum (www.gridforum.org) as distributed computing over a network of heterogeneous resources across domain boundaries and enabled by open standards. Although the industry has used server cluster technology and distributed computing over networks for nearly two decades, these technologies cannot in themselves constitute grid computing. What makes grid computing different is the use of open source middleware to virtualize resources across domains.

Grids are based on policies created to define job scheduling, security, resource availability, and workload balancing across multiple applications and user domains. The first case study in Chapter 11, "Worldwide Green IT Case Studies," discussed the World Community Grid made up of a million user laptops, desktops, and so on. That grid is about as heterogeneous as you can get.

The concept of grid computing is shown in Figure B.2. Notice that everything is considered virtualized: processing, storage, I/O, applications, data, and operating system.

Grid Computing — The Ultimate in Virtualization

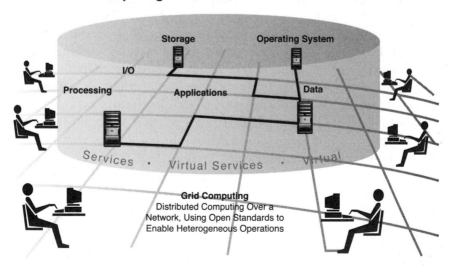

Source: IBM Grid Computing

Figure B.2 Grid computing—the ultimate in IT virtualization

The major risk of moving to grid computing is that the technology is only starting to be used by commercial enterprises for mission-critical operations. To date, the primary use of grid computing has been at universities (where every student's desktop or laptop computer is considered a candidate for the grid) or in government research organizations.

It is important to consider grid computing in your company's IT strategy because it is the future direction for IT organizations to dramatically improve percentage-utilization of dedicated IT resources that are now typically "pinned" to an application or platforms, either within or between enterprises. Also, current technologies are making significant steps in the direction of grid computing for corporations.

Potential Advantages

Potential advantages of any cloud or grid computing approach include the following:

- Location of infrastructure in areas with lower costs of space and electricity.
- Sharing of peak-load capacity among a large pool of users, improving overall utilization.
- Separation of infrastructure maintenance duties from domain-specific application development.
- Separation of application code from physical resources.
- Ability to use external assets to handle peak loads (for example, so you don't have to engineer for highest possible load levels).
- Not needing to purchase assets for one-time or infrequent intensive computing tasks.

It is probable that organizations would look to have a mixture of data and applications that live in the data center and in the cloud. Small and medium-sized enterprises would entertain the notion of a higher percentage of data and applications in the cloud because of cost factors, whereas it would be much lower in the case of large enterprises because of reliability, security, and trust issues. Large enterprises might consider cloud infrastructure for small projects and specific development stage work and move them to the data center once they are ready for production. Also, this approach may be considered if the ease of using a cloud offering for a particular short-term project offsets the effort required to set-up the same on the on-premise data center. Because of their large-scale operations, it can be reasoned that large enterprises may obtain the same economies of scale provided by cloud offerings; however the cloud offering may be spread across heterogeneous customers, whereas for a large enterprise, the sharing is across the different divisions and departments of the enterprise.

References

Because of the significant amount of activity on cloud computing, this chapter contains a list of references.

"About Application Service Provider" from Wikipedia, http://en.wikipedia.org/wiki/Application_service_provider

"About Cloud Computing" from Wikipedia, http://en.wikipedia.org/wiki/Cloud_computing

About Grid Computing from Wikipedia, http://en.wikipedia.org/wiki/Grid_computing

"About Internet Service Provider" from Wikipedia, http://en.wikipedia.org/wiki/Internet_service_provider

Amazon Web Services, http://aws.amazon.com/

"Cloud Computing Brought to You with the Power of Joyent Accelerator," http://www.joyent.com/

"Get Off My Cloud: Private Cloud Computing Takes Shape," http://www.eweek.com/c/a/Cloud-Computing/Why-Private-Cloud-Computing-Is-Beginning-to-Get-Traction/

Google Apps for Business, http://www.google.com/apps/intl/en/business/index.html

Google and the Wisdom of Clouds, "A Lofty New Strategy Aims to Put Incredible Computing Power in the Hands of Many," http://www.businessweek.com/magazine/content/07_52/b4064048925836.htm

"IBM Launches Cloud Services Initiative," http://www-03.ibm.com/press/us/en/pressrelease/25341.wss

"IBM Joins The 'Cloud Computing' Bandwagon," http://www.zdnetasia.com/news/software/0,39044164,62046886,00.htm

IBM Remote Data Protection Services, http://www-935.ibm.com/services/us/index.wss/offering/bcrs/a1029249

"IBM Unveils Cloud Computing Center at Bangalore," http://infotech.indiatimes.com/Enterprise_IT/IBM_unveils_cloud_computing_centre/articleshow/3525082.cms

"Linux on zSeries" from Wikipedia, http://en.wikipedia.org/wiki/Linux_on_zSeries

Sachet marketing, http://trendwatching.com/trends/SACHET_MARKETING.htm

"Salesforce Ascends Beyond SaaS Into Cloud Computing," http://www.intelligententerprise.com/showArticle.jhtml?articleID=212001542

Spider, http://whatis.techtarget.com/definition/0,,sid9_gci213035,00.html

C

Comparison of Different Power-Generation Methods

"Pocketbook environmentalism is powerful. If marketers can help consumers understand the hidden costs in products and services that are not environmentally friendly, they can grab consumers' attention."

—Joel Makower, Author of *Strategies for the Green Economy*

The comparisons in this appendix include renewable methods—for example, wind turbines, solar, geothermal, and so on. Although the topic of establishing green IT should be independent of methods used to generate electricity—with the possible exception of fuel cells that have been proposed as a potential part of green data center technology—power-generation technology is having an impact on the location of data centers. Here's an example. If the cost of electricity is 22 cents/KWH in New York City and only 4.5 cents/KWH in Charleston, West Virginia, the location of a large new data center in West Virginia could potentially save millions of dollars in electricity costs each year. With high-speed networks (including the Internet) available all over the United States and, for a large part, all over the world, data centers can now be located almost anywhere. And it's not only the location of data networks. High-speed networks have made global resourcing feasible so that computer programmers, analysts, project managers, and so on can now easily be in India or in Chicago. Usually the time zone differences are a bigger impediment to using global resources than any aspect on data communications or network performance.

The global economic meltdown of the last half of 2008 continuing on into 2009 will continue to have an impact on the economics of power-generation methods. The huge rise in oil prices during the first half of 2008, along with government incentives and advances in solar voltaic and wind power technologies, made those alternative energy sources much more attractive. Then the global economic meltdown drove down oil prices. However, stimulus spending in 2009 will undoubtedly include large sums for alternative energy as part of the push to create millions of "green" jobs. As noted earlier in this book, the recession will also continue to provide a substantial additional motivation to move to green data centers because of the promise of significant economic savings in addition to the societal necessity of reducing energy consumption in order to benefit the environment.

As indicated in Appendix D, "Worldwide Electricity Costs for IT with Projections," the cost per KWH and emissions estimates can vary widely on a worldwide basis. This appendix includes some information on the costs to generate electric power based on power-generation methods (for example, coal fired, hydro-electric, gas fired, and such). This appendix also has information on how estimates on emissions vary based on a power-generation method. The Appendix D tables give estimates for cost per KWH based on averages for the region.

Cost and Emissions Comparisons for Different Power-Generation Methods

The information for Tables C.1 and C.2 was taken from the Web site http://peswiki.com/energy/Directory:Cents_Per_Kilowatt-Hour that was compiled by Pure Energy Systems (PES) Network. PES acknowledges http://www.coldenergy.com/difference.htm for their compilation of the data based on 2005 information.

Traditional Power Generation

Table C.1 lists traditional power-generation methods, along with the 2005 cost range to generate electricity for each method.

Table C.1 Traditional Power Generation—Lowest Price Listed First

Method	Cents/KWH	Limitations and Externalities
Gas Currently supplies around 15% of the global electricity demand.	3.9–4.4 cents/ KWH	Gas-fired plants are generally quicker and less expensive to build than coal or nuclear, but a relatively high percentage of the cost/KWH is derived from the cost of the fuel. Due to the current (and projected future) upward trend in gas prices, there is uncertainty around the cost / KWH over the lifetime of plants. Gas burns more cleanly than coal, but the gas itself (largely methane) is a potent greenhouse gas. Some energy conversions to calculate your cost of natural gas per KWH: 100 cubic feet (CCF) ~ 1 Therm = 100,000 BTU ~ 29.3 KWH.
Coal Currently supplies around 38% of the global electricity demand.	4.8–5.5 cents/ KWH	It is increasingly difficult to build new coal plants in the developed world, due to environmental requirements governing the plants. There is growing concern about coal-fired plants in the developing world (China, for instance, imposes less environmental overhead, and has large supplies of high sulfur content coal). The supply of coal is plentiful, but the coal-generation method is perceived to make a larger contribution to air pollution than the rest of the methods combined.

Table C.1 Traditional Power Generation—Lowest Price Listed First

Method	Cents/KWH	Limitations and Externalities
Nuclear Currently supplies around 24% of the global electricity demand.	11.1–14.5 cents/ KWH	Political difficulties in using nuclear in some nations. Risk of widespread (and potentially lethal) contamination upon containment failure. Fuel is plentiful, but problematic. Waste disposal remains a significant problem, and de-commissioning is costly (averaging approximately US $320 million per plant in the U.S.).

Conventional, Renewable Power Generation

Table C.2 lists conventional, renewable power-generation methods along with the 2005 cost range to generate electricity for each method.

Table C.2 Conventional, Renewable Power Generation

Method	Cents/KWH	Limitations and Externalities
Wind Currently supplies approximately 1.4% of the global electricity demand. Wind is considered to be about 30% reliable.	4.0–6.0 cents/ KWH	Wind is currently the only cost-effective alternative energy method, but has a number of problems. Wind farms are highly subject to lightning strikes, have high mechanical fatigue failure, are limited in size by hub stress, do not function well, if at all, under conditions of heavy rain, icing conditions or very cold climates, and are noisy and cannot be insulated for sound reduction due to their size and subsequent loss of wind velocity and power.

Method	Cents/KWH	Limitations and Externalities
Geothermal		
Currently supplies approximately 0.23% of the global electricity demand. Geothermal is considered to be 90-95% reliable.	4.5–30 cents/KWH	New low temperature conversion of heat to electricity is likely to make geothermal substantially more plausible (more shallow drilling possible) and less expensive. Generally, the bigger the plant, the less the cost, and cost also depends upon the depth to be drilled and the temperature at the depth. The higher the temperature, the lower the cost per KWH. Cost may also be affected by where the drilling is to take place as concerns distance from the grid and another factor may be the permeability of the rock.
Hydro		
Currently supplies around 19.9% of the global electricity demand. Hydro is considered to be 60% reliable.	5.1–11.3 cents/KWH	Hydro is currently the only source of renewable energy making substantial contributions to global energy demand. Hydro plants, however, can (obviously) only be built in a limited number of places, and can significantly damage aquatic ecosystems.
Solar		
Currently supplies approximately 0.8% of the global electricity demand.	15–30 cents/KWH	Solar power has been expensive, but soon is expected to drop to as low as 3.5 cents/KWH. Once the silicon shortage is remedied through artificial silicon, a solar energy revolution is expected.

Worldwide Aspects of Hydroelectricity

Because hydro is currently the only source of renewable energy making substantial contributions to global energy demand, we'll take a further look at this source of electricity. From the previous table, hydro currently supplies around 20 percent of global electricity demand. Hydro plants, however, can (obviously) be built in only a limited number of places and can significantly damage aquatic ecosystems.

Hydropower produces no waste and does not produce carbon dioxide (CO2), a greenhouse gas. Much of the following information comes from the Web site http://en.wikipedia.org/wiki/Hydroelectricity.

Although large hydroelectric installations generate most of the world's hydroelectricity, small hydro schemes are particularly popular in China, which has more than 50 percent of world small hydro capacity. Some jurisdictions do not consider large hydro projects to be a sustainable energy source due to human and environmental impacts, though this judgment depends on the definition of sustainability used.

Most hydroelectric power comes from the potential energy of dammed water driving a water turbine and generator. In this case, the energy extracted from the water depends on the volume and on the difference in height between the source and the water's outflow. This height difference is called the **head**. The amount of potential energy in water is proportional to the head. To obtain very high head, water for a hydraulic turbine can be run through a large pipe called a **penstock**.

Pumped storage hydroelectricity produces electricity to supply high-peak demands by moving water between reservoirs at different elevations. At times of low electrical demand, excess generation capacity is used to pump water into the higher reservoir. When there is higher demand, water is released back into the lower reservoir through a turbine. Pumped storage schemes currently provide the only commercially important means of large-scale grid energy storage and improve the daily load factor of the generation system. Hydroelectric plants with no reservoir capacity are called run-of-the-river plants, because it is not then possible to store water. A tidal power plant makes use of the daily rise and fall of water due to tides; such sources are highly predictable, and if conditions permit, construction of reservoirs can also be dispatchable to generate power during high-demand periods.

Annual electric energy production depends on the available water supply. In some installations, the water flow rate can vary by a factor of 10:1 over the course of a year.

Small-Scale Hydroelectric Plants

Small hydro plants are those producing up to 10 megawatts, although projects up to 30 megawatts in North America are considered small hydro and have the same regulations. A small hydro plant might be connected to a distribution grid or might provide power only to an isolated community or a single home. Small hydro projects generally do not

require the protracted economic, engineering, and environmental studies associated with large projects, and often can be completed much
more quickly. A small hydro development might be installed along with
a project for flood control, irrigation, or other purposes, providing extra
revenue for project costs. In areas that formerly used waterwheels for
milling and other purposes, often the site can be redeveloped for electric
power production, possibly eliminating the new environmental impact
of any demolition operation. Small hydro can be further divided into
mini-hydro, with units around 1 MW in size, and micro-hydro, with
units as large as 100 kW down to a couple of kW rating.

Small hydro units in the range of 1 MW to about 30 MW are often
available from multiple manufacturers using standardized water-to-wire
packages; a single contractor can provide all the major mechanical and
electrical equipment (turbine, generator, controls, switchgear), selecting
from several standard designs to fit the site conditions. Micro-hydro
projects use a diverse range of equipment; in the smaller sizes; industrial
centrifugal pumps can be used as turbines, with comparatively low purchase cost compared to purpose-built turbines.

Advantages

The major advantage of hydroelectricity is elimination of the cost of
fuel. The cost of operating a hydroelectric plant is nearly immune to
increases in the cost of fossil fuels, such as oil, natural gas, or coal. Fuel
is not required, and so it need not be imported. Hydroelectric plants
tend to have longer economic lives than fuel-fired generation, with some
plants now in service having been built 50 to 100 years ago. Operating
labor cost is usually low because plants are automated and have few personnel onsite during normal operation.

Where a dam serves multiple purposes, a hydroelectric plant can be
added with relatively low construction cost, providing a useful revenue
stream to offset the costs of dam operation. It has been calculated that
the sale of electricity from the Three Gorges Dam will cover the construction costs after 5 to 8 years of full generation.

Greenhouse Gas Emissions

Because hydroelectric dams do not burn fossil fuels, they do not
directly produce carbon dioxide (a greenhouse gas). Although some carbon dioxide is produced during manufacture and construction of the
project, this is a tiny fraction of the operating emissions of equivalent
fossil-fuel electricity generation.

Related Activities

Reservoirs created by hydroelectric schemes often provide facilities for water sports and become tourist attractions in themselves. In some countries, farming fish in the reservoirs is common. Multi-use dams installed for irrigation can support the fish farm with relatively constant water supply. Large hydro dams can control floods, which would otherwise affect people living downstream of the project. When dams create large reservoirs and eliminate rapids, boats may be used to improve transportation.

Disadvantages

Recreational users must exercise extreme care when near hydroelectric dams, power plant intakes, and spillways.

Environmental Damage

Hydroelectric projects can be disruptive to surrounding aquatic ecosystems both upstream and downstream of the plant site. For instance, studies have shown that dams along the Atlantic and Pacific coasts of North America have reduced salmon populations by preventing access to spawning grounds upstream, even though most dams in a salmon habitat have fish ladders installed. Salmon spawn are also harmed on their migration to sea when they must pass through turbines. This has led to some areas transporting smolt downstream by barge during parts of the year. In some cases, dams have been demolished, (for example, the Marmot Dam was demolished in 2007) because of the impact on fish. Turbine and power-plant designs that are easier on aquatic life are an active area of research. Mitigation measures such as fish ladders might be required at new projects or as a condition of relicensing of existing projects.

Generation of hydroelectric power changes the downstream river environment. Water exiting a turbine usually contains little suspended sediment, which can lead to scouring of river beds and loss of riverbanks. Because turbine gates are often opened intermittently, rapid or even daily fluctuations in river flow are observed. For example, in the Grand Canyon, the daily cyclic flow variation caused by Glen Canyon Dam was found to be contributing to erosion of sand bars. Dissolved oxygen content of the water might change from preconstruction conditions. Depending on the location, water exiting from turbines is typically much warmer than the pre-dam water, which can change aquatic faunal populations, including endangered species, and prevent natural freezing processes from occurring. Some hydroelectric projects also use canals to divert a river at a shallower gradient to increase the head of the scheme. In some cases, the entire river can be diverted, leaving a dry riverbed. Examples include the Tekapo and Pukaki Rivers.

A further concern is the impact of major schemes on birds. Since damming and redirecting the waters of the Platte River in Nebraska for agricultural and energy use, many native and migratory birds, such as the Piping Plover and Sandhill Crane, have become increasingly endangered.

Greenhouse Gas Emission

The reservoirs of power plants in tropical regions might produce substantial amounts of methane and carbon dioxide. This is due to plant material in flooded areas decaying in an anaerobic environment, and forming methane, a very potent greenhouse gas. According to the World Commission on Dams report, where the reservoir is large compared to the generating capacity (less than 100 watts per square meter of surface area) and no clearing of the forests in the area was undertaken prior to impoundment of the reservoir, greenhouse gas emissions from the reservoir may be higher than those of a conventional oil-fired thermal generation plant. These emissions represent carbon already in the biosphere, not fossil deposits that had been sequestered from the carbon cycle.

In boreal reservoirs of Canada and Northern Europe, however, greenhouse gas emissions are typically only 2 percent to 8 percent of any kind of conventional fossil-fuel thermal generation. A new class of underwater logging operation that targets drowned forests can mitigate the effect of forest decay.

Population Relocation

Another disadvantage of hydroelectric dams is the need to relocate the people living where the reservoirs are planned. In many cases, no amount of compensation can replace ancestral and cultural attachments to places that have spiritual value to the displaced population. Additionally, historically and culturally important sites can be flooded and lost. Such problems have arisen at the Three Gorges Dam project in China, the Clyde Dam in New Zealand, and the Ilısu Dam in Southeastern Turkey.

Comparison with Other Methods of Power Generation

Hydroelectricity eliminates the flue gas emissions from fossil fuel combustion, including pollutants such as sulfur dioxide, nitric oxide, carbon monoxide, dust, and mercury in the coal. Hydroelectricity also avoids the hazards of coal mining and the indirect health effects of coal emissions. Compared to nuclear power, hydroelectricity generates no nuclear waste and has none of the dangers associated with uranium mining, or nuclear leaks. Unlike uranium, hydroelectricity is also a renewable energy source.

Compared to wind farms, hydroelectricity power plants have a more predictable load factor. If the project has a storage reservoir, it can be dispatched to generate power when needed. Hydroelectric plants can be easily regulated to follow variations in power demand.

Unlike fossil-fueled combustion turbines, construction of a hydroelectric plant requires a long lead-time for site studies, hydrological studies, and environmental impact assessment. Hydrological data up to 50 years or more is usually required to determine the best sites and operating regimes for a large hydroelectric plant. Unlike plants operated by fuel, such as fossil or nuclear energy, the number of sites that can be economically developed for hydroelectric production is limited; in many areas, the most cost-effective sites have already been exploited. New hydro sites tend to be far from population centers and require extensive transmission lines. Hydroelectric generation depends on rainfall in the watershed and might be significantly reduced in years of low rainfall or snowmelt. Long-term energy yield might be affected by climate change. Utilities that primarily use hydroelectric power might spend additional capital to build extra capacity to ensure sufficient power is available in low water years.

In parts of Canada (the provinces of British Columbia, Manitoba, Ontario, Quebec, Newfoundland, and Labrador), hydroelectricity is used so extensively that the word **hydro** is often used to refer to any electricity delivered by a power utility. The government-run power utilities in these provinces are BC Hydro, Manitoba Hydro, Hydro One (formerly "Ontario Hydro"), Hydro-Québec, and Newfoundland and Labrador Hydro, respectively. Hydro-Québec is the world's largest hydroelectric-generating company, with a total installed capacity (2005) of 31,512 MW.

Countries with the Most Hydroelectric Capacity

The ranking of hydroelectric capacity is either by actual annual energy production or by installed capacity power rating. A hydroelectric plant rarely operates at its full power rating over a full year; the ratio between annual average power and installed capacity rating is the load factor. The installed capacity shown in Table C.3 is the sum of all generator nameplate power ratings.

Table C.3 Worldwide Annual Hydroelectric Energy Production

Country	Annual Hydroelectric Energy Production (TWH)	Installed Capacity (GW)	Load Factor
People's Republic of China (2007)	486.7	145.26	0.37
Canada	350.3	88.974	0.59
Brazil	349.9	69.080	0.56
United States	291.2	79.511	0.42
Russia	157.1	45.000	0.42
Norway	119.8	27.528	0.49
India	112.4	33.600	0.43
Japan	95.0	27.229	0.37
Venezuela	74	-	-
Sweden	61.8	-	-
France	61.5	25.335	0.25

Worldwide Aspects of Wind Power

From Table C.2, wind power supplies only about 1.5 percent of global electricity demand. However, because wind is currently the only cost-effective alternative energy method, this section gives an overview of worldwide development of this power source. Much of the following information comes from the Web site http://en.wikipedia.org/wiki/Wind_power.

As mentioned in Chapter 1, "The Importance of Green IT," some companies are looking at wind power as a major source of electric power generation for data centers. For example, in 2009, Google is planning to open one of its first sites in the upper Midwest in Council Bluffs, Iowa, close to abundant wind power resources for fulfilling green energy objectives and proximate to fiber optic communications links. In general, wind power refers to the conversion of wind energy into a useful form, such as electricity, using wind turbines. At the end of 2007, worldwide capacity of wind-powered generators was 94.1 gigawatts. Although wind produces just a little over 1 percent of worldwide electricity use, it accounts for approximately 19 percent of electricity production in Denmark, 9 percent in Spain and Portugal, and 6 percent in Germany and the Republic of Ireland (2007 data). Globally, wind power generation increased more than fivefold between 2000 and 2007. Because of the energy crunch that reached critical levels during 2008, wind power is getting a significant push worldwide, and that push includes television ads and investment by people such as Texas oilman T. Boone Pickens.

Most wind power is generated in the form of electricity. Large-scale wind farms are connected to electrical grids. Individual turbines can provide electricity to isolated locations. In windmills, wind energy is used directly as mechanical energy for pumping water or grinding grain. Wind energy is plentiful, renewable, widely distributed, clean, and reduces greenhouse gas emissions when it displaces fossil fuel-derived electricity. Therefore, it is considered by experts to be more environmentally friendly than many other energy sources. The intermittency of wind seldom creates problems when using wind power to supply a low proportion of total demand. Where wind is to be used for a moderate fraction of demand, additional costs for compensation of intermittency are considered to be modest.

The multibladed wind turbine atop a lattice tower made of wood or steel was, for many years, a fixture of the landscape throughout rural America. The modern wind turbine was developed beginning in the 1980s, although designs are still under development.

There is an estimated 72 TW of wind energy on the Earth that potentially can be commercially viable. Not all the energy of the wind flowing past a given point can be recovered.

Distribution of Wind Speed and Grid Management

The strength of wind varies, and an average value for a given location does not alone indicate the amount of energy a wind turbine could produce there. To assess the frequency of wind speeds at a particular location, a probability distribution function is often fit to the observed data.

Different locations will have different wind-speed distributions. The Rayleigh model closely mirrors the actual distribution of hourly wind speeds at many locations.

Because so much power is generated by higher wind speed, much of the energy comes in short bursts. The 2002 Lee Ranch sample is telling; half of the energy available arrived in just 15 percent of the operating time. The consequence is that wind energy does not have as consistent an output as fuel-fired power plants; utilities that use wind power must provide backup generation for times that the wind is weak. Making wind power more consistent requires that storage technologies must be used to retain the large amount of power generated in the bursts for later use.

Grid Management

Induction generators often used for wind power projects require reactive power for excitation, so substations used in wind-power collection systems include substantial capacitor banks for power factor correction. Different types of wind turbine generators behave differently during transmission grid disturbances, so extensive modeling of the dynamic electromechanical characteristics of a new wind farm is required by transmission system operators to ensure predictable stable behavior during system faults. In particular, induction generators cannot support the system voltage during faults, unlike steam or hydro turbine-driven synchronous generators. (However, properly matched power factor correction capacitors along with electronic control of resonance can support induction generation without grid.) Doubly fed machines, or wind turbines with solid-state converters between the turbine generator and the collector system, have generally more desirable properties for grid interconnection. Transmission systems operators will supply a wind farm developer with a grid code to specify the requirements for interconnection to the transmission grid. This will include power factor, constancy of frequency, and dynamic behavior of the wind farm turbines during a system fault.

Because wind speed is not constant, a wind farm's annual energy production is never as much as the sum of the generator nameplate ratings multiplied by the total hours in a year. The ratio of actual productivity in a year to this theoretical maximum is called the capacity factor. Typical capacity factors are 20 percent to 40 percent, with values at the upper end of the range in particularly favorable sites. For example, a 1 megawatt turbine with a capacity factor of 35 percent will not produce 8,760 megawatt-hours in a year (1x24x365) but only 0.35x24x365 = 3,066 MWh, averaging to 0.35 MW. Online data is available for some locations, and the capacity factor can be calculated from the yearly output.

Unlike fueled generating plants, the capacity factor is limited by the inherent properties of wind. Capacity factors of other types of power plant are based mostly on fuel cost, with a small amount of downtime for maintenance. Nuclear plants have low incremental fuel cost, and so are run at full output and achieve a 90 percent capacity factor. Plants with higher fuel cost are throttled back to follow load. Gas turbine plants using natural gas as fuel might be very expensive to operate and might be run only to meet peak power demand. A gas turbine plant might have an annual capacity factor of 5 percent to 25 percent due to relatively high energy production cost.

According to a 2007 Stanford University study published in the *Journal of Applied Meteorology and Climatology*, interconnecting ten or more wind farms allows 33 percent to 47 percent of the total energy produced to be used as reliable, baseload electric power, as long as minimum criteria are met for wind speed and turbine height.

Intermittency and Penetration Limits

Because instantaneous electrical generation and consumption must remain in balance to maintain grid stability, this variability can present substantial challenges to incorporating large amounts of wind power into a grid system. Intermittency and the nondispatchable nature of wind energy production can raise costs for regulation, incremental operating reserve, and (at high penetration levels) could require energy-demand management, load shedding, or storage solutions. At low levels of wind penetration, fluctuations in load and allowance for failure of large generating units require reserve capacity that can also regulate for variability of wind generation.

Pumped-storage hydroelectricity or other forms of grid energy storage can store energy developed by high-wind periods and release it when needed. Stored energy increases the economic value of wind energy because it can be shifted to displace higher cost generation during peak demand periods. The potential revenue from this arbitrage can offset the cost and losses of storage; the cost of storage might add 25 percent to the cost of any wind energy stored, but it is not envisaged that this would apply to a large proportion of wind energy generated. Thus, the 2 GW Dinorwig pumped storage plant adds costs to nuclear energy in the UK for which it was built, but not to all the power produced from the 30 or so GW of nuclear plants in the UK.

Peak wind speeds might not coincide with peak demand for electrical power. In California and Texas, for example, hot days in summer can have low wind speed and high electrical demand due to air conditioning. In the UK, however, winter demand is higher than summer demand, and so are wind speeds. Solar power tends to be complementary to wind because on most days, with no wind, there is sun, and on most days with no sun, there is wind. A demonstration project at the Massachusetts Maritime Academy shows the effect. A combined power plant linking solar, wind, bio-gas, and hydrostorage is proposed as a way to provide 100 percent renewable power. The 2006 Energy in Scotland Inquiry report expressed concern that wind power cannot be a sole source of supply and recommends diverse sources of electric energy.

A report from Denmark noted that its wind power network was without power for 54 days during 2002. Wind power advocates argue that these periods of low wind can be dealt with by simply restarting existing power stations that have been held in readiness. The cost of keeping a power station idle is, in fact, quite low because the main cost of running a power station is the fuel.

Wind energy "penetration" refers to the fraction of energy produced by wind compared with the total available generation capacity. There is no generally accepted "maximum" level of wind penetration. The limit for a particular grid depends on the existing generating plants, pricing mechanisms, capacity for storage or demand management, and other factors. An interconnected electricity grid already includes reserve generating and transmission capacity to allow for equipment failures; this reserve capacity can also serve to regulate for the varying power generation by wind plants. Studies have indicated that 20 percent of the total electrical energy consumption can be incorporated with minimal difficulty. These studies have been for locations with geographically dispersed wind farms, some degree of dispatchable energy, or hydropower with storage capacity, demand management, and interconnection to a large grid area export of electricity when needed. Beyond this level, there are few technical limits, but the economic implications become more significant.

At present, few grid systems have penetration of wind energy above 5 percent: Denmark (values over 18 percent), Spain and Portugal (values over 9 percent), and Germany and the Republic of Ireland (values over 6 percent). The Danish grid is heavily interconnected to the European electrical grid, and it has solved grid management problems by exporting almost half of its wind power to Norway. The correlation between electricity export and wind power production is very strong.

Denmark has active plans to increase the percentage of power generated to more than 50 percent. A study commissioned by the state of Minnesota considered penetration of up to 25 percent and concluded that integration issues would be manageable and have incremental costs of less than one-half cent ($0.0045) per KWH.

ESB National Grid, Ireland's electric utility, in a 2004 study concluded that to meet the renewable energy targets set by the EU in 2001 would "increase electricity generation costs by a modest 15%."

Good selection of a wind turbine site is critical to economic development of wind power. Aside from the availability of wind itself, other factors include the availability of transmission lines, value of energy to be produced, cost of land acquisition, land use considerations, and environmental impact of construction and operations. Off-shore locations might offset their higher construction cost with higher annual load factors, thereby reducing cost of energy produced. Wind farm designers use specialized wind energy software applications to evaluate the impact of these issues on a given wind farm design.

Offshore Windfarms

On December 21, 2007, Q7, a 120 MW offshore wind farm with a construction budget of €383 million, exported first power to the Dutch grid, which was a milestone for the offshore wind industry. Q7 was the first offshore wind farm to be financed by a nonrecourse loan (project finance). The project comprised of 60 2 MW V80 Vestas machines and features monopile foundation to a depth of between 18–23 meters at a distance of about 23 km off the Dutch coast.

Utilization of Wind Power

Many thousands of wind turbines now operate with a total capacity of 73,904 MW, of which wind power in Europe accounts for 65 percent (2006). Wind power was the fastest-growing energy source at the end of

2004. World wind generation capacity more than quadrupled between 2000 and 2006. Eighty-one percent of wind power installations are in the United States and Europe, but the share of the top five countries in terms of new installations fell from 71 percent in 2004 to 62 percent in 2006.

Countries with the Most Installed Wind Power Capacity

In 2007, the countries with the highest total installed capacity were Germany, the United States, Spain, India, and China. Table C.4 lists the rankings.

Table C.4 Worldwide Installed Wind Power Capacity (2005–2007)

Worldwide Installed Wind Power Capacity (MW)

Rank	Nation	2005	2006	2007
1	Germany	18,415	20,622	22,247
2	United States	9,149	11,603	16,818
3	Spain	10,028	11,615	15,145
4	India	4,430	6,270	8,000
5	China	1,260	2,604	6,050
6	Denmark (& Faeroe Islands)	3,136	3,140	3,129
7	Italy	1,718	2,123	2,726
8	France	757	1,567	2,454
9	United Kingdom	1,332	1,963	2,389
10	Portugal	1,022	1,716	2,150
11	Canada	683	1,459	1,856
12	Netherlands	1,219	1,560	1,747
13	Japan	1,061	1,394	1,538
14	Austria	819	965	982
15	Greece	573	746	871
16	Australia	708	817	824
17	Ireland	496	745	805
18	Sweden	510	572	788
19	Norway	267	314	333
20	New Zealand	169	171	322
21	Egypt	145	230	310
22	Belgium	167	193	287
23	Taiwan	104	188	282

continues

Table C.4 Worldwide Installed Wind Power Capacity (2005–2007)   continued

Worldwide Installed Wind Power Capacity (MW)

Rank	Nation	2005	2006	2007
24	Poland	83	153	276
25	Brazil	29	237	247
26	South Korea	98	173	191
27	Turkey	20	51	146
28	Czech Republic	28	50	116
29	Morocco	64	124	114
30	Finland	82	86	110
31	Ukraine	77	86	89
32	Mexico	3	88	87
33	Costa Rica	71	74	74
34	Bulgaria	6	36	70
35	Iran	23	48	66
36	Hungary	18	61	65
	Rest of Europe	129	163	
	Rest of Americas	109	109	
	Rest of Asia	38	38	
	Rest of Africa & Middle East	31	31	
	Rest of Oceania	12	12	
	World (MW) Total	59,091	74,223	93,849

By 2010, the World Wind Energy Association expects 160GW of capacity to be installed worldwide, up from 73.9 GW at the end of 2006, implying an anticipated net growth rate of more than 21 percent per year.

Denmark generates nearly one-fifth of its electricity with wind turbines—the highest percentage of any country—and is fifth in the world in total wind power generation. Denmark is prominent in the manufacturing and use of wind turbines, with a commitment made in the 1970s to eventually produce half of the country's power by wind.

In recent years, the United States has added more wind energy to its grid than any other country; U.S. wind power capacity grew by 45 percent to 16.8 gigawatts in 2007. Texas has become the largest wind energy-producing state, surpassing California. In 2007, the state expects to add

2 gigawatts to its existing capacity of approximately 4.5 gigawatts. Iowa and Minnesota are expected to each produce 1 gigawatt by late-2007. Wind power generation in the United States was up 31.8 percent in February 2007 from February, 2006. The average output of one megawatt of wind power is equivalent to the average electricity consumption of about 250 American households. According to the American Wind Energy Association, wind will generate enough electricity in 2008 to power just over 1 percent (4.5 million households) of total electricity in United States, up from less than 0.1 percent in 1999. U.S. Department of Energy studies have concluded wind harvested in Texas, Kansas, and North Dakota could provide enough electricity to power the entire nation, and that offshore wind farms could do the same job. Because the author grew in North Dakota (50th of the fifty states in tourist attraction), this is an opportunity to put in a plug for my home state because it is number one in wind-energy potential.

Top Wind States (North Dakota #1)

With the push started in 2008 by Texas oilman, T. Boone Pickens, to cut the U.S.'s demand for foreign oil, wind energy has been significantly promoted in television ads. As stated previously, Texas, Kansas, and North Dakota alone could provide via wind power for all the electricity needed to power the entire United States. Table C.5 gives the top 20 states in wind power potential. North Dakota (the author's home state) is listed as number 1, followed by Texas and Kansas.

Table C.5   Top Wind States—Annual Wind-Energy Potential in Billions of Kilowatt Hours

Rank	State	Annual Potential (Billion KWH)
1	North Dakota	1,210
2	Texas	1,190
3	Kansas	1,070
4	South Dakota	1,030
5	Montana	1,020
6	Nebraska	868
7	Wyoming	747
8	Oklahoma	725
9	Minnesota	657
10	Iowa	551
11	Colorado	481

Table C.5 Top Wind States—Annual Wind-Energy Potential in Billions of Kilowatt Hours

Rank	State	Annual Potential (Billion KWH)
12	New Mexico	435
13	Idaho	73
14	Michigan	65
15	New York	62
16	Illinois	61
17	California	59
18	Wisconsin	58
19	Maine	56
20	Missouri	52

India ranks fourth in the world with a total wind power capacity of 8,000 MW in 2007, or 3 percent of all electricity produced in India. The World Wind Energy Conference in New Delhi in November 2006 has given additional impetus to the Indian wind industry. The wind farm near Muppandal, Tamil Nadu, India, provides an impoverished village with energy.

In 2005, China announced it would build a 1000-megawatt wind farm in Hebei for completion in 2020. China reportedly has set a generating target of 20,000 MW by 2020 from renewable energy sources—it says indigenous wind power could generate up to 253,000 MW. Following the World Wind Energy Conference in November 2004, organized by the Chinese and the World Wind Energy Association, a Chinese renewable energy law was adopted. In late 2005, the Chinese government increased the official wind energy target for the year 2020 from 20 GW to 30 GW.

Mexico recently opened La Venta II wind power project as an important step in reducing Mexico's consumption of fossil fuels. The 88 MW project is the first of its kind in Mexico and will provide 13 percent of the electricity needs of the state of Oaxaca. By 2012, the project will have a capacity of 3,500 MW.

Another growing market is Brazil, with a wind potential of 143 GW. The federal government has created an incentive program, called Proinfa, to build production capacity of 3,300 MW of renewable energy for 2008, of which 1,422 MW is through wind energy. The program seeks to produce 10 percent of Brazilian electricity through renewable sources.

South Africa has a proposed station situated on the West Coast north of the Olifants River mouth near the town of Koekenaap, east of Vredendal in the Western Cape province. The station is proposed to have a total output of 100 MW, although there are negotiations to double this capacity. The plant could be operational by 2010.

France has announced a target of 12,500 MW installed by 2010.

Canada experienced rapid growth of wind capacity between 2000 and 2006, with total installed capacity increasing from 137 MW to 1,451 MW, and showing an annual growth rate of 38 percent. Particularly rapid growth was seen in 2006, with total capacity doubling from the 684 MW at end-2005. This growth was fed by measures including installation targets, economic incentives, and political support. For example, the Ontario government announced that it will introduce a feed-in tariff for wind power, referred to as "Standard Offer Contracts," which can boost the wind industry across the province. In Quebec, the provincially owned electric utility plans to purchase an additional 2,000 MW by 2013.

Small Scale Wind Power

Small wind-generation systems with capacities of 100 kW or less are usually used to power homes, farms, and small businesses. Isolated communities that otherwise rely on diesel generators might use wind turbines to displace diesel fuel consumption. Individuals purchase these systems to reduce or eliminate their electricity bills, or simply to generate their own clean power.

Wind turbines have been used for household electricity generation in conjunction with battery storage over many decades in remote areas. Increasingly, U.S. consumers are choosing to purchase grid-connected turbines in the 1 to 10 kilowatt range to power their whole homes. Household generator units of more than 1 kW are now functioning in several countries, and in every state in the United States.

Grid-connected wind turbines might use grid energy storage, displacing purchased energy with local production when available. Off-grid system users either adapt to intermittent power or use batteries, photovoltaic, or diesel systems to supplement the wind turbine.

In urban locations, where it is difficult to obtain predictable or large amounts of wind energy, smaller systems might still be used to run low power equipment. Equipment such as parking meters or wireless Internet gateways can be powered by a wind turbine that charges a small battery, replacing the need for a connection to the power grid.

References: See the large list of reference at http://en.wikipedia.org/wiki/Wind_power.

Worldwide Aspects of Solar Power

From Table C.2, solar power supplies less than 1 percent of global electricity demand. The term **solar energy** refers to the utilization of the radiant energy from the Sun. Solar power is used interchangeably with solar energy but refers more specifically to the conversion of sunlight into electricity, either by photovoltaics and concentrating solar thermal devices, or by one of several experimental technologies such as thermo-electric converters, solar chimneys, or solar ponds. Because solar power, along with wind power, are the alternative power-generation methods currently receiving most attention, this section gives an overview of worldwide development of this power source. Much of the following information comes from the Web site http://en.wikipedia.org/wiki/Solar_energy.

The Earth receives 174 petawatts (PW) of incoming solar radiation (insolation) at the upper atmosphere. Approximately 30 percent is reflected back to space while the rest is absorbed by clouds, oceans, and land masses. The spectrum of solar light at the Earth's surface is mostly spread across the visible and near-infrared ranges with a small part in the near-ultraviolet.

Solar radiation along with secondary solar resources, such as wind and wave power, hydroelectricity, and biomass, account for more than 99.9 percent of the available flow of renewable energy on Earth. The total solar energy absorbed by Earth's atmosphere, oceans, and land masses is approximately 3,850 zettajoules (ZJ) per year. In 2002, this was more energy in one hour than the world used in one year. Photosynthesis captures approximately 3 ZJ per year in biomass. The amount of solar energy reaching the surface of the planet is so vast that in one year, it is about twice as much as will ever be obtained from all the Earth's nonrenewable resources of coal, oil, natural gas, and mined uranium combined.

Applications of Solar Energy Technology

Average insolation showing land area (small black dots) is required to replace the total world energy supply with solar electricity. Insolation for most people is from 150 to 300 W/m^2 or 3.5 to 7.0 kWh/m^2/day. Solar energy technologies use solar radiation for practical ends. Technologies that use secondary solar resources such as biomass, wind, waves, and ocean thermal gradients can be included in a broader description of solar energy, but only primary resource applications are discussed here. Because the performance of solar technologies varies widely between regions, they should be deployed in a way that carefully considers these variations.

Solar technologies are broadly characterized as either passive or active depending on the way they capture, convert, and distribute sunlight. Active solar techniques use photovoltaic panels, pumps, and fans to convert sunlight into useful outputs. Passive solar techniques include selecting materials with favorable thermal properties, designing spaces that naturally circulate air, and referencing the position of a building to the Sun. Active solar technologies increase the supply of energy and are considered supply-side technologies, whereas passive solar technologies reduce the need for alternate resources and are generally considered demand-side technologies.

Solar Electricity

Sunlight can be converted into electricity using **photovoltaics** (PV), concentrating solar power (CSP), and various experimental technologies. PV has mainly been used to power small and medium-sized applications, from the calculator powered by a single solar cell to off-grid homes powered by a photovoltaic array. For large-scale generation, CSP plants like SEGS have been the norm, but recently multimegawatt PV plants are becoming common. Completed in 2007, the 14 MW power station in Clark County, Nevada, and the 20 MW site in Beneixama, Spain, are characteristic of the trend toward larger photovoltaic power stations in the United States and Europe.

Photovoltaics

A solar cell, or (PV, is a device that converts light into direct current using the photoelectric effect. The first solar cell was constructed by Charles Fritts in the 1880s. Although the prototype selenium cells converted less than 1 percent of incident light into electricity, both Ernst Werner von Siemens and James Clerk Maxwell recognized the importance of this discovery. Following the work of Russell Ohl in the 1940s, researchers Gerald Pearson, Calvin Fuller, and Daryl Chapin created the silicon solar cell in 1954. These early solar cells cost 286 USD/watt and reached efficiencies of 4.5 percent to 6 percent.

The earliest significant application of solar cells was as a backup power source to the Vanguard I satellite, which allowed it to continue transmitting for more than a year after its chemical battery was exhausted. The successful operation of solar cells on this mission was duplicated in many other Soviet and American satellites, and by the late 1960s, PV had become the established source of power for them. Photovoltaics went on to play an essential part in the success of early commercial satellites such as Telstar, and they remain vital to the telecommunications infrastructure today.

The high cost of solar cells limited terrestrial uses throughout the 1960s. This changed in the early 1970s when prices reached levels that made PV generation competitive in remote areas without grid access. Early terrestrial uses included powering telecommunication stations, off-shore oil rigs, navigational buoys, and railroad crossings. These off-grid applications have proven to be very successful and accounted for more than half of worldwide installed capacity until 2004.

Building-integrated photovoltaics cover the roofs of an increasing number of homes. The 1973 oil crisis stimulated a rapid rise in the production of PV during the 1970s and early 1980s. Economies of scale, which resulted from increasing production along with improvements in system performance, brought the price of PV down from 100 USD/watt in 1971 to 7 USD/watt in 1985. Steadily falling oil prices during the early 1980s led to a reduction in funding for photovoltaic R&D and a discontinuation of the tax credits associated with the Energy Tax Act of 1978. These factors moderated growth to approximately 15 percent per year from 1984 through 1996.

Since the mid-1990s, leadership in the PV sector has shifted from the United States to Japan and Germany. Between 1992 and 1994, Japan increased R&D funding, established net metering guidelines, and introduced a subsidy program to encourage the installation of residential PV systems. As a result, PV installations in the country climbed from 31.2 MW in 1994 to 318 MW in 1999, and worldwide production growth increased to 30 percent in the late 1990s.

Germany has become the leading PV market worldwide since revising its feed-in tariff system as part of the Renewable Energy Sources Act. Installed PV capacity has risen from 100 MW in 2000 to approximately 4,150 MW at the end of 2007. Spain has become the third-largest PV market after adopting a similar feed-in tariff structure in 2004, while France, Italy, South Korea, and the United States have seen rapid growth recently due to various incentive programs and local market conditions. World solar photovoltaic (PV) market installations reached a record high of 2.8 gigawatts peak (GWp) in 2007.

The three leading countries (Germany, Japan, and the U.S.) represent nearly 89 percent of the total worldwide PV installed capacity. On Wednesday, August 1, 2007, word was published of construction of a production facility in China, which is projected to be one of the largest wafer factories in the world, with a peak capacity of around 1,500 MW. Germany was the fastest growing major PV market in the world during 2006 and 2007. In 2007, more than 1.3 GWp of PV was installed. The German PV industry generates over 10,000 jobs in production, distribution, and installation. By the end of 2006, nearly 88 percent of all solar PV installations in the EU were in grid-tied applications in Germany. The balance is off-grid (or stand-alone) systems. Photovoltaic power capacity is measured as maximum power output under standardized test conditions (STC) in "Wp" (Watts peak). The actual power output at a particular point in time may be less than or greater than this standardized, or "rated," value, depending on geographical location, time of day, weather conditions, and other factors. Solar photovoltaic array capacity factors are typically under 25 percent, which is lower than many other industrial sources of electricity. Therefore, the 2006 installed base peak output would have provided an average output of 1.2 GW (assuming 20 percent × 5,862 MWp). This represented 0.06 percent of global demand at the time.

Countries with the Most Installed Photovoltaic Peak Power Capacity

In 2007, the countries with the highest photovoltaic peak power capacity were Germany, Japan, the United States, Spain, and Italy. Table C.6 lists the rankings based on photovoltaic peak power capacity estimated at the end of 2007. This information is from http://en. wikipedia.org/wiki/Photovoltaics. In addition to the total capacity at the end of 2007, the table includes estimates for capacity installed during 2007. Because of the ongoing drop in costs for photovoltaic power and worldwide push for alternative power-generation methods, we would expect continuous and significant changes to this type of table. Note that the Wp/capita (Watts peak per capita) is far higher for Germany than for any other country.

Table C.6   Worldwide Photovoltaic Peak Power Capacity (End of 2007)

Country/ Region	Installed off Grid in 2007	Installed on Grid in 2007	Total Installed in 2007	Total off Grid	Total on Grid	Total End of 2007	Wp/ Capita Total
World	127.86	2,129.778	2,257.638	662.34	7,178.392	7,840.732	
Germany	35	1,100	1,135	35	3,827	3,862	46.8
Japan	1.562	208.8	210.395	90.15	1828.744	1918.894	15
United States	55	151.5	206.5	325	505.5	830.5	2.8
Spain	22	490	512	29.8	625.2	655	15.1
Italy	0.3	69.9	70.2	13.1	107.1	120.2	2.1
Australia	5.91	6.28	12.19	66.446	16.045	82.491	4.1
South Korea	0	42.868	42.868	5.943	71.658	77.601	1.6
France	0.993	30.306	31.299	22.547	52.685	75.232	1.2
Netherlands	0.582	1.023	1.605	5.3	48	53.3	3.3
Switzerland	0.2	6.3	6.5	3.6	32.6	36.2	4.9
Austria	0.055	2.061	2.116	3.224	24.477	27.701	3.4
Canada	3.888	1.403	5.291	22.864	2.911	25.775	0.8
Mexico	0.869	0.15	1.019	20.45	0.3	20.75	0.2
United Kingdom	0.16	3.65	3.81	1.47	16.62	18.09	0.3
Portugal	0.2	14.254	14.454	2.841	15.029	17.87	1.7
Norway	0.32	0.004	0.324	7.86	0.132	7.992	1.7
Sweden	0.271	1.121	1.392	4.566	1.676	6.242	0.7
Denmark	0.05	0.125	0.175	0.385	2.69	3.075	0.6
Israel	0.5	0	0.5	1.794	0.025	1.819	0.3

Concentrating Solar Power

Solar troughs are the most widely deployed and the most cost-effective CSP technology. Concentrated sunlight has been used to perform useful tasks since the time of ancient China. A legend claims that Archimedes used polished shields to concentrate sunlight on the invading Roman fleet and repel them from Syracuse. Auguste Mouchout used a parabolic trough to produce steam for the first solar steam engine in 1866, and subsequent developments led to the use of concentrating solar-powered devices for irrigation, refrigeration, and locomotion.

Concentrating Solar Power (CSP) systems use lenses or mirrors and tracking systems to focus a large area of sunlight into a small beam. The concentrated light is then used as a heat source for a conventional power plant. A wide range of concentrating technologies exists; the most developed are the solar trough, parabolic dish, and solar power tower. These methods vary in the way they track the Sun and focus light. In all these systems, a working fluid is heated by the concentrated sunlight and is then used for power generation or energy storage.

The PS10 concentrates sunlight from a field of heliostats on a central tower. A solar trough consists of a linear parabolic reflector that concentrates light onto a receiver positioned along the reflector's focal line. The reflector is made to follow the Sun during the daylight hours by tracking along a single axis. Trough systems provide the best land-use factor of any solar technology. The SEGS plants in California and Acciona's Nevada Solar One near Boulder City, Nevada, are representatives of this technology.

A parabolic dish system consists of a stand-alone parabolic reflector that concentrates light onto a receiver positioned at the reflector's focal point. The reflector tracks the Sun along two axes. Parabolic dish systems give the highest efficiency among CSP technologies. The 50 kW Big Dish in Canberra, Australia, is an example of this technology.

A solar power tower uses an array of tracking reflectors (heliostats) to concentrate light on a central receiver atop a tower. Power towers are less advanced than trough systems but offer higher efficiency and better energy storage capability. The Solar Two in Barstow, California, and the Planta Solar 10 in Sanlucar la Mayor, Spain, are representatives of this technology.

Experimental Solar Power and Storage Methods

A solar updraft tower (also known as a solar chimney or solar tower) consists of a large greenhouse that funnels into a central tower. As sunlight shines on the greenhouse, the air inside is heated and expands. The expanding air flows toward the central tower, where a turbine converts the air flow into electricity. A 50 kW prototype was constructed in Ciudad Real, Spain, and operated for eight years before decommissioning in 1989.

Space solar power systems would use a large solar array in geosynchronous orbit to collect sunlight and beam this energy in the form of microwave radiation to receivers (rectennas) on Earth for distribution. This concept was first proposed by Dr. Peter Glaser in 1968, and since then a wide variety of systems have been studied, with both photovoltaic and concentrating solar thermal technologies being proposed. Although still in the concept stage, these systems offer the possibility of delivering power approximately 96 percent of the time.

Energy Storage Methods

Solar Two's thermal storage system generated electricity during cloudy weather and at night. Storage is an important issue in the development of solar energy because modern energy systems usually assume continuous availability of energy. Solar energy is not available at night, and the performance of solar power systems is affected by unpredictable weather patterns; therefore, storage media or backup power systems must be used.

Thermal mass systems can store solar energy in the form of heat at domestically useful temperatures for daily or seasonal durations. Thermal storage systems generally use readily available materials with high specific heat capacities such as water, earth, and stone. Well-designed systems can lower peak demand, shift time-of-use to off-peak hours, and reduce overall heating and cooling requirements.

Phase change materials such as paraffin wax and Glauber's salt are another thermal storage media. These materials are inexpensive, readily available, and can deliver domestically useful temperatures (approximately $64°C$). The Dover House (in Dover, Massachusetts) was the first to use a Glauber's salt heating system, in 1948.

Solar energy can be stored at high temperatures using molten salts. Salts are an effective storage medium because they are low-cost, have a high specific heat capacity, and can deliver heat at temperatures compatible with conventional power systems. The Solar Two used this method of energy storage, allowing it to store 1.44 TJ in its 68 m^3 storage tank with an annual storage efficiency of about 99 percent.

Off-grid PV systems have traditionally used rechargeable batteries to store excess electricity. With grid-tied systems, excess electricity can be sent to the transmission grid. Net metering programs give these systems a credit for the electricity they deliver to the grid. This credit offsets electricity provided from the grid when the system cannot meet demand, effectively using the grid as a storage mechanism.

Pumped-storage hydroelectricity stores energy in the form of water pumped when energy is available from a lower-elevation reservoir to a higher-elevation one. The energy is recovered when demand is high by releasing the water to run through a hydroelectric power generator. See the large list of references at http://en.wikipedia.org/wiki/Solar_energy.

D

Worldwide Electricity Costs for IT with Projections

"Green is not simply a new form of generating electric power. It is a new form of generating national power—period."

—Thomas L. Friedman, author of *Hot, Flat, and Crowded*

Electricity costs have a significant impact on the location of new data centers. This appendix gives information on how the cost of electricity varies around the world and within countries such as the United States.

Of course, the cost of electricity goes beyond the data center in its impact on green IT. Thomas Friedman, in his book *Hot, Flat, and Crowded: Why We Need a Green Revolution and How It Can Renew America*, sees the fusion of IT and energy technologies, envisioning all the power systems in your home as communicating with all the information systems in your home and that they had all merged into one big seamless platform for using, storing, generating, and even buying and selling clean electronics. Friedman sees the need to have information technology and energy technology, IT and ET, merged into a single system that he calls an Energy Internet (ET). He envisions how professionals with IT skills will be needed to build integral components of this clean-energy Web.

Getting back to data centers, here's an example of how the cost of electricity can have an impact on the location of data centers. If the cost of electricity is 22 cents/KWH in New York City and only 4.5 cents/KWH in Charleston, West Virginia, the location of a large, new data center in West Virginia could potentially save millions of dollars in electricity costs each year. With high-speed networks (including the Internet) available throughout the United States and, for a large part, worldwide, data centers can now be located almost anywhere.

As indicated in this appendix, the cost per KWH and emissions estimates can vary widely on a worldwide basis. This appendix is intended to give information on how the cost of electricity varies around the world—and how this could impact the location choice for new data centers.

U.S. Average Electricity Prices by State

Electrical prices can vary significantly within the United States. Based on Table D.1, average electrical prices per KWH during 2006 ranged from a low of 4.92 cents/KWH in Idaho to a high of 20.72 cents/KWH in Hawaii. The average U.S. price per KWH during 2006 was 8.9 cents/KWH.

Table D.1   U.S. Average Electricity Prices by State
U.S. Department of Energy EIA (Energy Information Agency) released November 2007.
(http://www.eia.doe.gov/cneaf/electricity/st_profiles/e_profiles_sum.html)

State Electricity Profiles—Alphabetical   DOE/EIA-0348   Date of Data: 2006
Data Release Date: November 2007

Name	Avg. Retail Price (cents/KWH)	Summer Capability (megawatts)	Net Generation (megawatthours)	Total Retail Sales (megawatthours)
Alabama	7.07	30,664	140,895,441	90,677,695
Alaska	12.84	1,884	6,674,197	6,182,291
Arizona	8.24	25,608	104,392,528	73,252,776
Arkansas	6.99	14,507	52,168,703	46,635,624
California	12.82	63,213	216,798,688	262,958,528
Colorado	7.61	11,156	50,698,353	49,733,698
Connecticut	14.83	7,882	34,681,736	31,677,453
Delaware	10.13	3,374	7,182,179	11,554,672
District of Columbia	11.08	806	81,467	11,396,424
Florida	10.45	53,206	223,751,621	228,219,544
Georgia	7.63	36,499	138,010,208	134,834,168

Name	Avg. Retail Price (cents/KWH)	Summer Capability (megawatts)	Net Generation (megawatthours)	Total Retail Sales (megawatthours)
Hawaii	20.72	2,414	11,559,174	10,567,912
Idaho	4.92	3,210	13,386,085	22,761,749
Illinois	7.07	42,289	192,426,958	142,447,811
Indiana	6.46	26,990	130,489,788	105,664,484
Iowa	7.01	11,143	45,483,462	43,336,835
Kansas	6.89	11,124	45,523,736	39,751,302
Kentucky	5.43	20,047	98,792,014	88,743,435
Louisiana	8.30	26,786	90,921,829	77,467,748
Maine	11.80	4,187	16,816,173	12,284,768
Maryland	9.95	12,500	48,956,880	63,173,143
Massachusetts	15.45	13,932	45,597,775	55,850,090
Michigan	8.14	30,189	112,556,739	108,017,697
Minnesota	6.98	12,651	53,237,789	66,769,931
Mississippi	8.33	16,620	46,228,847	46,936,437
Missouri	6.30	20,599	91,686,343	82,015,230
Montana	6.91	5,437	28,243,536	13,814,980
Nebraska	6.07	7,071	31,669,969	27,276,292
Nevada	9.63	9,648	31,860,022	34,586,260
New Hampshire	13.84	4,340	22,063,695	11,094,343
New Jersey	11.88	18,971	60,700,139	79,680,947
New Mexico	7.37	7,102	37,265,625	21,434,957
New York	15.27	39,550	142,265,432	142,238,019
North Carolina	7.53	27,061	125,214,784	126,698,979
North Dakota	6.21	4,839	30,881,137	11,245,238
Ohio	7.71	33,877	155,434,075	153,428,844
Oklahoma	7.30	20,085	70,614,880	54,905,314
Oregon	6.53	12,333	53,340,695	48,069,265
Pennsylvania	8.68	45,005	218,811,595	146,150,358
Rhode Island	13.98	1,771	5,967,725	7,799,126
South Carolina	6.98	22,782	99,267,606	80,877,321
South Dakota	6.70	2,933	7,132,243	10,056,387
Tennessee	6.97	20,905	93,911,102	103,931,744
Texas	10.34	100,754	400,582,878	342,724,213
Utah	5.99	6,712	41,263,324	26,365,716
Vermont	11.37	1,117	7,084,344	5,795,029
Virginia	6.86	22,648	73,069,537	106,721,241

continues

Table D.1   U.S. Average Electricity Prices by State   continued

Name	Avg. Retail Price (cents/KWH)	Summer Capability (megawatts)	Net Generation (megawatthours)	Total Retail Sales (megawatthours)
Washington	6.14	28,224	108,203,155	85,033,335
West Virginia	5.04	16,443	93,815,804	32,312,126
Wisconsin	8.13	16,415	61,639,843	69,820,749
Wyoming	5.27	6,707	45,400,370	14,946,612
U.S. Total	8.90	986,215	4,064,702,227	3,669,918,840

Worldwide Electricity Prices for Industry by Country

Table D.2 shows a "snapshot" of electricity prices for industry by country posted by the U.S. Department of Energy (DOE) on June 7, 2007. Additional information on sources is given at the end of the table. The DOE Web site with this table is http://www.eia.doe.gov/emeu/international/elecprii.html.

Use this table for comparison purposes of average electricity costs for industry per country. Use the actual costs per KWH hour for your data center area for server power cost estimates. Electrical prices can vary significantly throughout the world. Based on the following table, average industry electrical prices per KWH during 2006 ranged from a low of 2.4 cents/KWH in Kazakhstan to a high of 16.7 cents/KWH in Cyprus. Notice that the average price per KWH for 2006 was not available for many countries—with 2004 having the most data. Average price in the United States during 2006 for industry was 6.1 cents/KWH. Notice that the electricity cost for industry in the United States in 2006 was significantly less than the overall average cost in the United States. Use the DOE Web site listed previously for more recent data.

Table D.2   Worldwide Electricity Prices for Industry by Country

Electricity Prices for Industry[1] (U. S. Dollars per KWH)

Country	1998	1999	2000	2001	2002	2001	2004	2005	2006
Argentina	NA	NA	NA	NA	NA	NA	0.033	NA	NA
Australia	0.047	0.050	0.045	0.044	0.049	0.054	0.061	NA	NA
Austria	0.078	0.057	0.038	NA	NA	NA	0.096	0.102	0.109
Barbados	NA	NA	NA	NA	NA	NA	0.197	NA	NA
Belgium	0.061	0.056	0.048	NA	NA	NA	NA	NA	NA
Bolivia	NA	NA	NA	NA	NA	NA	0.051	NA	NA

Country	1998	1999	2000	2001	2002	2001	2004	2005	2006
Brazil	NA	NA	NA	NA	NA	NA	0.047	NA	NA
Canada	0.038	0.038	0.039	0.042	0.039	0.047	0.049	NA	NA
Chile	NA	NA	NA	NA	NA	NA	0.057	NA	NA
China	NA	NA	NA	NA	NA	NA	NA	NA	NA
Chinese Taipei (Taiwan)	0.058	0.059	0.061	0.056	0.053	0.053	0.055	0.057	0.056
Colombia	NA	NA	NA	NA	NA	NA	0.081	NA	NA
Costa Rica	NA	NA	NA	NA	NA	NA	0.069	NA	NA
Cuba	NA	NA	NA	NA	NA	NA	0.078	NA	NA
Cyprus	0.072	0.074	0.087	0.079	0.082	0.104	0.107	0.125	0.167
Czech Republic	0.052	0.048	0.043	0.043	0.049	0.056	0.066	0.081	0.094
Denmark	0.068	0.066	0.058	0.060	0.070	0.092	0.096	NA	NA
Dominican Republic	NA	NA	NA	NA	NA	NA	0.120	NA	NA
Ecuador	NA	NA	NA	NA	NA	NA	0.089	NA	NA
El Salvador	NA	NA	NA	NA	NA	NA	0.120	NA	NA
Finland	0.050	0.046	0.039	0.038	0.043	0.065	0.072	0.070	NA
France	0.047	0.044	0.036	0.035	0.037	0.045	0.050	0.050	0.051
Germany	0.067	0.057	0.041	0.044	0.049	0.065	0.077	0.084	NA
Greece	0.050	0.050	0.042	0.043	0.046	0.056	0.063	0.067	NA
Grenada	NA	NA	NA	NA	NA	NA	0.188	NA	NA
Guatemala	NA	NA	NA	NA	NA	NA	0.116	NA	NA
Guyana	NA	NA	NA	NA	NA	NA	0.078	NA	NA
Haiti	NA	NA	NA	NA	NA	NA	0.085	NA	NA
Honduras	NA	NA	NA	NA	NA	NA	0.035	NA	NA
Hungary	0.056	0.055	0.049	0.051	0.059	0.078	0.093	0.096	0.105
India	0.082	0.081	0.080	NA	NA	NA	NA	NA	NA
Indonesia	0.025	0.029	0.040	NA	NA	NA	NA	NA	NA
Ireland	0.060	0.057	0.049	0.060	0.075	0.094	0.096	0.099	0.122
Italy	0.095	0.086	0.089	0.107	0.113	0.147	0.162	0.174	NA
Jamaica	NA	NA	NA	NA	NA	NA	0.130	NA	NA
Japan	0.128	0.143	0.143	0.127	0.115	0.122	0.127	0.121	NA
Kazakhstan	0.030	0.018	0.013	0.014	0.014	0.015	0.018	0.020	0.024
Korea, South	0.039	0.046	0.052	0.048	0.047	0.051	0.053	0.059	0.065
Mexico	0.038	0.042	0.051	0.053	0.056	0.063	0.078	0.088	0.099
Netherlands	0.062	0.061	0.057	0.059	C	C	C	C	C

continues

Table D.2 Worldwide Electricity Prices for Industry by Country   continued

Country	1998	1999	2000	2001	2002	2001	2004	2005	2006
New Zealand	0.038	0.033	0.028	0.028	0.033	0.046	0.051	0.055	0.053
Nicaragua	NA	NA	NA	NA	NA	NA	0.128	NA	NA
Norway	NA	NA	0.019	0.025	0.031	0.046	0.043	0.043	0.055
Panama	NA	NA	NA	NA	NA	NA	0.099	NA	NA
Paraguay	NA	NA	NA	NA	NA	NA	0.039	NA	NA
Peru	NA	NA	NA	NA	NA	NA	0.079	NA	NA
Poland	0.037	0.037	0.037	0.045	0.049	0.056	0.060	0.070	0.073
Portugal	0.090	0.078	0.067	0.066	0.068	0.083	0.093	0.098	0.110
Romania	0.045	0.037	0.044	0.042	0.053	0.067	0.071	0.096	NA
Russia	NA	NA	NA	0.021	0.024	0.029	NA	NA	NA
Slovak Republic (Slovakia)	0.049	0.041	0.042	0.043	0.047	0.070	0.083	0.086	0.098
South Africa	0.020	0.017	0.017	0.013	0.012	0.019	NA	NA	NA
Spain	0.057	0.049	0.043	0.041	0.048	0.054	0.060	0.083	0.091
Suriname	NA	NA	NA	NA	NA	NA	0.123	NA	NA
Sweden	NA	NA	NA	NA	NA	NA	NA	NA	NA
Switzerland	0.101	0.090	0.069	0.069	0.073	0.081	0.085	0.083	0.080
Thailand	0.053	0.054	0.057	0.056	0.057	0.060	0.063	NA	NA
Trinidad and Tobago	NA	NA	NA	NA	NA	NA	0.037	NA	NA
Turkey	0.075	0.079	0.080	0.079	0.094	0.099	0.100	0.107	0.100
United Kingdom	0.065	0.064	0.055	0.051	0.052	0.055	0.067	0.087	NA
United States[3]	0.045	0.044	0.046	0.051	0.049	0.051	0.053	0.057	0.061
Uruguay	NA	NA	NA	NA	NA	NA	0.055	NA	NA
Venezuela	NA	NA	NA	NA	NA	NA	0.032	NA	NA

[1]   Energy end-use prices including taxes, converted using exchange rates.

[2]   Price excluding tax (currently all prices in the table include tax).

[3]   Price includes state and local taxes, energy or demand charges, customer service charges, environmental surcharges, franchise fees, fuel adjustments, and other miscellaneous charges applied to end-use customers during normal billing operations. Prices do not include deferred charges, credits, or other adjustments, such as fuel or revenue from purchased power, from previous reporting periods.

NA=Not available.

C=Confidential.

Sources: United States—Energy Information Administration, *Monthly Energy Review*, May 2007, Table 9.9.

Other Countries—International Energy Agency, *Energy Prices & Taxes—Quarterly Statistics, First Quarter 2007*, Part II, Section D, Table 21, and Part III, Section B, Table 18, 2007. The Paris-based International Energy Agency (IEA) maintains annual and quarterly time series of this price data that begin with the year 1978 and that also include the most recent quarterly prices. Information on purchasing this data online from the IEA is available at http://data.iea.org/ieastore/default.asp.

Projections for Worldwide Clean Energy Cost Comparisons

What are projections for the future? Each of us knows from personal experience that electricity costs keep going up. However, costs for renewable/sustainable power generation are projected to go down. Appendix C, "Comparison of Different Power-Generation Methods," includes information on the continuing significant progress in reducing costs for electric generation by wind power and solar power. Hydro is currently the only source of renewable energy making substantial contributions to global energy demand (refer to Figure C.1). However, hydro plants, clearly have limited growth potential and can significantly damage aquatic ecosystems. Other traditional power generation methods such as nuclear are seeing resurgence. Nuclear, although clean from a CO_2 perspective, will continue to bring up concerns on safe disposable of spent fuel and overall safety concerns. From a cost per KWH standpoint, however, nuclear power generation has definite advantages. This section looks at projections for costs to generate electricity from nuclear, wind, and solar power.

The global increase in oil and gasoline prices in mid-2008 had a significant impact on the global economy. The increase in oil prices had a positive impact on the market dynamics for clean energy alternatives like solar, wind, and geothermal. It made those energy alternatives more attractive financially and spurred research. Of course, the turn-around of oil prices during the second half of 2008 changed the market again.

Based on history, the price of oil will go up again—probably in 2009. At the same time that natural gas and coal prices will be going up in price, the costs of solar and wind should continue to come down. Improved technologies and better manufacturing efficiencies (as solar panel and wind turbine makers scale up production) are lowering and stabilizing clean energy prices.

Some studies in 2008 concluded that solar power will reach cost parity with most electric rates in the United States in less than a decade, by 2015. In general, as solar prices continue to fall and utilities embrace solar power more aggressively, the United States could generate 10 percent of its electric power (up from less than one percent today) from the sun by 2025. In 2008, the U.S. Department of Energy released a report detailing a realistic path for wind power to contribute 20 percent of the nation's electricity by 2030. It is a complex economic situation, but as oil, coal, and natural gas get more expensive, clean energy looks better by comparison—not even taking into account the environmental, climate, and domestic job creation benefits.

In the United States, the new administration has indicated a big push to create green energy jobs. That push will help accelerate the price crossover point, where clean alternative energy becomes cost-competitive with carbon-based energy.

Glossary

AEM (Active Energy Manager)
An IBM tool to measure energy use on each server and other IT devices.

AFCOM (Association for Computer Operations Management)
An organization that provides education and resources for data center managers.

AIX (Advanced Interactive Executive)
AIX is IBM's version of UNIX.

Alliance to Save Energy
An organization that promotes energy efficiency worldwide.

AMD (Advanced Micro Devices)
A microprocessor manufacturer and the main competitor to Intel.

APC (American Power Conversion)
A company that deals with data center efficiency.

ASHRAE (American Society of Heating, Refrigerating, and Air Conditioning Engineers)
An engineering society that has always been involved in the design of efficient plumbing to heat and cool buildings and data centers.

bandwidth
The amount of data that can be transmitted across a particular network. Basic Ethernet has a 10-Mbps bandwidth; however, 100-Mbps Ethernet and recently Gigabit Ethernet are common for corporate LANs and server farm infrastructure.

BIOS

In computing, BIOS is an acronym that stands either for the Basic Input/Output System or for Built In Operating System. BIOS usually refers to the firmware code run by a PC when first powered on. The primary function of the BIOS is to identify and initialize system component hardware (such as the video display card, hard disk, and floppy disk) and some other hardware devices.

blade server

A chassis housing that contains multiple, modular electronic circuit boards (blades), each of which includes processors, memory, and storage and network connections and can act as a server on its own. The thin blades can be added or removed, depending on needs for capacity, power, cooling, or networking traffic.

bps (bits per second)

The rate of data transmission across a network.

browser

See Web browser.

BTU (British Thermal Unit)

The BTU is a unit of energy used in the power, steam generation, and heating and air conditioning industries. A BTU is defined as the amount of heat required to raise the temperature of one pound of liquid water by one degree Fahrenheit.

CDU (Cabinet Power Distribution Unit)

An intelligent Power Distribution Unit (PDU) with local input current monitoring to allow precise measurement of the electric current (in amps) that network devices (for example, computer room air-conditioning units, servers, and so on) are drawing on the power circuit.

CEO (Chief Executive Officer)

The head of a corporation.

CERN

The European Organization for Nuclear Research (acronym, originally from the French: Conseil Européen pour la Recherche Nucléaire). CERN is the world's largest particle physics laboratory, situated in the northwest suburbs of Geneva on the Franco-Swiss border. CERN requires high-performance computing and represents a real and a virtual workplace for many scientists and engineers, representing 500 universities and 80 nationalities.

CHP Combined Heat and Power
Distributed technologies used for data centers.

CIO (Chief Information Officer)
The lead IT executive at a corporation.

cloud computing
The name used for a subset of grid computing that includes utility computing and other approaches to the use of shared computing resources. Cloud computing is an alternative to having local servers or personal devices handling users' applications. Essentially, it is an idea that the technological capabilities should "hover" over everything and always be available for users.

cogeneration
The use of a heat engine or a power station to simultaneously generate both electricity and useful heat. In the United States, Con Edison distributes 30 billion pounds of 350°F/180°C steam each year through its seven cogeneration plants to 100,000 buildings in Manhattan—the biggest steam district in the world.

CPU (central processing unit)
The "brains" of a computer.

CRAC (computer room air conditioner)
A device that controls humidity through humidification or dehumidification as required, both of which consume energy.

Cricket
A system for monitoring trends in time-series data, initially developed to help network managers visualize and understand the traffic on their networks (http://cricket.sourceforge.net/).

data centers
Facilities that primarily contain electronic equipment used for data processing, data storage, and communications networking.

DCiE (Data Center Infrastructure Efficiency)
The DCiE = (IT Equipment Power × 100%) / Total Facility Power. This is the reciprocal of the Green Grid's PUE (Power Usage Effectiveness). The DCiE is considered to be a more intuitive metric than the PUE

because the DCiE can range from 0 percent to 100 percent, where 100 percent would be the ideal efficiency. The PUE can range from 1 to a large number, where 1 is considered ideal. So, a PUE of 1.1 is good, whereas a PUE above 3 is not. A DCiE below 33 percent is considered inefficient.

DG (Distributed Generation)
Include fuel cells and other clean, efficient distributed technologies used in data centers.

DOE (Department of Energy)
A U.S. governmental department with a mission to advance the national, economic, and energy security of the United States and to promote scientific and technological innovation in support of that mission.

DOE DC Pro Tool Department of Energy Data Center Profiler Tool
An online software tool designed to help industries worldwide quickly "diagnose" how energy is used by their data centers and how they might save energy and money. The tool is available at http://www1.eere.energy. gov/industry/saveenergynow/printable_versions/partnering_data_ centers.html.

EDUCAUSE
A nonprofit association with a mission to advance higher education by promoting the intelligent use of information technology (http://www. educause.edu/).

EEC (European Energy Community)
A regulatory framework for trading energy in Europe.

ensemble
A pool of homogenous systems within a grid or cloud computer system that is compatible with one another.

EPA (Environmental Protection Agency)
A U.S. governmental agency with a mission to protect human health and the environment.

EPEAT (Electronic Product Environmental Assessment Tool)
EPEAT was created through an Institute of Electrical and Electronics Engineers (IEEE) council because companies and government agencies wanted to put green criteria in IT requests for proposals. EPEAT's energy-consumption criteria are based on the EPA's Energy Star requirements for PCs, and the "sensitive material" criteria require companies to

meet the European Union's tough standards for limiting the hazardous chemicals and components used to make them.

ESPC (Energy Services Performance Contract)
An incentive envisioned by the U.S. federal government for efficiency upgrades for data centers.

EUI (Energy Use Intensity)
The EPA uses EUI (kBTU/square foot) to determine building Energy Star ratings. See www.energystar.gov for the range of EUI Energy Star (green buildings) ranges depending on building type.

Fibre Channel
The technology commonly used to connect a server to external data storage (SAN).

GB (Gigabyte)
A billion bytes of computer or hard-disk memory.

GIPC (Green IT Promotion Council)
An organization established in Japan in 2008 to address global warming by electronics firms, related industry bodies, and other groups.

Green Grid, The
A consortium of IT professionals working to improve data-center energy efficiency.

green washing
Projects or processes that appear to be greener than they are; similar concept to "white washing."

Greenpeace
A group originally founded in Vancouver, British Columbia, Canada, in 1971 to oppose the United States testing of nuclear devices in Alaska. The focus of the organization later turned to other environmental issues: whaling, bottom trawling, global warming, old growth, and nuclear power. Greenpeace has national and regional offices in many countries. It also has a big presence worldwide, all of which are affiliated to the Amsterdam office of Greenpeace International.

grid computing
A major evolutionary step that virtualizes an IT infrastructure. It's defined by the Global Grid Forum (www.gridforum.org) as distributed computing over a network of heterogeneous resources across domain boundaries and enabled by open standards.

GUI (Graphical User Interface)
A pictorial way of representing to a user the capabilities of a system and the work being done on it.

host
In the TCP/IP sense, a computer that enables users to communicate with other host computers on a network. Individual users communicate by using application programs, such as electronic mail and FTP. Also, refers to a large computer system, such as a mainframe.

HPC (High Performance Computing)
Uses supercomputers and computer clusters to solve advanced computation problems.

HTML (Hypertext Markup Language)
The language used to write World Wide Web documents, or pages. It is a subset of ISO SGML.

HTTP (Hypertext Transfer Protocol)
The protocol used by the World Wide Web to transfer documents between clients and servers.

HVAC (Heating, Ventilating, and Air Conditioning)
The engineering discipline related to heating, ventilating, and cooling buildings.

Hyper-V
A Microsoft Windows Server 2008 hypervisor-based server virtualization technology. Allows separate virtual machines (VMs) running on a single physical machine. Like other virtualization software (for example, VMware), Hyper-V also can run multiple different operating systems—Windows, Linux, and others-in parallel—on a single server.

IDC (International Data Corporation)
A market research and analysis firm specializing in information technology, telecommunications, and consumer technology.

Insight Control
A tool from HP for measuring and managing energy use in servers and other IT equipment. Insight Control allows management of HP ProLiant and BladeSystem infrastructure systems. The management includes power measurement and power capping.

Intel
The major microprocessor manufacturer of CPUs used in Windows PCs and servers.

Internet
A set of connected networks. The term "Internet" refers to the large and growing public domain Internet developed by DARPA that uses TCP/IP. It is shared by universities, corporations, and private individuals.

intranet
A Web network that connects computers within the same company or organization over a private network. An intranet offers higher security than an Internet Web site because of the private nature of the network.

IP (Internet Protocol)
The network-layer protocol for the Internet protocol suite.

IT (Information Technology)
The study, design, development, implementation, support, or management of computer-based information systems, particularly software applications and computer hardware.

ITIL (Information Technology Infrastructure Library)
A set of concepts and policies for managing information technology (IT) infrastructure, development, and operations.

Ivy Plus technology consortium
A consortium of top universities (Ivy League plus other universities, such as MIT, Duke, and Stanford) that fosters collaboration to help drive future growth and use of technology.

KWH or kWh (kilowatt hour)
A basic unit of electric energy based on using power of 1,000 watts for one hour. The kilowatt hour is the energy delivered by electric utilities that is usually expressed and charged for in kWh. Note that the kWh is the product of power in kilowatts multiplied by time in hours; it is not kW/h.

Large Hadron Collider
The Large Hadron Collider (LHC) is the world's largest and highest-energy particle accelerator. Built by CERN, the LHC drives much of the need for performance computing (HPC) at hundreds of universities and laboratories around the world.

LEED (Leadership in Energy and Environmental Design)
A Green Building Rating System, developed by the U.S. Green Building Council (USGBC), which provides a suite of standards for environmentally sustainable construction.

Liebert Corporation
An American manufacturer of environmental, power, and monitoring systems for mainframe computer, server racks, and critical process systems. Liebert is an Emerson Network Power Company.

LPAR (Logical Partition)
A subset of a computer's hardware resources, virtualized as a separate computer.

MIB (Management Information Base)
A MIB stems from the OSI/ISO network management model and is a type of database that manages the devices (such as routers and switches) in a communications network.

Moore's Law
Describes a long-term trend in the history of computing hardware. Since the invention of the integrated circuit in 1958, the number of transistors that can be placed inexpensively on an integrated circuit has increased exponentially, doubling approximately every two years. The trend was first observed by Intel cofounder Gordon E. Moore in a 1965 paper. It has continued for almost half of a century and is not expected to stop for another decade at least and perhaps much longer.

NAGIOS
A popular open source computer system and network monitoring application software that watches hosts and services, alerting users when things go wrong and again when they get better (http://www.nagios.org/).

NEDC (New Enterprise Data Center)
A concept announced by IBM in 2008 that is a vision for energy-efficient data centers based on lessons learned from working with customers on hundreds of data centers on best-practice ways to approach energy efficiency for both existing and new data centers.

NYSERDA (New York State Energy Research and Development Authority)
A public benefit corporation created in 1975. NYSERDA's earliest efforts focused solely on research and development with the goal of reducing the state's petroleum consumption. Subsequent research and development

projects focused on topics including environmental effects of energy consumption, development of renewable resources, and advancement of innovative technologies can be found at http://www.nyserda.org/.

NYSERNet (New York State Education and Research Network)
This organization includes a shared data center in Syracuse, NY, members of the NYSGrid, members of K-12 schools, colleges, universities, libraries, and corporate research labs.

NYSGrid (New York State Grid)
A New York State High Performance Computing (HPC) consortium.

OSI (Open Systems Interconnection)
The OSI Reference Model is an abstract description for layered communications and computer network protocol design.

PDU (Power Distribution Unit)
A device that distributes electric power. Large industrial units are used for taking high voltage and current and reducing it to more common and useful levels—for example, from 240V 30A single phase to multiple 120V 15A or 120V 20A plugs. PDUs are used in computer data centers, stage shows, and in other electrically intensive applications.

PSSC (Products and Solutions Support Center)
The IBM PSSC at Montpelier, France, is focused on benchmarking, performance, and sizing.

PUC (Public Utility Commission)
The general name for the state regulatory body charged with regulating utilities.

PUE (Power Usage Effectiveness)
PUE = Total Facility Power/IT Equipment Power. A PUE of 1.5 for a data center is excellent (a green data center), whereas a PUE above 3.0 is considered quite inefficient. To make a more intuitive metric, the Green Grid defined the DCiE (Data Center Infrastructure Efficiency) that is the reciprocal of the PUE × 100%. So, a DCiE of 100 percent is considered ideal, whereas a DCiE of 33 percent (a PUE of 3) is considered quite inefficient.

ROI (Return On Investment)
The amount, expressed as a percentage, which is earned on a capital investment in a project. For example, an investment virtualized for your data center may have a 33 percent ROI or approximately a three-year payback.

SAN (Storage Area Network)
A high-speed subnetwork of shared storage devices.

server
A computer system that has been designated for running a specific server application or applications.

SNMP (Simple Network Management Protocol)
An Internet standard network monitoring protocol used in network management systems to monitor network-attached devices.

SPEC (Standard Performance Evaluation Corporation)
A nonprofit corporation formed to establish, maintain, and endorse a standardized set of benchmarks that can be applied to the newest generation of high-performance computers.

server cluster
A group of linked servers, working together closely so that in many respects, it forms a single server (computer). Clusters are usually deployed to improve performance and availability over that provided by a single server, while typically being much more cost-effective than single servers of comparable speed or availability.

sustainability
The U.S. EPA defines sustainability as "meeting the needs of the present without compromising the ability of future generations to meet their own needs."

TCP/IP (Transmission Control Protocol/Internet Protocol)
The set of applications and transport protocols that uses IP (Internet Protocol) to transmit data over a network. TCP/IP was developed by the Department of Defense to provide telecommunications for internetworking.

ton (air conditioning)
One ton of air conditioning capacity equals 12,000 BTUs per hour.

UAT (User Acceptance Test)
An IT test environment that is usually designed to be identical or as close as possible to the user's production environment. This test environment is used for final verification before a system goes to production mode.

UESC (Utility Energy Service Contract)

An incentive envisioned by the U.S. federal government for efficiency upgrades for data centers.

UNIX

The operating system originally designed by AT&T and enhanced by the University of California at Berkeley and others. Because it was powerful and essentially available for free, it became popular at universities. Many vendors made their own versions of UNIX available—for example, IBM's AIX, based on OSF/1. The UNIX trademark and definition have since come under the control of X/Open, which will issue a unifying specification.

UPS (Uninterruptible Power Supply)

UPS, also known as a battery backup, provides emergency power. A UPS typically protects computers, telecommunication equipment, or other electrical equipment where an unexpected power disruption could cause injuries, fatalities, serious business disruption, or data loss. A UPS can provide uninterrupted power to equipment, typically for 5–15 minutes, until a generator can be turned on or utility power is restored.

URL (Universal Resource Locator)

World Wide Web name for a document, file, or other resource. It describes the protocol required to access the resource, the host where it can be found, and a path to the resource on that host.

VMware

A developer of virtualization software. The company is based in Palo Alto, California. VMware's enterprise software, VMware ESX Server, runs directly on server hardware without requiring an additional underlying operating system.

WAN (Wide Area Network)

A long-distance network for the efficient transfer of voice, data, and video between local, metropolitan, campus, and site networks. WANs typically use lower transfer rates (64Kbps) or higher-speed services such as T3, which operates at 45Mbps. WANs also typically use common-carrier services (communications services available to the general public) or private networking through satellite and microwave facilities.

watt

A basic unit of electric power. Electric energy used is measured in kilowatt hours (KHW) that equate to using 1,000 watts of power for one hour.

Web browser

An application that provides an interface to the World Wide Web.

Webmaster

A person who manages a Web site—similar to the network administrator.

X86

A generic term that refers to the processor architecture commonly used in personal computers and servers. It is derived from the model numbers, ending in "86," of the first few processor generations backward-compatible with the original Intel 8086. The architecture has been implemented in processors from Intel, Cyrix, AMD, VIA, and many others.

Xen

A free (open source) software virtual machine monitor for IA-32, x86-64, IA-64, and PowerPC® 970 architectures. It allows several guest operating systems to be executed on the same computer hardware at the same time.

Bibliography

Ainsworth, Phil, et al. "Going Green with IBM Active Energy Manager," IBM Redpaper, http://www.redbooks.ibm.com, 2008.

CDW white paper. "Blade Servers and Virtualization: A Perfect Match," http://www.webbuyersguide.com/resource/resourceDetails.aspx ?id=11136, May 2008.

Ebbers, Mike, et al. "The Green Datacenter: Steps for the Journey," IBM Redpaper, http://www.redbooks.ibm.com, 2008.

Emerson/Liebert white paper. "Five Strategies for Cutting Data Center Energy Costs Through Enhanced Cooling Efficiency," Emerson/Liebert, http://www.energyefficientdatacenters.techweb.com/ login.jhtml?_requestid=882321, 2008.

Environmental Protection Agency—U.S. "Report to Congress on Server and Data Center Energy Efficiency—Public Law 109-431," ENERGY STAR Program, August 2, 2007, http://www.energystar.gov/ index.cfm ?c=prod_development.server_efficiency_study.

Esty, Daniel C. and Andrew S. Winston. *Green to Gold: How Smart Companies Use Environmental Strategy to Innovate, Create Value, and Build Competitive Advantage*, Yale, University Press, 384 pages, 9780300119978, 2006.

European Commission, Institute for Energy. "Code of Conduct on Data Centres Energy Efficiency," Version 1.0, October 30, 2008, http://re.jrc.ec.europa.eu/energyefficiency/pdf/CoC%20data%20 centres%20nov2008/CoC%20DC%20v%201.0%20FINAL.pdf.

Friedman, Thomas L. *Hot, Flat, and Crowded: Why We Need a Green Revolution—and How It Can Renew America* (Hardcover), Farrar, Straus, and Giroux, 2008.

Gartner Conference. "The Data Center Power and Cooling Challenge," Las Vegas, November 2007.

Gore, Al. *An Inconvenient Truth: The Crisis of Global Warming* (Paperback), Penguin, 2007.

Harris, Jason. *Green Computing and Green IT Best Practices on Regulations and Industry Initiatives, Virtualization, Power Management, Materials Recycling, and Telecommuting*, Emereo Pty Ltd, 2008.

Harvard Business School. *Harvard Business Review on Green Business Strategy*, Harvard Business School Press, 2007.

Hiremane, Radhakrishna. "Using Utility Rebates to Minimize Energy Costs in the Data Center," *The Data Center Journal*, http://datacenterjournal.com/index.php?option=com_content&task=view&id=1475&Itemid=41, February 2008.

Hoover, Nicholas. "Next-Gen Data Centers," *Information Week* white paper, http://www.findwhitepapers.com/whitepaper2244/, February 2008.

IBM Global Business Services. "Attaining Sustainable Growth Thorough Corporate Social Responsibility," IBM Institute for Business Value, February 2008.

IBM point-of-view white paper. "IBM's Vision for the New Enterprise Data Center," March 2008.

IBM Software. "A Green Strategy for Your Entire Organization," IBM Software Division, http://www-306.ibm.com/software/solutions/green/, June 2008.

Koomey, Jonathan G., Ph.D. "Data Center Electricity Use," Lawrence Berkeley National Laboratory and Stanford University. Presented at the EPA stakeholder workshop at the Santa Clara Convention Center, February 16, 2007.

Koomey, Jonathan G. "Estimating Total Power Consumption by Servers in the U.S. and the World," http://enterprise.amd.com/Downloads/svrpwrusecompletefinal.pdf, February 15, 2007.

Koomey, Jonathan G. "Worldwide Electricity Used in Data Centers," *Environmental Research Letters*, http://stacks.iop.org/1748-9326/3/034008, September 23, 2008.

LBNL. "High-Performance Buildings for High-Tech Industries, Data Centers," Lawrence Berkeley National Laboratory, http://hightech.lbl.gov/datacenters.html, January 12, 2009.

Loper, J. and S. Parr. "Energy Efficiency in Data Centers: A New Policy Frontier," Alliance to Save Energy, http://www.ase.org/content/article/detail/4071, January 2007.

Makower, Joel. *Strategies for the Green Economy: Opportunities and Challenges in the New World of Business*, U.S. Green Building Council, 312 pages, 9780071600309, 2008.

Mitchell, Robert. "Seven Steps to a Green Data Center," *Computerworld*, April 21, 2007.

Molloy, Chris. "Project Big Green: The Rest of the Story," IBM Technical Leadership Conference (TLE), Orlando, Florida, April 2008.

NYSERDA. "Next-Generation Emerging Technologies for End-Use Efficiency: Program Opportunity Notice 1105," New York State Energy Research and Development Administration, http://www.nyserda.org/funding/funding.asp?i=2, 2007.

NYSERDA. "The NYSERDA / DOE Joint Energy Storage Initiative," NYSERDA and DOE, http://www.storagemonitoring.com/ nyserda-doe/storage-home.shtml, January 12, 2009.

Pacific Gas & Electric (PG&E), "Data Center Energy Management," http://hightech.lbl.gov/DCTraining/, 2008.

Pacific Gas & Electric (PG&E), "High-Performance Data Centers," http://hightech.lbl.gov/documents/DATA_CENTERS/06_DataCenters-PGE.pdf, January 2006.

Patterson, M.K., D. Costello, P. Grimm, and M. Loeffler. "Data Center TCO; A Comparison of High-Density and Low-Density Spaces," THERMES 2007, Santa Fe, New Mexico, 2007.

Patterson, M.K., A. Pratt, and P. Kumar. "From UPS to Silicon, an End-to-End Evaluation of Data Center Efficiency, Proceedings of the EPA Event: Enterprise Servers and Data Centers: Opportunities for Energy Savings," http://www.energystar.gov/ia/products/downloads/MPatterson_APratt_Case_Study.pdf, February 2006.

Pernick, R. and C. Wilder. "The Clean Tech Revolution: Discover the Top Trends, Technologies, and Companies to Watch," *Collins Business*, 336 pages, 9780060896249, 2008.

Rassmussen, N. "Electrical Efficiency Modeling of Data Centers," white paper #113, APC, http://www.apcmedia.com/salestools/NRAN-66CK3D_R1_EN.pdf, 2005.

Rodriguez, Jean-Michel. "Green Data Center of the Future—Architecture," IBM Technical Leadership Conference (TLE), Orlando, Florida, April 2008.

The Green Grid. "The Green Grid Data Center Power Efficiency Metrics: PUE and DCiE," The Green Grid, http://www.thegreengrid.org/en/sitecore/content/Global/Content/TechnicalForumPresentation/How%20to%20Measure%20and%20Report%20PUE%20and%20DCiE.aspx, 2009.

Velte, T.J., A.T. Velte, and R. Elsenpeter. *Green IT: Reduce Your Information System's Environmental Impact While Adding to the Bottom Line*, McGraw-Hill, 2008.

Walsh, Bryan. "Al Gore's Bold, Unrealistic Plan to Save the Planet," *Time*, July 18, 2008, http://www.time.com/time/health/article/0,8599,1824132,00.html?xid=newsletter-weekly.

Index

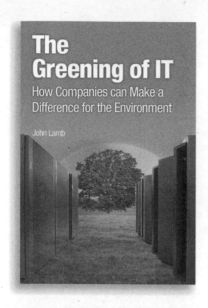

The
Greening of IT
How Companies can Make a
Difference for the Environment

John Lamb

FREE Online Edition

Your purchase of *The Greening of IT* includes access to a free online edition for 45 days through the Safari Books Online subscription service. Nearly every IBM Press book is available online through Safari Books Online, along with more than 5,000 other technical books and videos from publishers such as Addison-Wesley Professional, Cisco Press, Exam Cram, O'Reilly, Prentice Hall, Que, and Sams.

SAFARI BOOKS ONLINE allows you to search for a specific answer, cut and paste code, download chapters, and stay current with emerging technologies.

Activate your FREE Online Edition at
www.informit.com/safarifree

> **STEP 1:** Enter the coupon code: XBDDIWH.

> **STEP 2:** New Safari users, complete the brief registration form. Safari subscribers, just log in.